S0-BSD-372

William Dean Howells

William Dean Howells

William Dean Howells

A STUDY

BY

OSCAR W. FIRKINS

NEW YORK
RUSSELL & RUSSELL · INC
1963

REISSUED, 1963, BY RUSSELL & RUSSELL, INC.
BY ARRANGEMENT WITH HARVARD UNIVERSITY PRESS
L. C. CATALOG CARD NO: 63—11030

PRINTED IN THE UNITED STATES OF AMERICA

To GEORGE EDGAR VINCENT

WHOSE KINDNESS IS UNFORGETTABLE AND UNFORGETTING

THIS BOOK IS INSCRIBED

CONTENTS

William Dean Howells

CHAPTER I

Life

I

I WAS born," says William Dean Howells, in "Years of My Youth," "on the 1st of March, 1837, at Martin's Ferry, Belmont County, Ohio. My father's name was William Cooper Howells, and my mother's was Mary Dean; they were married six years before my birth, and I was the second child in their family of eight."

The father's ancestors were Welsh; they made clocks and watches, first in Wales and later in London, from which capital a descendant afterward returned to Wales to found a homelier repute on the excellence of his flannel. In 1808, the novelist's grandfather, with his young wife and year-old son, landed in America, where his flannels were already prized; but his Welsh savings melted away in American enterprise, and a series of ventures, ending mostly as misadventures, brought him to anchor at last in Hamilton, Ohio. Here, as owner of the local book and drug store, he alleviated the bodily ills and mental hungers of his townsfolk. Meanwhile, the year-old son had grown to manhood, and in Wheeling, West Virginia, had met and married Mary Dean. This gave the future novelist an Irish grandfather, and a grandmother whose German phlegm (she sprang from the thrifty Pennsylvania Germans) was a needed offset to the Celtic yeast. Relative ignorance and advanced culture are but a step or two apart in our progressive country; the boy who was to rise to the headship of American letters had two grandparents who dropped their *h*'s and a third who could not read English and asked, "What fur a tay is it?"

The father of William Dean Howells began his career by ruining himself with the publication of a book that no one wanted, and this disaster was the fit, if sad, prelude to a wandering and straitened life as editor and printer in various sections of Ohio. Prosperity would never have failed him if humane and tender wisdom or a craftsman's skill in knacks and ingenuities could have supplied the absence of commercial insight. But even with ten mouths to feed, he could not deny himself the luxury of sustaining the Free-Soil and Anti-Slavery movements with a vigor which lost him many a subscriber. He had a character almost beyond praise, perfect in the great essentials, yet not without the due allowance of engaging or enraging foibles. His sunny humor brightened the responsibilities which it never shirked, and made his family forgive him for the share they were all forced to take in repaying the debts which his hopefulness contracted.

I will set down briefly the migrations and occupations of the family from the birth of William Dean Howells in 1837 to his appointment to the Venetian consulship in 1861.

From 1837 to 1840, the family lived in Martin's Ferry, in eastern Ohio, where the father built a small brick house "with his own capable hands," and, after a physical breakdown, painted houses in the experiments of convalescence.

From 1840 to 1848, in Hamilton, the "Boy's Town," the father edited a Whig paper, which he sold in the latter year in displeasure at the nomination of Taylor for the presidency.

From 1848 to 1850, in Dayton, another newspaper ran a swift course through hardship to disaster.

From 1850 to 1851, the family shared in an attempt to convert lumber and flour mills into mills for the making of cloth and paper on a coöperative basis. The failure was complete, but the undertaking had fruits, long afterward, in the materials it afforded for "My Year in a Log Cabin" and "New Leaf Mills."

From 1851 to 1852 comes a winter in Columbus, where the son, now fourteen, is compositor on the "Ohio State Journal," to which the father supplied reports of the proceedings of the legislature.

From 1852 to 1861, the family is settled in northeastern Ohio, where a journal, after six months' tentative establishment at Ashtabula, is removed to Jefferson, the county seat. During this period the father and son are often engaged in Columbus: the father as clerk for the legislature, 1856–1858, the son as reporter, 1856–1858, later as exchange editor and editorial writer, on the "Ohio State Journal," 1858–1861.

II

Four currents are traceable in the first twenty-four years of the life of William Dean Howells. There is the vocational life as printer and editor; there is the self-education in literature; there is the social life with boys or fellow-craftsmen, or social acquaintance; and there are the intimacies of the family bond and the inwardness of private feeling. These currents may be separately traced.

Mr. Howells remembered when he could not read, but not when he was unable to set type; he typed and printed his own first essay in literature. His father's theory that boys must either work or attend school resulted, not very unnaturally, in a maximum of work and a paucity of schooling. The tiny boy eked out his meagre inches with a chair, and the sarcastic good-nature of the printers dubbed him The Old Man. At thirteen years his proficiency was a matter of knowledge and an object of desire to country editors. A winter's reporting for the "Cincinnati Gazette" issued in the offer to the lad, now twenty years of age, of a place as city editor at a salary of one thousand dollars — a large sum, if measured by the scale of the times or the needs of the family. He recoiled from police work and declined the offer; it is not often that a penniless lad of twenty has the courage or the delicacy to poise sensibilities against dollars. About a year later, he was called to the editorial staff of the "Ohio State Journal," where he supervised exchanges and wrote anti-slavery editorials for a period lasting, with an intermission, from 1858 to 1861. The importance of the editorials of that journal in that nation-shaping epoch was attested by a rebuke in person from the autocratic Horace Greeley.

That the young man's efficiency was large, and was, to a surprising extent, recognizable and marketable, are facts which Mr. Howells, with all his skill in masking his own virtues, cannot hide from the alert reader. The boy who had spent his thirteenth year in a log cabin was only twenty-one when he was invited to dinner by the governor of the state, and his talents alone had favored his ascent. The continuity of his vocational life is remarkable. With the exception of a week or two of abortive apprenticeship in an uncle's drug store, a month in a law office, and the considerately rare intrusions of politics on the scholarly leisure of the four-year consulship at Venice, Mr. Howells's work for nearly eighty years consisted solely of verbal intercourse with the public in the several capacities of type-setter, journalist, and author.

He was a faithful and useful son, contributing to the family support in the ratio of his powers rather than his years, and of the necessities rather than the wishes of an affectionate and partial father. Once, at least, the stringency became cruel. For a brief period in Dayton, before he was thirteen, the long days, which began with the delivery of papers before five o'clock in the morning and closed with the typing of the telegraphic despatches at eleven at night, allowed the growing lad barely six hours of sleep. The experience made him perennially "tender of those who overwork, especially the children who overwork."

Realism has its ground in respect for the fact, and it was undoubtedly fostered in Mr. Howells by competence and responsibility, two things which acquaint a boy with realities. He did not lose the dreams and visions proper to the boy; in fact, his boyhood and his manhood flowed on together in his early life, and he was fortunate in forming a love for the actual long before he had ceased to prefer the romantic.

III

The second current in boyhood and youth is the private self-discipline in literature. The formal education of the man whom great institutions were to court was limited to a few brief terms of passable instruction in common-school branches. That fact might well disturb the sleep of universities. He did not repine in youth at the restrictions which his maturity politely regretted. He acquiesced patiently in the family edict which decided that a session at an academy was impracticable. An offer on the part of a kind Scotch farmer to be one of three or four to send to Harvard a stripling in whom the county foresaw its own distinction was put by with a disdain which the years chastened into thankfulness.

Meanwhile, the boy was passionately and tirelessly clearing his own path. The father was eager to share his enthusiasm for letters with the son whose companionship he valued and whose power he divined. William read and wrote with eagerness. He conceived a passion for languages. He flung himself upon Spanish in scorn of helps, and learned to read that seignorial tongue with ease and competence. He was attracted and victimized by "a sixteen-bladed grammar" which included all the Romance tongues; he studied Latin half-heartedly with the questionable aid of a kindly and sleepy old minister; he learned German more effectually from a little bookbinder of Hanoverian origin, as the preparation for an immersion in Heine which ended, logically enough, in a saturation. At one period he was studying five languages.

Composition had already begun. The first poem which his father surreptitiously offered to an editor made his young heart tumultuous with shame and pride. A luckless serial which he began to publish in the family paper broke his heart and quenched his ambition when a farmer said about it the very word he had been painfully saying to himself. But his aspirations at this period were mainly poetic; he mimicked the authors whom he loved, and pursued false ideals with ardor and sincerity. The morning and the early afternoon were consumed by the exacting office; but from three o'clock till supper-time and from supper-time till ten or eleven at night, the boy gave himself to his studies in the windowed nook under the stairs which housed his desk and guarded his privacy. This was his workshop for six or seven years. His labor was solitary; one of those deep reserves known even to affectionate families kept his studies at a distance which he chooses to term "savage." Later he could not review those early struggles without "a faint, or perhaps more than faint, heartache for the boy who strove so fervently to realize a false ideal of beauty in his work."

His relations with magazines were marked by the inconsistency from which even success is not exempt in that world of shine and shower. His early successes were incredibly prompt; the confirmation of his position after his embarkation for Europe was strangely belated. He was twenty or little more when he scored his first acceptance from the "Atlantic Monthly," a magazine whose favors at that epoch rarely scaled the Alleghanies. The kindness was repeated, and the "Saturday Review" of New York opened its columns more freely than its purse to the solicitations of the young Westerner. "I can sell, now, just as much as I will write," he confides to his sister in the Columbus period.

He was twenty-two when he published, in conjunction with John J. Piatt, the volume entitled "Poems of Two Friends," and his modesty almost triumphs in the commercial failure of the book and the superiority, as he stoutly affirms, of the contributions of his associate. A life of Lincoln which he compiled from meagre material gathered by another hand sold freely in the West, and prepared the way for kindnesses from Washington. A hovering consulate, which after poising irresolutely between Munich and Rome, split the geographical difference by descending opportunely upon Venice, was offered to the Western journalist. The young consul, who embarked for Italy in 1861, after consuming the entire Waverley Novels in the leisure of the preceding month, was already an expert newspaper man and man of letters, not yet known to an extensive public, but discerned and trusted by the prescient few.

IV

An average boy would have found it hard to practise a trade, pursue an ideal, and mix at the same time with his boyish fellows; but the elasticity of time is miraculous, and Mr. Howells seems, at all periods, to have mingled freely and happily with his kind. The handicraft begat fellowships; study implied the tutor; literature in that hour and spot was less insulative than it has latterly and elsewhere been; and humor, which ripened early in the boy, established a passing brotherhood between persons to whom even cousinship on other terms would have been impossible. His curiosity was alert, and his sympathies the reverse of inactive. In the "Boy's Town" days at Hamilton, he was a boy among other boys; he possessed a fortunate plasticity, all the more fortunate that it never deliquesced into suppleness. "Swimming, fishing, foraging at every season, with the skating which the waters of the rivers and canals afforded, were my joy; I took my part in the races and the games, in football and in baseball, then in its feline infancy of Three Corner Cat; and though there was a family rule against fighting, I fought like the rest of the boys, and took my defeats as heroically as I knew how; they were mostly defeats."

He tells us that he loved play even better than reading. I allow myself to think, nevertheless, that the lure of these sports was social rather than athletic; at least, the early and final shedding of these pursuits which apparently took place might be referred to the speedy rise of other forms of fellowship. His power of friendship was an endowment in itself; it was strongly evoked in Jefferson by two young men whose names appear only in the twilight of initials; and the journalism, in the "State Journal" office became the inducement to close and tender friendships, with the flush of which, after more than fifty years, his page is roseate.

At the same time the capital opened its drawing-rooms to the young editor. The gulf between journalism and fashion is readily bridged by the intervention of political magnates to whom journalism is necessary and fashion obsequious. The world to which he was now admitted, with its dinners, its dances, its music, its frank and cordial women, its eagerness in the pursuit of literature, its bright informality and fearless trust, apparently yielded him a delight which the larger opportunities of riper years could not induce in his maturity. "Those two happy winters in Columbus, when I was finding opportunity and recognition, were the heyday of life to me. There has been no time like them since, though there have been smiling and prosperous times a plenty." The reverse side of the picture, the charm which made him instantly precious to his associates, is visible through all the folds of his reserve.

V

The fourth strand of experience comprises the more intimate emotions. He lived largely and closely with his father in a commerce of the heart which found an outlet and a screen in full communication on literary and philosophic topics. His love for his mother was simpler, more passionate and elemental; her tenderness warmed his life, and it was separation from her that darkened and usually shortened the infrequent absences from home in the boyhood period before Columbus. His was an elastic temperament, mainly cheerful and abidingly humorous, with an "habitual gravity" broken by "bursts of wild hilarity," and a great readiness to enjoy, tempered by a large capacity to suffer. The double strain of handicraft and literature racked his constitution at one period, and he was forced to seek in muscular work and in field sports a refuge from the fears and distresses that haunted his unrest.

I do not know whether this episode concurs in time with another period of anguish for which a separate cause is assigned in "Years of My Youth." A bite from a dog, and long afterward, a casual remark about postponed and suddenly outbreaking hydrophobia, enmeshed the lad in a hypochondria from which he was extricated in the course of months or years by his father's discretion, his own sense, and the great restorative of time. The experience was so penetrating that after sixty years he could not write or speak the sinister word without a "shutting of the heart." It is quite clear that the equipoise of the boy's mind in these overstressed and probing years was both delicate and precarious, and his parents, with all their overflowing love, seem to have viewed the case with that curious calmness by which parental love defends itself from the number and weight of its responsibilities.

They were concerned for the "mistaken piety" of childhood, expressed in the remark that the central aisle of the Methodist church was a place where one might die with the prospect of a prompt ascent to heaven. There were times when the boy's conscience was morbidly exigent, and happier times of relaxed authority when it permitted him to fight and to call names. A death which he knew only through his brother's eyes and voice plunged him into consternation, and he was harassed at one period by the foreboding that he should die at the age of sixteen. His imagination had its happier and saner outlets. The "vain and ridiculous dreamer," as he calls himself in a not untender self-disparagement, was "inwardly all thrones, principalities, and powers, the foe of tyrants, the friend of good emperors, and the intimate of magicians, and magnificently apparelled." "He could not help revealing sometimes to the kindness of his father and mother the world of foolish dreams half of him lived in, while the other half swam, and fished, and hunted, and ran races, and played tops and marbles, and squabbled and scuffled in the 'Boy's Town.'" The experience is normal enough; I record it because of its normality.

He tells us that his temper was hot and his disposition vengeful — to which the reader can only reply in the words of Hamlet to Horatio: "I would not hear your enemy say so." It is possible to sum up his boyhood in the assertion that he was an imaginative, dreamy, plastic, affectionate lad, less remarkable for these not uncommon traits than for their rare combination with a latent affinity for realism and an exceptional capacity for work.

VI

From the time of the departure for Venice, the thread of these records will be mainly chronological. In the fall of 1861, after an evening in which the reading aloud of "Christie Johnstone" served as anæsthetic to the ache of separation, with the kiss of the young brother whom he was never to see again still warm upon his lips, he parted with his family at the gate, under the pale sky of the October night. He spent four years at Venice; he had a salary of fifteen hundred dollars; and the Confederate privateers which he was commissioned to watch forbore to infringe on the tranquillities of scholarship. He read Dante with a genial priest, acquired a ready if not a blameless Italian, and planned reading and writing in Italian history and literature on the Utopian scale of youth. In actual product the period was relatively infertile, and his ventures found scanty acceptance in the press. The early cordiality of the magazines was an April warmth, to be followed by one of those chills which give even to successful contributorship the fickleness and shaking of an ague. The spell was partly broken by Lowell's acceptance of an essay on "Recent Italian Comedy" for the "North American Review," and by the appearance in the "Boston Advertiser" of a series of letters predestined to literary favor and commercial success under the attractive title of "Venetian Life."

Meanwhile, other inspirations had quickened his soul. On December 24, 1862, he had married Elinor G. Mead of Brattleboro, Vermont, whose acquaintance he had formed amid the suavities and vivacities of the unforgettable sojourn in Columbus. I set down the few words he devotes to this relation in "Years of My Youth."

> Very likely those dances lasted through the winter, but I cannot be sure; I can only be sure that they summed up the raptures of the time, which was the most memorable of my whole life; for now I met her who was to be my wife. We were married the next year, and she became with her unerring artistic taste and conscience my constant impulse toward reality and sincerity in my work. She was the first to blame and the first to praise, as she was the first to read what I wrote. Forty-seven years we were together here, and then she died. But in that gayest time when we met it did not seem as if there could be an end of time for us, or any time less radiant.

A daughter was born in Venice, and "Venetian Life" offers a pleasing picture of her association, in the unreserve of infancy, with the half-mystic, nocturnal conclave of servants in the lower regions of the house.

We are told in "My Literary Passions" that the influence of Venice changed the whole course of the young consul's literary life. "My literary life, almost without my willing it, had taken the course of critical observance of books and men in their actuality." No stranger recipe for converting idealism into realism could have proved the whimsicality of fact than the transfer of the subject from an American newspaper office at the outbreak of the Civil War to the most dream-like city of a land of dreams, the asylum of fleeing romance from the pursuit of relentless actuality. There may be some pertinence in the remark that truth in its most romantic aspect, in other words, truth in Italy, might furnish a young romanticist with the most available thoroughfare from dream to verity. Another fact in the explanation is more tangible. The intending contributor found the tempest-tossed America of his day receptive of his observations, but deaf to his verse; though doubtless the appeal to self-interest would have been fruitless, had not the mounting observer in Mr. Howells already set himself against the waning poet. The change, and the discernment of the change, required time, and this explains why, even in 1866, when he joined the staff of the "Atlantic Monthly," his career, at twenty-nine, was still unsettled in a degree which the spectator of his early endeavors and precocious successes would hardly have foreseen.

It was in 1865 that he returned from Venice to recover his lost foothold in American journalism. He was not spared the tests to which fortune is prone to resubject the metals she has already tempered in the furnace of uncertainty; but, after various rebuffs in Boston, Columbus, Cincinnati, and New York, the ordeal ended happily in his establishment in the office of the New York "Nation," under E. L. Godkin, at forty dollars a week. Here he printed "Italian Journeys," wrote critiques (which his riper judgment disavowed), disported himself in a department of social phases and events which was his offspring and nursling, and formed for his new chief one of those precipitate but imperishable friendships which clothed routine with the grace of an idyl. "I worked with joy, with ardor, and I liked so much to be there, in that place and in that company, that I hated to have each day come to an end." But his stay in this Elysium was cut short;

he received in January, 1866, from James T. Fields, the Boston publisher, the invitation which resulted in his fifteen years' service on the "Atlantic Monthly," as assistant under Mr. Fields from 1866 to 1872, as editor-in-chief from 1872 to 1881.

Let me advert briefly to a chain of incidents which I purposely left untouched in my narrative of the pre-consular life. In 1860, in the period of recess from the "Ohio State Journal," he had made a brief trip to New England by way of Niagara and Canada, having rashly promised a sanguine publisher to visit factories and compile or edit a work on the "distinctive mechanical inventions of our country." He escaped the penalties of this indiscretion (for he was equally ignorant and impatient of mechanics) through the reluctance of manufacturers to expose their processes to the imaginable perfidy of an unknown visitor. This freed him for an excursion to Cambridge, where he enjoyed an exquisite and memorable hour with Lowell and Fields and Holmes, the last of whom made his young heart glow with a gracious word about the apostolic succession and the laying-on of hands. After that it was all Olympus or Valhalla. He breakfasted with Fields, and a tea with the Autocrat was the happy presage of inestimable years of friendly intercourse to follow. Hawthorne was glimmeringly benevolent in the Old Manse in Concord, and wrote "I find this young man worthy" on a card which the amused but ecstatic bearer was to present to Emerson. He left the door of the kind philosopher in abysmal humiliation at the infelicity with which he chose to imagine that he had conducted himself in that momentous interview. The glance and the touch of Whitman was the signal incident in the later visit to New York.

The foundation was already laid for the offer from the "Atlantic Monthly" no less than for the trustful and tender friendships which shed their glamour over the fifteen years of faithful service to which that offer was the key. Mr. Howells had never edited a magazine, but the fact shrank into irrelevance in face of the instant trust which all men felt in a presence that exhaled capacity. He sifted manuscripts, read proofs, and wrote the book notices; his pay was fifty dollars a week. He had the type of efficiency which makes employers secure if not lazy, and in 1872, when he became full editor, Fields had doubtless little to relinquish but the name. The "Atlantic," still only eight years old in 1866, had at that time both reserves and intrepidities, and no person could be better qualified to mediate between old and new, between East and West, than the young man who divided his worship pretty impartially between two such antipodes as Mark Twain and Henry James. Nor had he any difficulty in reconciling these antithetic modernisms with the loyalty which he owed to the founders and guarantors of the periodical. His heart indorsed and forestalled the honor which his position obliged him to pay to Longfellow, Whittier, Lowell, Hawthorne, Emerson, and Holmes.

His own contributions speedily overflowed from the book reviews into the magazine proper, taking form in sketches, critiques, short stories, and, finally, the novels, in which the irresolutions of his poising genius matured into certainty and repose. His fame was as modest as his disposition, and its leisurely, though secure, advance left him even in 1880 a writer inaudible to the masses.

On May 1, 1866, he moved into a "carpenter's box" on Sacramento Street, Cambridge, the ownership of which was a cheering possibility dimly seen through the rifts in a cloud of mortgages. There was an arbor-vitæ hedge in front, and a tall board fence in the rear, and the pears, grapes, and currants with which the little lot was almost too densely planted lent a savor of gentility to a kitchen-garden. Here the young couple began their participation in the favored life of Cambridge, "that life so refined, so intelligent, so gracefully simple" that Mr. Howells doubted if the world could show its parallel. His admission to the literary adyta was certified by an invitation to the Dante evenings, to hear Longfellow read installments of his version of the "Divine Comedy" at Craigie House; and Lowell, after a moment of coyness, became liberal, even bountiful, of his high companionship.

After four years came a removal to a larger house near Harvard Square, and in 1878 a further removal from Cambridge to Belmont, where another four years of "amplest quiet" terminated in a serious illness of seven or eight weeks' duration. This misfortune tested both the strength of the patient's constitution and the constancy of his friends, with vindications on both points.

The illness was apparently the chief exception to the fortunate uniformity of a health which, having once outlived the stresses of boyhood, "has never since failed me under any reasonable stress of work." I may mention here three privileged years of neighborship to Dr. Holmes in Beacon Street in Boston, which include the year 1886, and therefore fall outside of the term of editorship in the "Atlantic" office.

VII

After 1881, the autobiographies begin to forsake us and details become spare and colorless. In the early eighties Mr. Howells wrote novels for the "Century Magazine," and from 1886 to 1891 he conducted the department of "Editor's Study" in "Harper's Monthly," arousing an indignation to which celebrity was the adjunct and offset. This editorship was the first step in that fraternization with "Harper and Brothers" in which that house evinced a true instinct for its own honor, and which only in 1916 relaxed far enough to allow the name of Howells to reappear in the magazines and book-lists of competing publishers. In 1900, he undertook the editorship of the intermitted "Easy Chair" in "Harper's Monthly," from which combination of cell and turret he exercised a strengthening and widening influence on public opinion in literary and extra-literary fields to the hour of his death. The practice of criticism in the "North American Review," the reversion to poetry, and the excursions into drama hardly slackened the quiet outpour, or rather efflux, of novels and briefer tales.

European journeys checkered the monotony of authorship. There were visits to Switzerland and Germany, and a new outreach or outbreak of itineracy in his eighth decade proved how far he still was from the hairy gown and mossy cell which Milton counseled for the weariness of age. In company with Miss Howells, who shared his travels after the death of her mother in or about 1909, he visited Rome; returned to the hearth of the Anglo-Saxon race, to read its history in the unextinguished coals; reclasped the links of amity and ancestry with Wales; and, by a brief but happy tour in the Spanish peninsula, interwove his last wanderings with his earliest dreams.

The later years were prodigal of honors. Universities did not hesitate to indorse a career which belied their necessity and almost impugned their value. Harvard, Yale, and Columbia conferred degrees, and a doctorate of literature from Oxford in 1904 affixed the seal of the centuries to the American's fame. He was privileged in the reception, fortunate perhaps in the refusal, of three offers of professorships from the highest institutions of America. For many years he was president of the American Academy of Arts and Letters. He died on May 11, 1920, at his home in New York.

The writings of Mr. Howells are chary of allusions to the members of his household. The daughter, Mildred Howells, is not unknown to literature. There is a son, an architect, designer of a house for Mark Twain at Stormfield, with which that exigent person declared himself to be blissfully content. A grandson appears briefly in "Familiar Spanish Travels," as the absent occasion for the purchase of a jaunty headstall for a supposititious donkey; and there is a granddaughter whom I suppose to be authentic in "Imaginary Interviews," who wields the sceptre of granddaughtership with contemporary rigor.

VIII

A handful of specifications as to habits, tastes, and opinions may be set down without indiscretion in this place.

In a "Boy's Town," my boy, as he is affectionately called, hunts, fishes, swims, skates, and plays games, in a word, puts on the livery of boyhood. Of these amusements only one seems to have outlasted adolescence: the swimming, which was first among childish raptures, had its sequel in the tri-weekly bath at Venice. He admitted that he was a bad shot, and his failures with the gun no doubt relieved his heart almost as much as they stung his vanity. Even in inexorable boyhood, he could restore a captured duckling to its pond. His interest in sports and games seems to have suddenly declined; at least, in later days, he rarely mentions a muscular sport like golf or tennis, even in the sedulous and impartial portraiture of the society which those diversions permeate. To less active exercises, like driving, sleighing, or sailing, he was more addicted, and the emphasis which he withholds from cards and checkers is bestowed on picnics and theatricals. He preferred moderation in walking, and it is clear that he liked to sit in parks and watch squirrels and study types and talk philosophy. If this habit savors too much of senescence or quiescence, let us temper it by his own avowal that he used the axe and scythe on his summer estate.

A misadventure with tobacco in early life resulted in an antipathy which steeled him for all time to come against the insinuations of the drug. Of beer, also, he was apprehensive, in youth at least, but he acquired a taste for vintages. The tuition of his palate, by his own testimony, remained imperfect, and he deplores some very bad sherry of his own which "the better envyned" Longfellow drank with the serenity of a martyr. He pursued tea, especially in his travels, with an ardor that was partly jocular. He was far from insensible to the attractions of a well-cooked and well-served meal, but the Altrurian, in whom his ideals found a voice, is loud in his denunciations of the swinish abundance of the fashionable table. Toward the "dinner" in the social sense, the attitude of Mr. Howells vacillated from enthusiasm to disgust; the first dinner of a season brightened his anticipations for weeks in advance; the last darkened his memory for a fortnight afterward.

His fear of dogs enclosed a fondness, and the dogs reciprocated the fondness without heeding the fear. The ugliest and dreadest of bull-dogs used to climb into his buggy and couch at the novelist's feet "with a confidence in my reciprocal tenderness which I was anxious not to disturb by the least movement." With cats his relations were unclouded, though they partook of the ceremony which that self-respecting animal exacts as the price of its intercourse with a feebler species. He professed an estrangement from horses, which he grounds a little fantastically on the low-bred men whom the high-bred horses admit to their companionship; the Yahoos discredit the Houyhnhnms. The dislike was clearly superficial, for in the "Quality of Mercy" there is a passage that would have stirred the equine sympathies of Walter Scott, and, in his latter days in England, his aversion crumbled in the gusto of a visit to a horse-race. His affection for birds matched Spenser's or Stevenson's.

He was fond of the public spectacle — the show, as Americans term it. He had a twofold relation to the theatre. Between its appeal to his love of public entertainment, and its perpetual checkmate to his literary and realistic expectations, it became both a delight and a despair. He liked anything simple and popular; in boyhood he loved the circus; he formed a liking for Venetian marionettes; he admitted that he "always loved the films and their measureless possibility for good";[1] he could find play for his sympathies in the antics of a dime museum, the more readily, perhaps, in that the place silenced that demand for literature which kept him restless in the legitimate theatre, and strewed with misgivings his reading of the comedies of Shakespeare. He was so little of a convert to *laissez-faire* that he favored a municipal theatre supported by a tax. His judgments of actors were more than friendly; they were fond.

The senses, from eye to palate, were alert. His nose, in particular, had an almost chemic aptitude for the resolution of a smell into its abstruse constituents. On the other hand, he resented the American habit of giving to that organ an ascendency in speech commensurate with its prominence in the visage; and a Scotchman whose own bur was incredible assured him that he had never known another American voice untainted with nasality.

Toward dress his attitude was unvaryingly respectful. In early youth he envied Mr. Stedman his fortune in tailors, and so late as 1916 he conceded without irony that "the art of dressing well, or fashionably, comes from deep and earnest study." In the coolness of retrospect, he could admit that the majority of fashions have been ugly, but "style" in the present tense was his captor and tyrant from the start.

I glance at certain opinions. He mentions in one place "the misgivings that beset the beholder who looketh upon the woman when she is New." But his objections to newness in this field either did not include, or ceased to include, the franchise; for, after various wavering or hovering allusions, he tells us flatly in the "Daughter of the Storage" that he "voted for

[1] See, however, an arraignment of the "insensate reel" in the Easy Chair for June, 1916.

woman's suffrage the other day." He calls Americans "the best-hearted and worst-mannered of mankind," vituperates our hotel clerks in 1872, and denounces our tram-conductors in 1900. In one place he assigns to America "the most beautiful and glorious of all civilizations"; but the difference between the world's actual best and a perfect, or even a respectable, economic order is searchingly probed in "A Traveler from Altruria" and "Through the Eye of the Needle." I must defer the exposition of his economy, but even at this point I may specify his adhesion to a social order in which the state employs and supports all its citizens, in which labor for the common good is the universal obligation and subsistence from the common store the universal right. He was mildly censorious of the trades-unions and faintly apologetic for the trusts. He disapproved of anyone "who owns more of the earth than he knows how to use," and there is one sentence which implies, rather distantly and unhopefully, the acceptance of free trade and a land tax.

He abhorred flogging in schools, and believed that the effect of incarceration is to sentence a man, not only to prison, but to crime. The whole fabric of criminal justice affected him with pity and horror. He was emphatic and persevering in his arraignment of the death penalty. His bold plea against the execution of the Chicago anarchists excited that popular disapprobation which is the index, almost the recompense, of courage. He was not less prompt and precise in his condemnation of the summary and drastic justice administered by Great Britain to Sir Roger Casement and his associates in 1916. He was old enough in 1846 to be divided in soul between the paternal and avuncular hate of the Mexican War and the popularity of that enterprise among his boyish companions; and he was young enough in 1914 to write with bitter energy against Germany's selfish rashness in the precipitation of the world-conflict. He frankly "detested" the Spanish War, and he deprecated the annexation of the Philippines.

The veil which the modesty of Mr. Howells interposes between his good deeds and the reader is occasionally lifted, or, let us say, rifted, in the candor of autobiography. He gave to the cause, to the friend, to the servant. In his hand the tip was unfailing; he observed the habit while he deplored the custom. He sometimes gave to a random beggar in the streets, his social qualms imparting a zest to his personal gratification. When beggars with imposing retrospects or prospects asked for ten dollars, his practice was to offer five, a proposition which the modest hope that underlay the bold demand incontinently accepted. It is very pleasant to learn from his own mouth in "Seven English Cities" that neither age nor fame could deter him from offering help to an old woman with a bundle.

I doubt if the religious problem ever challenged him with a peremptory demand for an instant and final settlement; he was always in a condition to await the advent of a clearer vision or the dawn of a second life. He read the Bible sparingly in childhood, and the paternal Swedenborgianism dropped insensibly from his expanding manhood. His visits to churches commonly involved the Baedeker rather than the prayer-book, and he notes the resumption of church-going habits in his seventy-ninth year as an interesting departure. He distrusted Eddyism, and in England he recoiled from what seemed to him tasteless and tawdry in the external fashions of the Salvation Army. With all these drawbacks or furtherances, as the reader pleases to describe them, he retained rather more of effective piety than is customary in the class of men to whom he was allied by celebrity, modernity, worldly knowledge, and cosmopolite training. The beliefs to which he clung were simple and hereditary; he never recast them in the dialect of science. They consisted mainly in the double hope — I use the word advisedly in preference to doctrine or conviction — of a pilotage in this errant universe using wisdom and goodness as its final compass and lodestar, and of a harbor offering reunion to those whom the storm has divided and peace to those whom it has buffeted and misled.

CHAPTER II

"Memories and Portraits"

THE previous section includes the more important facts in Mr. Howells's life, for the truth of which and for the utterance of which we have the warrant of his own record. The present section reviews the works in which those records are embodied. The material is grouped in the order of publication. It includes "A Boy's Town" (1890), "My Year in a Log Cabin" (1893), "My Literary Passions" (1895), "Literary Friends and Acquaintance" (1900), "My Mark Twain" (1910), "New Leaf Mills" (1913) (a "chronicle" in name, a novel in aspect, and a biographical fragment in essence), and "Years of My Youth" (1916).

I

A Boy's Town

"A Boy's Town," written in the early nineties of the last century for "Harper's Young People," is a simple record of boyish life and manners in the town of Hamilton, Ohio, in the early eighteen-forties. The style and matter are adapted to young readers, though I suspect that the absence of adventure and the paucity of anecdote might attenuate the interest for very young or very stolid boys. An obvious task has been performed with obvious skill, and this success would have contented the average writer. Mr. Howells has gone further: he has secreted a book within a book; a profound thing has been done with occult skill, and "A Boy's Town" abounds in curious and pointed contrasts. Three or four of these should be specified.

With the possible exception of two very late pictures of life in the same region, "A Boy's Town" is the homeliest of the author's prose works. There is nothing anomalous in this fact; the anomaly lies in the associated fact that, being the homeliest, it should also be the most poetic.

Again, the book is skillfully adapted to boys, yet its maturity shames the adult.

Yet again, while it gets within the boy, dramatizes his attitude, employs the vocabulary of his thought, it retains the power to survey him from a thoughtful eminence.

Still further, it is, in a quiet way, exultantly and healthily animal, yet its pathos is clinging and profound.

The world painted in this little volume, in which phrases like The Canal and its Basin, Schools and Teachers, Manners and Customs, Plays and Pastimes, Circuses and Shows, introduce the homely chapters, is the world of everyday and everybody, as distinguished from the world of the strong person and the rare event. The psychology is generic; deed and doer are each referred to its class. "My boy," as the author calls his earlier and elder self with a pathos which steadily accumulates, is one boy among others. He plainly wanted to be of his *kind*, though I fancy that he liked his world less than the sense of being of his world. The boys cling together in the great, the almost frightening, loneliness which divides their little clan from the encompassing adult world in which they move like waifs and refugees.

The self-centred life of the boy, his *ad hominem* or *ad puerum* view of the universe, is reflected with a clearness that blames and pardons in the same breath. "Like the savage, he dwells on an earth round which the whole solar system revolves, and he is himself the centre of all life on the earth."

The fatalism of society, the certainty of fusion with one's associates, is not less poignantly set forth. Much of the humor springs out of the finality, the adamantine and monumental aspect, which provisional and perishable things present to the frailty of the unproved intelligence. To that strange beginning known as childhood, all things are ultimata. The pathos is as genuine as the humor. Men have been wont to mourn the recession of that felicity and innocence which discriminates childhood from the sins and shadows of later life; for Mr. Howells the pathos of boyhood is its resemblance to maturity. The errors of the child are inevitable, but they are serious, not trivial or diverting. They are the prologue and the parable of man's later groping, or rather of man's jostling and buffeting at the hands of an unceremonious and close-mouthed universe. The core of meaning is that voiced by Maeterlinck at the close of "Pelléas and Mélisande": "'T was a poor little mysterious being, like everybody."

Maeterlinck has set his moral in a world of fantasy in which one might be a poor little mysterious being as reasonably and congruously as anything else. The art of Mr. Howells is finer and subtler in so far as it extracts the same meaning from a plain record of unvarnished actualities.

I have no doubt that a reader unfamiliar with the book would form an altogether erroneous notion of its tenor and content from the paragraphs in which I have abridged its purport. Its usual tone is suggested by the following extract:

> To run off was held to be the only way for a boy to right himself against the wrongs and hardships of a boy's life. As far as the Boy's Town was concerned, no boy had anything to complain of; the boys had the best time in the world there, and in a manner they knew it. But there were certain things that they felt no boy ought to stand, and these things were sometimes put upon them at school, but usually at home. In fact, nearly all the things that a fellow intended to run off for were done to him by those who ought to have been the kindest to him. Some boys' mothers had the habit of making them stop and do something for them just when they were going away with the fellows. Others would not let them go in swimming as often as they wanted, and, if they saw them with their shirts on wrong-side-out, would not believe that they could get turned in climbing a fence.

> Others made them split kindling and carry in wood, and even saw wood. None of these things, in a simple form, was enough to make a boy run off, but they prepared his mind for it, and when complicated with whipping, they were just cause for it. Weeding the garden, though, was a thing that, almost in itself, was enough to make a fellow run off.

The style is tanned, barefooted, straw-hatted, with stubbed hands and brown finger-nails. It is not first made homely and afterward artistic; it is kept homely, or, if the two elements meet, the homeliness reaps three fourths of the profits of the compact.

The style of the above passage is impersonative; its view is concentric with the boy's. But I have already shown that the pathos and poetry which signalize the work are the result of an antipodal method — the contemplation of the boy from an eminence. I am by no means sure that the plan of combining these opposites was judicious, but I am sure that the result is happy.

"My Year in a Log Cabin," which appears in a tiny volume in the Black and White Series, is like "A Boy's Town" in the poetic cast it imparts to the recital of unburnished actualities. But the reconciliation, though not less cordial, is effected on easier terms from a shorter mutual distance. The author has not gone so far into the boy's consciousness to find his picture or so deep into the man's soul to obtain his poetry. The impersonation is dropped; the style is enriched; and the simple details borrow lustre and aroma from an atmosphere in which thought and affection, humor and melancholy, are mixed in proportions which tradition has familiarized and sanctioned. The experience was varied and prolific beyond that recounted in "A Boy's Town," and the minute volume is a confection of landscape, anecdote, manners, pathos, characterization, thought, religion, literature. Not much pains is taken to bind these diversities together, but they show no wish to fall apart. I think the sketch little short of perfect in its kind.

II

MY LITERARY PASSIONS

The biographical facts in "My Literary Passions" have been already summarized, and its literary judgments may be deferred to the section on Criticism. I am here concerned mainly with its worth as literature.

It is a book of one hundred and eighty-nine pages, in thirty-five sections, and its topic is the successive or simultaneous affection of Mr. Howells for some fifty or sixty authors of somewhat divergent epochs and widely scattered nationalities. The book is autobiography, not criticism, and the first twenty-seven sections, in which autobiography is sovereign, possess an interest which declines materially in the seven or eight terminal chapters, in which criticism takes the chair. The author calls his affections "passions," and he has put into his story, not only the earnestness, but the tremor, the glamour, and the ardor which other men reserve for the adventures of the heart. In "My Year in a Log Cabin," he tells how a duckling once came up in his very grasp, and how its wild heart bounded against his hand. The phrase almost describes the mingled sense of privilege and sacrilege with which the reader finds himself in contact with the palpitations of this youthful and aspiring heart. He is a stolid reader if his own heart is not stirred, shaken, wrung, by what he may guess to be the half-involuntary picture of the plain and frugal, but eager, tremulous, and glowing life reflected in these luminous and limpid pages. Nothing was wanting to make the work the most exquisite, the most appealing, of idyls, except the will to make it so; but the author, with an incorruptible honesty and modesty, refused to allow himself either the decoration or the prominence which the fulfillment of such a purpose would exact. In his own mind he is telling plain facts about an average stripling, and the warmth and poetry enter self-invited.

We are introduced to a nature seeking to disburden itself of the potential admiration and reverence that overflow and overcharge its life by the discovery of books on which it can lavish — I had almost said, wreak — its affection. We read it with that pity and terror which fill the spectator of any profound and quivering sensitiveness in the grotesque diversities and cruel maladjustments of the world. Chaucer's lines in "The Parlement of Foules" revisit the memory:

> The lyf so short, the craft so long to lerne,
> The assay so sharp, so hard the conquering,
> The dredful joye, that alwey slit so yerne.

The reader may think it strange, if he will, that the review of early aspiration from the peak of unexampled fulfillment should inspire any other sentiment than that of sympathetic exultation. Nevertheless, in the story of this groping lad, so pathetic in his triumphs and so enviable in the worst of his defeats, on whom the later Howells looked back with a humor and tenderness that complement and justify each other, the core of melancholy in "A Boy's Town" reappears: one is so tiny, so alone, in a world so great, which one can change so little.

The record is internal, but there is no dearth of objectivity. People and things are etched clearly, but always passingly, abstractedly, as the group of loafers on a station platform, the hurrying trucks, and the dismounting passengers might print themselves on the random glance of one who lifted his eyes momentarily from an engrossing book. The style is full of warmth and crispness, but there is an obvious intention to sacrifice elegance to sincerity. I should have liked it even better without the intention and without the sacrifice.

This youthful probation recalls two analogies to the thoughtful reader: one is reminded sometimes of the indomitableness of Stevenson, and sometimes of the vibrancy of Keats.

III

"LITERARY FRIENDS AND ACQUAINTANCE"

This book is a cluster of scattered papers, the authorship of which is itself dispersed over ten years, or twenty years, if "My Mark Twain" be reckoned in the list. They deal with possibly fifty persons, all, I think, Americans by birth or domicile, with degrees of fullness proportionate to the wide diversities in the length and closeness of propinquity. There is not an ill-natured or egotistic word in the volume, and it is improbable that the exclusion of these tempting materials cost the recorder a pang. Mr. Howells treats himself with the satirical indulgence appropriate to an incumbrance from whom escape is inconceivable. He has no more self-love than can make itself thoroughly agreeable under the double easement of an alert self-mockery and an unbounded and unsated interest in others. We like to hear a man who loves others talk about himself; modesty in the tents of egotism is exquisite beyond its wont.

The harvest of fact and anecdote hardly reaches the mark of anticipation. Memory has acted as a sieve even for Mr. Howells, if we reject the less probable theory that his taste has acted as a sieve for the accumulations of his memory. The slightness of some of the anecdotes confirms the impression that the store of facts is not extensive.

These sketches are touched more or less by an error which Mr. Howells delights to reprove in the fiction of others and to illustrate in his own: they explain and comment overmuch. Penelope Lapham's remark that she wished George Eliot would let you find out a little about the characters for yourself might be applied to these reminiscences by a grumbler, if the desire to grumble could outlast the perusal of the book.

The truth is that Mr. Howells seems subject to that rarest of compulsions in the mature American, the necessity for the continuous outpour of fondness on persons who are nothing more than friends. The book is courtly; it is sincere in courtliness. That rich, ample, diffused homage which we associate with ceremony or convention has become for once little less than an outflow of temperament, a voice of nature. I could wish that it had been wholly the voice of nature. The attitude is the man's impulse, but it is also his purpose, almost his formula. With so much kindness I could have got on with less circumspection. Possibly no man ever breathed in whom the dictates of frankness and of discretion would have so nearly coincided, and it seems a pity therefore that the final effect should be one of discretion rather than of frankness.

The supply of aureolas is apparently limitless. The praise is now and again lavished on a person whom one suspects Mr. Howells of not really liking, and it is piquant to detect the aloofness — it never amounts to an aversion — through the embowerment of eulogy in which it is punctiliously hidden. It is curious that the one damaging anecdote in a book which is reverent of ideals should relate to a man as to whom the world has made up its mind that there is nothing damaging to be said.

Sometimes Mr. Howells insists on the merits of a man whom we willfully and presumptuously feel that he has no business to like, or to like so unreservedly, and his picture fails to vindicate his theory. There is his favorite Bret Harte, for instance, of whom he has everything good to say and nothing good to tell. The final picture of Harte waving a valedictory cigar from the back platform of a train which his eagerness for tobacco has almost made him lose, so far from completing our enthrallment, is the touch which procures our liberation. Mr. Howells may be idyllic or pathetic to his heart's content (I disclaim the pun) in the ensuing paragraphs; we are glad that the train has moved off.

The success in individualization is very unequal, and seems unconditioned either by ardor of sympathy or breadth of canvas. Holmes is conveyed to us intact in an excellent full study, but Longfellow, with whom equal pains are taken, is caught by glimpses through the rifts in an aureate cloud. Boyesen, whose claims are stressed, remains a formless centre of panegyric. The earlier Lowell is not only distinctly charming, but charmingly distinct; but the Lowell of later life, while far from a blur, acquires a forlorn individuality by the removal of the edge from the salience of his former contours. He becomes a precisian in dress, an admirer of things English, a claimant of deference from inferiors, the victim of a sort of "baffle" in his moral idealism, a relaxed believer in the life to come. The process is full of nature and interest, and the record, though saddening, is pregnant.

Francis J. Child, though very briefly sketched, breathes humanly in his straitened limits, and a pulse-beat in the elder James is perceptible. In Hawthorne the clear thing is the dimness: he justifies the quoted remark of Holmes: "He is like a dim room with a little taper of personality burning on the corner of the mantel." Walt Whitman is made animate in a few clarifying words, and the wistfulness in the brief sketch of Lincoln is of photographic efficacy. Stedman comes out in black and white, but the Stoddards, on whom equal diligence and even greater love are spent, remain unthankfully nebulous.

I do not rank "Literary Friends and Acquaintance" with that conjuration of profound poetry out of bare commonplace, "A Boy's Town," or with that rare commixture of snow and flame which imparts its fervid and tremulous beauty to the picture of youthful aspiration in "My Literary Passions." But the later work is excellent of its kind, clear, interesting, judicious, the fruit of priceless, because unrecurring, opportunities, and informed with a taste and temper so impeccable that its faults seem merely the projections of its virtues.

IV

"MY MARK TWAIN"

The "Mark Twain" book is a sequel, if not more properly a section, of "Literary Friends and Acquaintance." The problem, as it appeared to Mr. Howells, might be phrased thus: to paint a great native force, generous, riotous, unscrupulous, with absolute candor, yet with a final effect of idealization. An earlier success in the not quite dissimilar problem offered by Fulkerson in "A Hazard of New Fortunes" might have pleaded for a fearless objectivity. But Mr. Howells shrank from a total objectivity in the Mark Twain case, where objectivity was hampered by the obligation of precise conformity to fact. He lacked the ultimate courage; he adduces the facts bravely, almost defiantly; but he wanted the final valor to stand aside and let the sum of the facts explain and justify his hero. He will not leave the reader alone with Mark Twain for five minutes. He qualifies, he adjusts, he tempers; he buries in glosses the text which he is too honest to emend. The reader who sees the precautions taken to avoid offence is half disposed to the inference that offence would be timely.

Mr. Clemens is obscene; in the Howells dialect, he is "Elizabethan." He is grossly profane; this is a "heritage from boyhood," an "impersonal" blasphemy. He tells lies; this is being not "stupidly truthful." He feigns a belief in immortality to relieve an apprehensive wife; this lying is "heroic." He dresses spectacularly before a Congressional committee; this is a "magnificent coup." When he is not wearing a sealskin coat with the fur out, or hiding a matutinal dress suit under an overcoat, he is triumphing in the gayety of an Oxford gown; this is having a "poet-soul." He is uproarious in jubilation at accumulating profits; he has "frenzies of resentment and suspicion"; he is implacable even to the dead; but, in the last analysis, he remains "exquisite."

All this seems very indiscreet. The facts are the best, if not the only, apologists for the facts. The care that Mr. Howells takes of Mark Twain is a virtual acknowledgment that Mark Twain cannot take care of himself. This concession is extreme and needless. Mark Twain would doubtless get into scrapes with the reader, as he got into scrapes in real life; but there is little doubt that his competence for self-extrication would approve itself in the one case as in the other. He was unmistakably a good fellow; he could be brave, tender, generous, regardful of the claims and wishes of inferiors. But Mr. Howells will not be content with this restricted eulogy: he will have it that Mark Twain is oracular and world-centred, a cosmic soothsayer, a Silenus, half-tipsy, half-inspired. But this is not the record, this is exegesis; and I, personally, question its truth.

I need hardly say that almost every word is interesting. Among the passages that attract me are the description of the physique in section VII, the list of good deeds in XIV, the visit to Grant in XVIII, and the end of XXIV, where the relief of a quiet interest betrays the strain to which that living hubbub known as Samuel Clemens has been subjecting us. The meeting of Matthew Arnold and Mark Twain is pregnant in its very whimsicality, and is deeply significant of the moral amplitude of a biographer whose nature was conterminous with both. The faithfulness of Mr. Howells to Mark Twain is a trait of rememberable beauty. It may seem occasionally that his motto in the enterprise is *Credo quia impossibile*, and we may wonder to what closet or *oubliette* of his divided consciousness he remanded his taste in his colloquies with his friend. Possibly Clemens was of so unqualified a crudity that taste died, or fled, at his advent, and forbore the outcries which attest its abiding presence and vitality. But it must not be forgotten that there was the nucleus of a Clemens in Mr. Howells; given a ruder nurture, a robuster make, and a hardier — I do not say a harder — conscience, and the smile which now curves the scholar's plastic lips might have been a paroxysm of the midriff. To call his life an hilarious martyrdom would seem a fantastic exaggeration to readers who find in his serenity and urbanity the refutation of both ends of the antithesis; but the phrase would keep its modicum of truth.

V

"NEW LEAF MILLS"

I have preferred to include among the autobiographies "New Leaf Mills," which, under the evasive appellation of "chronicle," reviews with more fullness and livelier drama the milling enterprise already noted — an enterprise which filled so large a place in the imagination of Mr. Howells's boyhood and the cherished memories of his later life. That the book is mainly true is evident; the line at which truth ceases and enlargement and alteration begin is nowhere palpable. The substitution of the name "Powell" for "Howells" suggests the wish to veil but not to mask the identity, and the o-w-e common to both names recalls the difficulties in which the enterprise had its birth.

I have read "New Leaf Mills" twice. On the first occasion I allowed reminiscences of "Silas Lapham," "Indian Summer," and their kind to govern expectation too exclusively, and I found the book slipshod and aimless. In a second attempt I knew the author better, and the simple beauty of the unaffected record became clear to a wiser preadjustment.

A house is built under the reader's eyes, and something of the cleanly and cheerful disarray of the constructive process, something of the heartening aroma of moist sawdust, is perceptible in its confiding pages. The people live in a log cabin, and the style and art have forgotten their courtly dress and urban ceremony. I should say that the steersmanship of the little craft was competent without being unassailable. I doubt if Mr. Howells has quite made up his mind whether a boy's intelligence or a man's is to regulate the exclusions and rejections. At the date in question he was a boy of thirteen, and to peep at life through chinks, as the boy of thirteen unquestionably does, has its ravishment for the imaginative senior; but a window is none the less a convenience for systematic observation, and Mr. Howells shifts from chink to window at his pleasure. Much of the looseness is not properly looseness, because it is inseparable from the theme and method; but a portion of it is avoidable and voluntary. The book is a family story, and the family knack of taking things for granted, of assuming everybody's wontedness and comprehension, is brought into play with the tact of a veteran.

In one respect the childish point of view has been a godsend to the work. It has kept the story not uncheerful in the face of an accumulation of mournful and baleful circumstances which might have equipped and inspired a tragedy. The enterprise completely fails; a bright-souled brother of Owen Powell dies of irreparable hemorrhages; there is a miller in whose soul hatreds fester under the nurture of gruesome fears and fiery waters; there is a man who is a peon to his neighbor, who is smitten with fatal disease, and whose young children drop one by one like leaflets upon their father's new-made grave; a sneaking lawyer is saved from the lynching plotted by indignant neighbors; a poor young girl is enticed away from security and innocence by the wiles of a terrible mother, to match whose dim grisliness I should be tempted to retrace the current of English literature back to the mother of Grendel in the well-head of the far-off Beowulf.

This is a curious aggregation of sinister events and possibilities for one year of authentic youthful experience on the part of a writer whose novels were to be rather famous for the alleged insufficiency of their happenings. Yet the childish point of view, though unequally sustained, has enabled the author to reconcile justice to all these distresses and malignities, with the retention of the vivacity — I had almost said the frolic — of adventure. The gloom is lightened by the fitful and freakish attention, the inversion of proportions, which imparts originality to that quaint universe which the child shapes out of stereotyped materials. There is, in the childish beholder, a mixture of indifference and awe, which cares less to divide the observed phenomena into goods and evils than to unify and simplify the mass under the common attribute of wonder.

The picture of Owen Powell is consummate. It required both attachment and detachment to be just to the charm of that subtly tempered nature, so mellow in its keenness, so lovable in the provocations it supplies, so helpless in its efficiency, so yielding in its incorrigible persistence. The material in the mother, Ann Powell, is less notable, but the workmanship is hardly less expert. The book, indeed, has everywhere a sharp distinctness; it is a rough-hewn but square-turned block of local and temporal reality, and it is both curious and pleasing that an emanation from senescence and from New York should vivify so keenly for us an hour of boyhood and a plot of Ohio when Mr. Howells and America were both on franker terms with life.

VI

"Years of My Youth"

"Years of My Youth," the latest of the autobiographies, has more of the bearing, the poise, of a classic than works of richer content and larger value, like "A Boy's Town" and "My Literary Passions." I account for this largely by the reasserted dominance of style. The sacrifice of grace to ease is remitted, and I cannot see that the ease appreciably suffers by a change by which the grace so largely benefits. The ovals of the sentences resume the delicacy of their pristine curve. Passages imported almost without change from the carefully written

"My Year in a Log Cabin" and "Impressions and Experiences" reflect no discredit on the modest beauty of their new setting.

The matter is supplemental, or interstitial, to earlier work. Nothing definable as a novel aspect or unforeseen posture is disclosed, unless we choose to except the gay insouciance and reckless buoyancy which mark the inspiriting Columbus days. With this doubtful proviso, it is the old veins that supply the new ore, and the yield is adequate rather than bountiful. We learn things that we prize about the ancestors and the household; the father was already clear, but the mother, the elder brother, and the elder sister emerge into fuller distinctness; the rest merely people the shadow. The curtain is unselfishly lifted from one or two phases of boyish hypochondria, the report of which both terrifies and consoles. There are considerate vignettes of Ohio statesmen of aging or expiring fame. The picture of the gayeties in the "Ohio State Journal" office in the shadow of the foreordained and onrushing Civil War recalls Brussels on the eve of Waterloo. There are fond reversions to early comradeships, the glow of which, even in memory, derides the feeble glimmer which passes for friendship among ordinary men. Mr. Howells speaks of old friends in the tone which other men allot to vanished loves. I have only to add that this book, written in the penumbra of the author's eighties, reveals a spirit in which youth is invincible.

I mention here, for want of a better place, three minor works adjacent to biography. "Stories of Ohio" sketches the picturesque and dramatic side of the annals of the state, with an adaptation to youthful readers the more perfect for the address which conceals the fact of adaptation. "A Little Girl among the Old Masters" is a series of drawings by a young child, presumably the novelist's daughter, to which the father furnished the explanatory letter-press. The thing is slight, but his friends could not spare it. It is handled with a deft politeness and winning deference, and the irony is demure enough to maintain its incognito for the youthful artist and censor, who insisted on the expurgation of jest. "The Flight of Pony Baker" is an example of that type of literary felicity of which Goethe's "Hermann and Dorothea" is the renowned and capital exemplar. Concern, in the pose of unconcern, arrives at mastery; or — by another version of the fact — a momentary relapse occurs to the ingenious and solicitous artist — a relapse into perfection. A few simple happenings in everyday boyhood are conveyed to us through the boy's eye and tongue, and the curious and charming result is a book which neither overshoots the capacities of boys nor undershoots the requirements of maturity. The obviousness in the child, which only subtlety in the man could recover and reproduce, evokes an original psychology in whose charm the subtle and the obvious cohere. The work resembles "A Boy's Town"; it is even stronger than "A Boy's Town" in its unerring maintenance of key, though it lacks the profound and touching under-note which gave poetry and distinction to that homespun idyl.

CHAPTER III

Journeyings and Parleyings

"THERE are some sorts of light literature," — says Mr. Howells in "Literature and Life," — "once greatly in demand, but now apparently no longer desired by magazine editors, who ought to know what their readers desire. Among these is the travel sketch, to me a very agreeable kind, and really to be regretted in its decline." His own work in this field, in which a broken pursuit is the witness of an unbroken attachment, began early in 1866 with "Venetian Life," and had not ended in 1913, the date of "Familiar Spanish Travels." To show the compass of this work in time and space, I shall list briefly the chief publications, including dates and places (wherever doubtful), and adding in parenthesis the novels of the road and rail.

Venetian Life, 1866.
Italian Journeys, 1872.
(*Their Wedding Journey*, 1872; Niagara and Canada).
(*A Chance Acquaintance*, 1873; Canada).
Three Villages, 1884; Lexington, Mass., Shirley, Mass., Gnadenhütten, Ohio.
A Little Swiss Sojourn, 1892.
Tuscan Cities, 1894.
(*Their Silver Wedding Journey*, 1899; Germany).
Literature and Life, 1902; in which a few papers, mostly American, deal with travel.
(*The Kentons*, 1902; Holland).
London Films, 1905.
Certain Delightful English Towns, 1906.
Roman Holidays, 1908.
Seven English Cities, 1910.
Familiar Spanish Travels, 1913.

An author's travels are commonly much of a piece, and justify the critic in enlarging on the general method and condensing on particular books. Three great merits are universal in these works: clearness of vision transmitted in equal clearness of voice, perennial sympathy, perennial humor. The books are all good, and yet perhaps not quite so good as might be inferred from their equal possession of what may be described with mild exaggeration as unceasing charm. I shall note their inequality as books, and shall try to explain how works can differ so much in satisfactoriness which differ so little, or so much less, in felicity.

I

THE VEHICLE

The method has three properties: it is subjective, it is emotional, and it is granulated. The centre is interior, in the traveller's consciousness. In general, he is to record only what he felt and felt distinctly, the æsthetic sense being counted among the feelings; though this rule is not to be construed so strictly as to shut out the brief record of a useful practical detail or pertinent reflection. Lastly, the order will be the order of experience, which means in travel the order of space and time; the chapters will stand for places, the paragraphs for hours or minutes. The writer will find both orders in his pocket, the first in his pocket-map, the second in his watch.

It is clear that, if one admits nothing or very little that does not markedly prick the sensibilities, and if one groups these punctures in the order, not of their affinities, but of their proximities by calendar or clock, the method implies detachment and almost favors disintegration. An impartial and dispersed enthusiasm — if such a thing exists — might countervail this difficulty; but Mr. Howells is a man whose enthusiasm is as selective as his curiosity is universal. I have, in some of the works, in "Italian Journeys," for instance, a feeling of slimness and poverty growing out of the very rigor of the exclusions that have been made in my behalf. Mr. Howells has gone through his orchard, and has cut out the single delectable morsel from the sunny side of every peach, and has feasted me with this compact and culled munificence; but when I see these morsels ranged together on my plate, I do not feel exultant — I feel forlorn. But for the thanklessness, I could almost say, "Give me a whole peach, stone and rind." This is true of "Italian Journeys" and its class; in luckier works, the difficulty, while never unfelt, is largely counteracted.

Another invariable factor and occasional fault is the space which is reserved in these condensed narratives for the waiter, the cabman, the guide, the porter, and other operators on the pocket of the American travelling public. The effect of these matters in actual travel is secondary and parenthetic, though it often happens, in life and letters both, that the parenthesis is the least forgettable member of the sentence. Does it follow that because these episodes are vivid in transit they should be salient in the retrospect? When an author throws aside one half or two thirds of the artistic material as trite or technical, but husbands and hoards every anecdote of traffic, proportions are seemingly displaced. I am reminded of the ingenious lover in Labiche who remarked of the painting by which he hoped to flatter the vanity of his bourgeois patron that he had ordered a very small Mont Blanc and an immense Perrichon.

Individually, the passages in question are often charming. No subject has furnished Mr. Howells with more jokes or better jokes than tipping. The gleam of his wit follows that of his silver with a regularity that seems the index in both kinds of an exhaustless plenty. If I undertook to blue-pencil the allusions to this topic, I should quail at the task of placating his readers even if I succeeded in forgiving myself. All this does not preclude a sense of incongruity in the final picture, in which I seem to behold an eccentric Spain or Italy with a baldric on its shoulders and a napkin on its arm.

The impression of detachment, tenuity, and disparity is absent or latent in the happier works. In "Venetian Life," for instance, to which four years of domicile have contributed, the experience has width and depth as well as length, and the author can block out his impressions of Venice instead of merely "chalking them out." He has Emerson's advantage in "English Traits," the advantage of writing a train of essays rather than a string of memoranda. In "London Films" and in "Familiar Spanish Travels" the effect of inconsequence is lessened by the eagerness and fervor of the tone. And here a crumb of explanation is imperative.

Lowell's sketch of Italy is in form quite as desultory as "Italian Journeys" or "Tuscan Cities." But the inconsequence is scarcely perceptible; the abounding lustihood, the tameless exuberance, of Lowell's temper suffices not only to fill the interstices but to cement the gaps. A similar, though slighter, effect is observable in Dickens's "Pictures from Italy." Mr. Howells, however, is of lighter make than Lowell or Dickens, and it is the lighter side of his constitution that is oftenest dominant in his books of travel. It is curious to compare the pictures of travel in his books of fact and books of fiction, to observe how a page of reality in Florence or Venice seems like lattice-work or wicker-work by the side of the firm grain and serried fibre of a page of fiction in the forgotten Saratoga of "An Open-Eyed Conspiracy" or the noteless Campobello of "April Hopes." One might almost say, if one did not say it too seriously, that reality is the dissipation by which Mr. Howells relieves a mind overtasked by the strenuosities of fiction. It is like that book over which Sarah Battle unbent her mind in the intervals of her activities at whist.

Mr. Howells himself, under cover of the third person, will tell us frankly what he thinks about travelling: —

Formerly he enjoyed travel with all its necessary concomitants. It amused him to check his baggage and depart from stations, to arrive at hotels and settle himself in new rooms; the very domiciliation in sleeping-cars or the domestication in diners had a charm which was apparently perennial; a trip on a river-boat was rapture; an ocean voyage was ecstasy. The succession of strange faces, new minds, was an unfailing interest, and there was no occurrence, in or out of the ordinary, which did not give him release from self and form a true recreation.

This "little glow" had its retributive "little shiver," to re-apply the phrases in Praed's ballad. The following is from "Their Silver Wedding Journey": "Suddenly he felt himself as tired as she looked, with that sense of the futility of travel which lies in wait for everyone who profits by travel." This was written after sixty; but at thirty-five, in the earlier "Wedding Journey," he had exposed the make-believe of travellers in the following sentence: "Here a whole empire had been lost and won, Basil reminded Isabel; and she said, 'Only think of it!' and looked to a wandering fold of her skirt, upon which the rain beat through a rent of the curtain." Two pages farther on, the satire cuts perhaps even more deeply in the nonchalant phrase, "some vague and patronizing intention to revere." Mr. Howells knows how often admiration must be nursed to keep it warm, how often nursing itself is ineffectual.

Mr. Howells is in love with Venice, yet his candor is anything but loverlike. He is irritated by its stagnation, averse to its writers, indifferent to its painting, nauseated by its Renaissance architecture, indignant at its filth, intolerant alike of the license and the dullness of its society. The reader's enthusiasm contends with these disenchantments as half-heartedly as the Venetian *scaldini* with the encroaching chill. The author loves Tuscany and Florence, but if you open "Tuscan Cities" to warm your soul with his outflowing ardor, you will bask with difficulty in that fitful and elusive sunshine. Here is an affection that has outlived — in part, at least — its secure faith in its own reasonableness. There is always the same alacrity of praise, the same revulsion of doubt, the heart hoodwinking the eyes, and the eyes, in their turn, unmasking the heart. If the latter phrases are excessive, let me hedge a little in the paragraph which follows.

Why is it that a meal which the traveller ate with surly patience becomes quite uneatable in the report of the menu which he amplifies for the amused listener? Why is it that a play which is far more bad than good may yield an evening which is rather good than bad, better certainly than an evening spent at home? Because, in the first case, the listener, balancing the cook's successes against his failures, ignores the counterweight which made the meal endurable to the consumer — the appetite. Because, in the second case, the evening is made tolerable by expectation, by the excitement which even disappointment affords, and by the amusement derived from one's skill in demonstrating that the evening was intolerable. The application to these books of travel is plain. In Mr. Howells the appetite is insatiable; it is not affected to-day by yesterday's bad meal; it is not affected by that doubt of its own genuineness which followed yesterday's good meal in a sequence to which satiation is always liable. His interest is forever renascent. But the reader who judges by the result without the prospect, or, if you please, by the palate without the stomach, feels a discouragement which outruns the mind of the author and the warrant of the facts. To rephrase the matter, Mr. Howells is a man subject to enchantment, to disenchantment, and to reënchantment; but in these books the second process is particularized, while the first and third are in a way assumed. This does not mean that happy moments are not plentiful and are not duly recorded; only there are enough disappointments and discomforts to cool the reader's wish for a replica of the experience.

The mood, then, in these works is powerful; in one aspect it is decisive. It cannot decide whether the book is good or bad; the merit of all the records is unquestionable. But it decides whether the admiration with which we close the volume shall expand into satisfaction, or shall absorb a tincture of unrest. The mood has been least helpful in "Tuscan Cities" and "Italian Journeys." It has been most bountiful, for reasons which I shall explain later, in "Familiar Spanish Travels" and in "London Films."

A word is due to the topics most often handled in this group of works. Landscape is touched with fondness, but not aggrandized; one is spared the picture — at any rate, the picture framed and hung. The weather, which has nourished so many conversations, does not refuse its aliment to this sprightly literature. The shrubs and trees are called up with a touch which is almost a greeting, and the songs of the birds are noted with a tender piety.

In the fine arts Mr. Howells expressly disclaims the authority which he virtually reclaims from time to time in the decisiveness of some repudiations. The meekest of us feel that there is an authority in our disgusts. He is divided, like many another able and sincere man, between the sense of his want of technique and his trust in a feeling for truth in which he suspects that he excels the technicians. Having told us roundly that Guido's Michael is ridiculous (in conception, not in execution), he adds repentantly: "I had little feeling about it and less knowledge." Among the arts his preference is architecture. The descriptions are humanely brief.

History and literature spot the composition with perpetual reference, but they are not taken too seriously. They are purveyors of admirable pretexts for trips to beguiling new places or beloved old places through smiling landscapes on benignant days. The author is courteous rather than obsequious to great names; the man is a new fragrance for the place. When he visits the house where Severn tended Keats, there is a tender, hushed moment of reminiscence, but there are no solemnities and no dissertation. Toward history his attitude is debonair. He affects a half-conscientious, half-whimsical interest in many persons whom he barely remembers, or remembers more lucidly by the aid of the guide-book. He laughs at his own ignorance or forgetfulness, and is candid as to the sources of his repaired knowledge; one suspects that in this matter, as elsewhere, he thinks ruin quite as respectable as restoration, and, after all, the knowledge which he mocks is wide enough to deter the wary reader from comparing it with his personal equipment. Occasionally, in "Venetian Life" and in "Tuscan Cities," for instance, Mr. Howells mounts the platform and unfolds a chapter of formal history to the perplexed hearer, questioning if the man behind the lectern be really his old playfellow.

On hotels and railway carriages he is fastidious and circumstantial; indeed, the emphasis on comfort is unvarying. He displays a redoubtable exigency offset by an exquisite patience. His fortune in meals is punctiliously reported, and his descriptions of unwarmed rooms in Italy and Spain fairly numb the fingers with which the indignant reader turns the leaves. Cleanliness is a major point, and the tribulations of the nose in European travel are set down with respectful diligence. I have spoken of his interest in fee-takers of all sorts; between people and things the choice falls normally on people. A mountain will do in default of a muleteer, and a cathedral may occupy a tolerant mind in the absence or quiescence of the sacristan. Travel- and table-companions are sedulously observed and conserved; his attitude toward the Latin races in the mass might be described as cupidity. He wants to capture them, and bear them off. His affection for certain Chilians whom he is always meeting in Spain becomes almost riotous, and the dark-eyed boy whom he has not thought of abducting and carrying off to America must have been visited by nature with some birth-mark or infirmity.

On the street his eye and heart are both open. Anecdotes visit him rather less often than the warmth of their reception would lead us to expect. Possibly the pointed incident declines to show itself to a wayfarer so hospitable to the incident that hardly achieves point. The following extract from "Roman Holidays" contains so much of Mr. Howells, so much of what estranges him from the foolish and endears him to the wise, that I quote it in full.

> Two pretty girls, smartly dressed in hats and gowns exactly alike, and doubtless sisters, if not twins, passed down to the same level. One was with a handsome young officer, and walked staidly beside him, as if content with her quality of captive or captor. The other was with a civilian of whom she was apparently not sure. Suddenly she ran away from him to the verge of the next fall of steps, possibly to show him how charmingly she was dressed, possibly to tempt him by her grace in flight to follow her madly. But he followed sanely and slowly, and she waited for him to come up, in a capricious quiet, as if she had not done anything or meant anything. That was all; but I am not hard to suit; and it was richly enough for me.

Responsibilities are slackened in these records of travel. Weighty reflections are inserted here and there, not with levity or nonchalance, but with a reduction of their weight which adapts them to a recreative setting. When an incident of travel reaches its probe into the sensitive tissue of the author's profoundest and saddest convictions, the ensuing comment is respectful of his graver mood without prejudice to his lighter errand. Travel at any age is youth for Mr. Howells, and it is amazing to note how little the large difference between an early and a ripe novel, "A Chance Acquaintance" and "April Hopes," for instance, is reflected in the far longer interval which separates "Venetian Life" from "Familiar Spanish Travels." Indeed, the sadder and weightier period is responsible for the sprightlier and nimbler book. The fact, which is no paradox, should have its weight in a final survey of the temperamental contrasts in Mr. Howells.

II

The Route

"Venetian Life," in the later and larger form which grew out of its marked success with the public, is rather too long for its effect of informality. I imagine Mr. Howells staying an hour and a half after a preliminary refusal to sit down. This effect does not exclude the impression of solidity arising from the cohesion of topics on which I have already dwelt.

In no book of its class is the mixture of illusion and disillusion so insistent. A strong initial prepossession has fraternized with an equally strong iconoclastic realism, and the co-heirs have divided the estate, without logic indeed, but without bickering. A reader exigent of simplicity might be disconcerted. He might even ask whether Mr. Howells stoned at night the image to which he knelt in the morning to pay his orisons.

I like best the sketches of modern Venetian character; here realism, insight, sympathy convene. The full-dress passages, the descriptions of land, water, and architecture, are sincere in the ethical sense, but they reflect moods that are unmistakably fostered and encouraged. They furnish the due muster of specifications, but they are not effectually, not rememberably, specific; the residuum in the mind is a hovering and dreamy pleasure. It is different with the popular modernities: the facts avail no less than the sentiments, because the sentiments lodge in the crannies of the facts.

"Italian Journeys" and "Tuscan Cities" are books in which disappointment variegates felicity. That is seemingly the author's view of Italy; that is the reader's impression of the books. Here again, the chief success is with the living people; they are idealized without being flattered — the form of idealization highest in itself and most congenial to Mr. Howells. I am uneasy at so much history; the recital is expert, but savors of a convention which is hardly dispelled by the frequent recurrence of the most sanely unconventional remarks. Siena furnishes the best chapter to "Tuscan Cities"; in "Italian Journeys" I prefer Pompeii, depicted with a pensive ardor which reaches finality in the sigh, "You cannot repeat great happiness." The book includes a trace of everything; there is a very sympathetic, or at least very laudatory, account of the Protestant ragged schools at Naples, and there is a record of some burlesque highway adventures at Forza Maggiore, in which the artistic means are so superior to the end as to circumvent it by their very distinction.

"Three Villages" need not detain us. "Lexington," written with punctilious care for an English periodical, is a concise miscellany marked by agreeable personalities and by a criticism of Matthew Arnold's "Word" which is charming in the suavity of its remonstrance. "Shirley," less solicitous of style, recurs respectfully to the Shakers, and is full of that brand of sympathy which might be defined as sympathy on its best behavior. "Gnadenhütten," in which the mature man goes back to one of the early calamities and infamies in the state of his birth, is an inspiriting proof that local affection may outlast the decay of the habits and tradition that were its cradle.

"A Little Swiss Sojourn" is one of those monographs to which the lapse of time is hardly favorable. The years convert journalism into chronicle, and the fragmentariness which is excusable, and even enjoyable, in news, seems volatile and debonair in history.

In most other points these sketches are praiseworthy. They neither deck nor disfigure the facts. The humor is very quiet, very suave, very demure in its slyness. The elastic pronoun "we," which leaves half or more than half its freightage in a gracious twilight, seems here to include both the wife and the children in its generous embrace.

In "Literature and Life," the reader has the exceptional advantage of observing critical essays and pictures of travel in instructive proximity. The preference falls to the critical essays. The only other point which claims notice is the great superiority of "Floating Down the River on the O-hi-o" to all the other travel sketches in the volume. Mr. Howells was here on the solid ground — solid ground none the less for being literally moving fluid — of vivid and vigorous youthful association, and the emotion integrates and vivifies the work.

It is for a similar reason that "London Films," published in 1905, is superior in force and attraction to "Tuscan Cities" and "Italian Journeys." It is not quite easy to say why this work, not distinguished from its kind by any obvious affluence of contents or compactness of adjustment, should impress us as "filled in" to an extent undiscoverable in most of its companions. The density of London possibly aids in stopping up the crevices in the portrayal. But I incline to lay more stress on the snugness of Mr. Howells's domiciliation in the subject. There is a lodged contentment, a seated and imbedded comity, which differs widely from the wayward, flitting eagerness of the Italian work. The author purrs (as Holmes would have said), or croons; he stretches himself like a dog upon the great rug of the peaceful and portly metropolis, with a cosy sense of littleness which includes a feeling of possession.

Mr. Howells narrows his field more and more evidently to the footway of personal experience. He tells us in a pregnant sentence that successive visits have confirmed him in a "diffident inconclusion on all important points to which I hope the pages following will bear witness." Hearsay and reading are sparingly consulted, and even the generalization which throws its light arch between particulars is put aside as an impertinence in two senses. His readers will thank him for not carrying his surrender to particulars so far as to exclude the following delectable generality. "I should say, with much fear of contradiction and scornful laughter, that it [London] was pretty, that it was endearingly nooky, cornery, curvy, with the enchantment of flowers and trees everywhere mixed with its civic turmoil, and the song of birds heard through the staccato of cabs, and the muffled bellow of omnibuses."

Mr. Howells's Americanism asserts itself healthily in the foreign capital by despatching him on commemorative errands to all the nooks and corners which had a share in the planting or rearing of colonies in the New World. He wishes to see the church in which Calvert, the founder of Maryland, was baptized, and the house or the street in which the wife of Elder Brewster of Plymouth Colony was born and bred. Patriotism could go no further.

It is curious that "Certain Delightful English Towns," which belongs to the same country and the next year, should be one of the works which I recall with misgiving. I suspect an inconsequence of attitude. Only a consuming passion for antiquities could justify the time that Mr. Howells spends in hunting up objects of major, of minor, of minute significance, or the space which he allots to the recital of these excursions. But when we probe the knowledge of this devout antiquarian, it is scant, and, when we analyze his manner, it is sportive. He has no business, we tell ourselves, to take so seriously things that he takes so airily. We are asked to accept things at Mr. Howells's valuation, while all the time he laughs at himself, and frisks and gambols about the monuments to which he has gravely insisted that we shall devoutly accompany him. The protestations of rapture are manifold, but moments come when we ask ourselves if these ardors do not resemble the English fire so often reprimanded in these pages — the spectrum of warmth without its actuality.

Yet, when all is said, few writers have equalled Mr. Howells in the clearness with which the compact density of English monuments and associations is conveyed. The plum-cake is more richly raisined than ever.

To make the treatment of English life consecutive, I shall speak here of "Seven English Cities" and "Stratford-on-Avon," in spite of the brief temporal priority of "Roman Holidays."

After "London Films" and "Certain Delightful English Towns," "Seven English Cities" may be said to gather up the fragments, that nothing be lost, but it would be calumny to imply that the fragments are unpalatable. Before industrial England, — Liverpool, Manchester, Sheffield, — the artist in Mr. Howells preserves a strange complacence, the social moralist a rare composure. The antiquary has his satisfactions in peeling York, if I may so word the process which penetrates to the ancient core of that historic town by stripping off its modern envelopes; and a chapter is piously allotted to that older Boston whose fame has been at once both assured and bedimmed by its transatlantic namesake. Two sketches of Welsh watering-places stretch themselves smilingly in the sun like indolent bathers, and the debonair volume surprises itself by a penetrating and pregnant final chapter, in which "English Character" is genially epitomized.

In "Seen and Unseen at Stratford-on-Avon," Mr. Howells has diversified the placid and equable record of visits, drives, and teas in that place and its environs by the bold device of the resuscitation of Shakespeare. The two worlds meet without embarrassment; a page of journal or its equivalent borders a page of fantasy, and the obvious nests in the rifts of the superhuman, like a sparrow in the nooks of a cathedral. Shakespeare is ease and good-nature itself, and waives his ghostship and his fame with a gayety before which awe and constraint incontinently vanish.

Devices of this kind have their peril as well as their spell. They offer seemingly a great initial advantage, but after this phantasm of help the artist is thrown back upon his normal resources to meet the abnormal expectations his device has aroused in the reader. A work of one hundred and twelve pages is long enough to incur these liabilities, and Mr. Howells is doubtless fortunate in the tact which has retrenched anticipation by humanizing his ghost and normalizing his celebrity. In another point his discretion is more questionable. It appears that spirits leave eternity for time, as nuns leave their convent for the street, only in pairs. Shakespeare's companion is Francis Bacon, a croaking and crotchety Bacon, the victim of a form of moral rheumatism, the Don John, as it were, to Shakespeare's Don Pedro, for whom the reader's comment is the phrase of Beatrice: "I can never see him but I am heart-burned an hour after."

Shakespeare himself resembles his American creator, or re-creator, in his power to dissemble an eventual seriousness. The "light, fantastic toe," the tripping sprightliness, with which he disallows the claim to reverence serve only to postpone the discovery that he is a Shakespeare remodelled in the image, or at least in the taste, of Mr. Howells. He protects the poor from injustice; his ridicule of the lower classes is imbued with the tenderness of self-mockery; he is the most delicately loyal of husbands, and his breaches of conjugal fidelity pursue him with remorse; he is even tractable to Mr. Howells in finding his own comedies censurable on the score of intermittent grossness, silliness, or horse-play. His modernity is immaculate; he can even furnish his auditor with points on the latest encroachments of the triumphant films in Venice; in fact, although this visit to earth is nominally episodic, we gather the impression that eternity is a vast auditorium in which the relation of the dead to the living is that of audience to performers. The coincidence of Shakespeare's ethics with those of Mr.

Howells is so precise that the poet is able to utter his personal views in the form of quotation from the works of his beaming interlocutor. It is part of the mixture of seriousness and truth in this decorously gamesome fantasy that Shakespeare — the imagined Shakespeare — and Mr. Howells should both really venerate the truth to which they conspire to give an enunciation so burlesque.

"Roman Holidays and Others" is, after "Venetian Life," the best of the Italian pictures. The wrappage of Spain and Madeira which encloses the parcel reveals, when untied, a rich, many-folded Roman fabric, with Naples and Tuscany as a broad selvage from which Genoa droops like a costly fringe. The book is of firmer tissue than "Italian Journeys" or "Tuscan Cities," and turns oftener to those weighty general topics — New Rome, the two-days strike, the present Italian government — which should compact and solidify a work of travel. Yet the treatment as a whole is far from rigid: in the succession of Roman topics it almosts basks in disorder; it abounds in straying and sportive reminiscence; it has nooks of sentiment in which one fancies a vague kinship to one's dusky recollections of "Paul and Virginia," or the "Sentimental Journey"; its humor, which spares nothing and wounds nothing, is a sprightliness that sometimes borders on giddiness, and is so irrepressible that it bubbles up gayly in a passage in which he asks kind people to show pity to neglected graves. The amiability of the book is superlative; the reader could not wish it less — or more.

"Familiar Spanish Travels," the latest work of its kind, if we omit "Stratford," is perhaps the foremost in attractiveness. The author, now progressing in the seventies, frankly assumes the part of an old man — a confession which has the grace of magnanimity, since his thought and style had agreed to guard the secret from the world. The tenderness quite unmixed with pity which the avowal excites in the reader blends pleasingly with the image of his daughter's companionship. Moreover, in these Spanish travels, a very early dream has found a very late fruition, and the years that had elapsed between hope and realization seemed at times to be swept from the calendar in the glow of rediscovered boyhood. Spain is viewed, now in the ungarnished clearness of realistic maturity, now through the double mirage to which those two romanticists, childhood and old age, have offered each its contribution. The book profits by that warmth of tone which serves as the common solvent, and therefore as the fitting cement, of otherwise inconsequent material.

III

SPY-GLASS AND EYE-GLASS

I shall consider in this section those sketches and essays which cannot properly be classed under either travel or criticism. They consist of three volumes widely separated in time: "Suburban Sketches" (1872), "Impressions and Experiences" (1896), and "Imaginary Interviews and Other Essays," extracted from the "Easy Chair" (1910). The Easy Chair papers contain some critical writing.

"Suburban Sketches" consists mainly of passing pictures of simple life in a Boston suburb. About half the sketches are modestly successful, with no enduring claim on the attention of criticism. Three or four are profoundly interesting to the student of literature and of human nature, as illustrations of the literary distemper which may arise when a man, not yet firm in his art, is resolved to be daringly simple and munificently literary in the same breath. The meritorious and forgettable sketches are "Mrs. Johnson," "A Doorstep Acquaintance" (keen drawings of mendicancy), "By Horse-Car to Boston," "A Romance of Real Life" (genuinely remarkable as to its facts), "Scene" (overwrought and perhaps under-felt tragedy), "Some Lessons from the School of Morals," and "Flitting."

The interesting scapegraces in the book are "A Day's Pleasure," "Jubilee Days," and, with less gravity in the offence, "A Pedestrian Tour." Were these sketches dateless, I should have supposed that they had been fished up out of that "standing water between boy and man" which yields so many curiosities to the literary naturalist; they were published, however, in book form, in 1872, when Mr. Howells was thirty-five, and had been for several years the competent editor of the "Atlantic Monthly."

The author has gallantly and yet tremulously essayed the task of portraying plain and simple things, and has sought a solace for his misgivings and an exit from his straits in every form of digression, transformation, and masquerade. The case demands a simile. Suppose that in "A Chance Acquaintance" Mr. Arbuton had really married Kitty; suppose that he magnanimously resolved to introduce her to the social aristocracy, but first made her over by insistent pressure to conform to his relentless taste. Kitty represents the everyday material in these sketches. If only the author would trust his fact enough to say it frankly and have done with it; if only the proportion of Howells to nature were less overwhelming! The felicities are incessant, but lack support; the stems do not hold up the blossoms. In "A Day's Pleasure," we have the fortune appropriate to pleasure-trips in finding ourselves knocked up by the strenuosities of the effort made, under the author's guidance, in the interest of agreeable relaxation. The style is not labored; it is easy. But the ease only aggravates the friction. The poor fact, obliged to yield up the last vestige of interest by the inhuman pressure to which it is subjected, is constrained to reply with a cheerful affirmative to the query, "You don't mind this, do you?" "Jubilee Days" is even worse in the addition of cloying panegyric to a literary form definable as journalism at once inspired and diseased.

These errors have no weight in the appraisal of Mr. Howells's output as a whole. They occupy at most a hundred and forty pages in a secondary and inconspicuous work, and the curious properties they exhibit never reappear. As pathology they interest the specialist.

"Impressions and Experiences" is a volume of eight essays. Exclusive of criticism and travel, they are the single book of essays produced by Mr. Howells in his meridian, and this fact gives point to their autobiographic tendency. The title, of course, professes or confesses this direction, but the title is a result rather than a purpose, and there is no complementary volume, if we except criticism, to redress the scale in favor of generalities. This fact is the key to a curious little antithesis. Nobody generalizes more persistently than Mr. Howells; the comprehensive reflection incrusts — some would say, infests — the later novels; yet, outside of criticism, his fidelity to the trail of individual experience is a valuable and noticeable fact. The explanation is not remote. Mr. Howells is passionately fond of the generality that borders the particular, the generality that is divided from the particular by a single step of the mind, and is still instinct with the aroma and warmth of the concrete world which it has barely and passingly forsaken. The *procreative* generality, the generality of the metaphysician and the geometer, which goes on fathering its kind and augmenting its distance from its source in the concrete, is alien both to his capacity and his desire. Government ownership of all property is a subject which evokes his gravest thought and deepest concern, but he has written no *essay* on government ownership; he cannot make a *web* of abstractions. An artist's task is with a different web. Moreover, the success of those who have engaged relays of abstractions to carry them in successive journeys further and further from their base in the particular will scarcely embitter our regret for the non-appearance of this trait in Mr. Howells.

The subjects of these papers are often light beyond expectation, and, where the subject is grave, the treatment propitiates by its blitheness. Five topics are local, that is, metropolitan. Central Park and the New York streets receive each the tribute of an essay. The East Side in New York is a sobering theme; the paper that depicts it is hardly gloomy. "Tribulations of a Cheerful Giver," mixing sorrow and cheer in its very title, is a profoundly compassionate man's exposition of beggary; it tingles and crepitates with humor. The most gloomy of the papers, "Police Report," is the most comic. A curious essay is that which nourishes thirty-five hungry pages on the scant nutriment afforded by the routine incidents in the closing of a summer hotel. I can hardly think for the moment of a parallel instance of literary thrift, and the sparely dieted essay, while certainly not plump, is far from puny, and a personal test has proved its susceptibility of re-perusal.

The method is sometimes narrative, more often descriptive or observant in the loosely clustering, lightly separable vein. The division into numbered sections is an improvement of the carriage of the essays, a reinforcement of their dignity. The *appearance* of method has half the effectiveness of the reality.

In "A Country Printer," reminiscent of boyhood, clearly grasped traits of the old-time newspaper office in the provinces are presented with modesty and tenderness. The remarkable narrative, "Police Report," is astonishing in two ways. In the first place, Mr. Howells's minutes of fact unfold a dialogue as superior in dramatic and humorous vividness to the reader's notion of fact as the conversation in his novels. In the second place, the reporter can extract the comic savor out of scenes by which his universe is darkened. His mercy and his rigor are both strikingly evinced in the passage in which he tries to show that a certain "old fool" and a "lost soul" and "the yet more fallen spirit who harbored her and traded at second-hand in her perdition" were — he says it "in all seriousness and reverence" — "not so very bad."

"I Talk of Dreams" is buoyant without cheerfulness; willingly anecdotic and recreative, it is remembered best for its gravest moments. "An East Side Ramble," in the search for moderation, has fallen into tameness.

"Tribulations of a Cheerful Giver" is a cluster of charming autobiographic fragments in which Mr. Howells smiles warily but winningly at the reader through thirty-nine sportive pages from which an ultimate melancholy is disengaged. If the ruefulness is mainly burlesque, the burlesque is eventually sad. I will not reopen the summer hotel which Mr. Howells has so ceremoniously closed. "Glimpses of Central Park" and "New York Streets" reveal the hand which practice has made very deft and perhaps a little weary. "Imaginary Interviews and Other Essays" is a selection from the author's contributions to the Easy Chair in "Harper's Monthly," a post in which he has less occasion than he thinks to be dismayed by the priority of George William Curtis. I have some reservations to make in relation to these papers, but their variety, their general sanity, their openness of mind, their vivacity, and the opulence of their unjaded humor are points which only the foolish would debate. Mr. Howells casts many papers in the form of dialogue in which the participants, as he informs us, are phases or multiples of self. I like these selves when they are kind and demure. Sometimes, for variety's or vivacity's sake, they are made bumptious, and bumptiousness is not the native or proper habitat of their creator's humor. Mr. Howells's proper humorous pose — if I may use the word without malice or offence — is of quite another kind: it is a make-believe of a quite unbelievable helplessness and meekness which had prototypes in Goldsmith and Emerson and finds a later parallel in Mr. Crothers. When two of his selves begin to recriminate, I feel a double pang; I am not quite pleased that Mr. Howells should say nagging things, and I am altogether grieved when nagging things are said to Mr. Howells. In cases where this give-and-take finds itself in company with the loosely aggregative, or snowball, type of sentence, and with an unconcern of method which suggests that the unity, if not broken, is extremely brittle, I have known my uneasiness to ripen almost into gloom. But this combination is not the rule.

The first paper which fully satisfies me is the "Magazine Muse," a marvel of succinctness, and an example of how a skilled hand may attain real efficiency in a task which permits neither finality nor completeness. There is true charm in "Qualities Without Defects," where a squirrel's dalliance with peanuts is made the cue, if not the key, to grave research into the mysteries of life, and where the autumn which brightens and despoils the trees in Central Park blends with the other autumn which exhales from the pensive, not unsmiling, meditations of the friends. The next of the beguiling papers is "A Niece's Literary Advice," where the theme is crisp and the situation dramatic, and the veteran novelist, reinstated in his lovable humility, permits himself to be bullied by his niece, like Lowell by the humming-bird in "My Garden Acquaintance." "Around a Rainy-Day Fire" supplies the grateful calm and social ease which its title implies, in combination with deeper and saner thinking than usually finds an inspiration in the flame or a solace in the raindrops. In "Reading for a Grandfather," the humor is again lovable, and the light material is touched with gleams of personality that the student of Mr. Howells would have been sorry to miss. If one of those allegorizing and personifying fables with which Addison diversified the Easy Chair papers of his own time were to enter into wedlock with one of Hawthorne's dreamier and more didactic sketches, their offspring might resemble the tender and pleasing "A Normal Hero and Heroine out of Work."

Among the essays that are not "Interviews," "Autumn" is almost a surprise, even from a pen that has made a commonplace of brilliancy. "The Counsel of Literary Age to Literary Youth" is an essay of what I shall venture to call a fine brunette type, excellent in its measured style, and its compassionate, its almost pleading, censure. "The Unsatisfactoriness of Unfriendly Criticism" is precious for its matter, and the "Summer Sojourn of Florindo and Lindora" is a happy instance of that vivific touch to which even the arithmetic and hygiene of domestic life must yield its toll of piquancy and animation.

In these essays there is range or fluctuation in at least four points. The thought ranges from excellence to merit, the tone from the superlatively enjoyable to the faintly rasping, the style from the point-device accoutrement of the middle period to the looser vestments of the later days, the method from forgivable unconcern to an incommodious laxity. When the paper wins in all four hazards, the result is delightful; when it loses in all or several, a feeling of disquiet may ensue.

NOTE. — Of the long series of uncollected Easy Chair papers in "Harper's Monthly" I shall offer no detailed criticism. I have criticized it, in a measure, by implication in my comment on "Imaginary Interviews"; and I own that I am unable to approach it with that cordiality which I grieve to withhold from any papers of Mr. Howells. I most gladly and eagerly concede an intellectual vigor and a literary faculty which would force themselves even on an inattentive or distrustful eye. I have merely to confess that the papers do not profit me in the ratio of their intellectual force, or please me in the measure of their skill.

CHAPTER IV

Novel and Tale

MR. HOWELLS wrote at least forty works of fiction. Thirty-one of these may without rigor of definition be called novels; the other nine are tales or novelettes. The deposition of literature in his case was unceasing because it was organic; he secreted it like ivory or pearl. Yet, while unceasing, it was hardly incessant; outflow never quickened into outpour; his very swiftness was unhurried, and he had the measure which chastens, almost disowns, abundance.

The travel, criticism, and autobiography of Mr. Howells were the extract of his own psychology and observation; his fiction had the same high parentage, and was subject to the same honorable restrictions. Literature and life in his case went hand in hand, and the transfer of the emphasis from the first to the second in his maturity merely shifted the leadership, leaving the fellowship intact. In his personal output he not only largely shared, he strongly advanced and signally illustrated, two leading biases of his time, the confinement of literature to experience and the conversion of experience into literature. The extent of his reservations is inscrutable, but I doubt if there be any man of our time except Tolstoi in whom life was so prevailingly articulate, in whom utterance has so nearly kept pace with sensibility.

He has proved impervious to those temptations to which the uprightness of other realists has succumbed; his is the rectitude of Turgénieff. His immaturity was undefiled by any "Chouans." He was not emulous of that "Turn of the Screw" which led his great coadjutor, Mr. James, into the boscage of the supernatural. Mr. Howells's "Questionable Shapes" are not of the kind which engender terror in the clown or contumely in the skeptic. He remains unseduced by those blandishments of earlier epochs which overcame the constancy of Miss Jewett in "The Tory Lover" and of Mrs. Wharton in "The Valley of Decision." He has kept to his own time; and, more than that, he is almost unique among realists in the fidelity with which he has reproduced the subdivisions of his own time. His novels change their equipage with the decades which they copy. In places, the correspondence is curiously exact. After his early Ohio experience, which finds a reflex mainly in his autobiography, the scenes of his fiction, initially Venetian, maturely Bostonian, autumnally New-Yorkian, dispersedly and interspersedly European and American, copy his migrations as precisely as if his imagination were a part of his luggage.

I

THE FIELD

What now are the actual themes of the forty volumes? They have very evident and very curious limitations. Mr. Howells restricts himself to an experience on which fortune and nature have laid their own restrictions. A prosperous and virtuous man of letters, living in good society, is shut out from many of those fluctuations which diversify the experience of less fortunate and less exemplary men. Mr. Howells's taste has also played the part of censor for his themes. In these forty volumes, adultery is never pictured; seduction never; divorce once and sparingly ("A Modern Instance"); marriage discordant to the point of cleavage, only once and in the same novel with the divorce; crime only once with any fullness ("The Quality of Mercy"); politics never; religion passingly and superficially; science only in crepuscular psychology; mechanics, athletics, bodily exploits or collisions, very rarely.

After so many excisions and curtailments, the anxious novice may inquire, what remains? The novice may temper his anxiety. There remains, first, the passion of love, treated with that vividness in innocence and ardor in purity which seem, in literature and life, to be the reward for abstinence from its distempers. Second, the interest in travel and foreign sojourn, which, in a bright group of early novels, supplies the warp through which the shuttle of the love-interest noiselessly and delicately plies. Third, literature and art, the pursuit of which is the inspiration of four novels. Fourth, ethics, dealing largely with the puritanized, the romanticized, and the commercially brutalized conscience, and essaying, not too often, with a shy daring, to lift an edge of the veil that hides the face of the secretive universe. Fifth, two volumes that fence rather than wrestle with the mysticism of psychology. Sixth, an important group of social problems, by which vague term I here denote subjects that might afford to economists or legislators the occasion for a study, a monograph, or a statute. In these fictions they are directed mainly to the problem of self-support and to those inequalities of fortune which divide and disgrace our industrial civilization.

This last group of fictions is an apt illustration of a quality in which all the novels share. They are, in a very real, though very peculiar, sense, novels of society. Mr. Howells, I need not say, is not so vulgar as to be "genteel"; he is responsible for no "Pelham" and no "Lothair." But the surprise lies in the fact that, while his concern for poverty is intense, it is impossible to conceive of him as writing a counterpart to Zola's "Germinal" or Mrs. Freeman's "Portion of Labor." He could hardly so far elude his own capacities, escape from the yoke of his powers, as Mrs. Wharton has done in the powerful novelette of "Ethan Frome." The centre, the "Golden Milestone" as it were, in Mr. Howells's world, is a cultivated, intellectual, privileged society, to which somehow, whether as appeal or menace or reproach or spectacle or even diversion, it is the business of the proletariat to relate itself. The proletariat exists in that relation. It is inseparable from its observers and critics and saviors. He cannot credit it with self-subsistence. Forms of life alien to his own may be obvious to his regard, but they are not pervious to his assimilative faculty. He is just to their deserts, he is tender to their shortcomings; but, in some elusive way, his justice, his tenderness, carries with it the implication of standards in whose delicacy more than in whose rigor their sentence is conclusively pronounced. We may have wandered hundreds of miles from the metropolis, but its presence, even in its material absence, controls our point of view.

II

THE FRAME

How far are these fictions possessed of form? It is felt that Mr. Howells's perceptions are subtle, and it is inferred that his structure is adept; but subtle perceptions need not be coherent any more than simple ones, except on the broad and lax hypothesis that the solicitude demonstrable at one point is presumable at another. There is no point in which criticism is more shiftless, less prone to concern itself with verifying particulars, more willing to take the aspect or effect of vigilance at its face value, than this matter of structural proficiency. Let us first try Mr. Howells by three distinct types of structure represented in three novels of the earliest group, "Their Wedding Journey," "A Chance Acquaintance," and "A Foregone Conclusion."

The plan of "Their Wedding Journey" barely evades the reproach of planlessness. Vignettes of Niagara, the St. Lawrence, Montreal, and Quebec are interspersed with light personalities referable to porters, cabmen, landlords, fellow travellers, and are overcast at one moment by a passing quarrel.

There is no logic, no issue, no process; we have narrative in its final simplification. Nevertheless, "Their Wedding Journey" is not formless. Such an excursion in life has its pattern, its physiognomy; and the reproduction in a book of its markings and veinings with an approach to completeness and a deference to proportion is plainly the solution of an artistic problem.

In "A Chance Acquaintance," the young man and woman, travelling in one party in French Canada, reappear; but a simple yet momentous variation in the circumstance lifts the novel to another plane of art. The principals are unmarried, and their successive encounters in spots of historic or natural interest are bound together by a growing mutual regard which issues in a delayed engagement and a hurried rupture. This may not be *better* art, — a diatom may be as perfect an instance of adaptation as a giraffe, — but it is unquestionably riper art. Succession has become process; cessation has become outcome. Narrative has evolved into story; if plot is still to seek, it is because the incidents have as yet no objective coherence — they cohere only in the lovers' minds.

"A Foregone Conclusion" is framed in Venice. An invalid American widow and her beautiful young daughter become objects of interest to two persons, an American painter masquerading as consul and an Italian technician who is formally a priest. Recommended by the consul, the priest becomes the young girl's tutor. From tutor he becomes lover. He confides his agnosticism to her sympathy, and she, in the strength of an imagined endorsement from the consul, urges him to forsake his vocation and his country, and offers him hospitality and encouragement in America. Misconstruing her charitable ardor, the priest reveals his passion, and, by the despair into which he is plunged by her rejection, the young girl is moved to an act of impulsive pity which the painter, hidden in the shrubbery, mistakes for an avowal of love. The priest, dying heart-broken, discloses the truth to the embittered painter, who refuses to believe, and expiates his disbelief in the long and dreary postponement of his reunion with the orphaned young girl in their common country.

We deal here plainly with an art still further evolved. Logic has been superadded to process and to outcome, and plot, in the traditional, prerealistic sense, is the result. Events are no longer generative of mere states of mind; they are generative of new events as concrete and tangible as themselves.

Mr. Howells's relation to the above types of structure may be readily epitomized: with the first, he is content; he exacts no more; with the second, he is richly satisfied; the third he views as a luxury which he admits or abandons according to the state of his means. One might add with much plausibility that the attitude of nature in this point agrees closely with that of Mr. Howells.

There is no real anomaly in the fact that, in the third or strongest of these relations, he should be most like other writers, while in the first or weakest he is most original. In art the strong ties are first grasped, because they are obvious, and the weaker connections wait for notice, because they are elusive.

The deftness of Mr. Howells's hand is visible in all three types, but in all three it is subject to an important limitation. In only one instance has he been able to transfer his aptness to a long novel, that is, a novel of approximately four hundred pages. That instance is "Indian Summer." In no case whatever has he been wholly fortunate in the conduct of a double or multiple plot.

I would not myself call into question the abstract legitimacy of the double or multiple plot; its guarantors are authoritative. I have never lived in a duplex, and I own to a kindliness for the simple-minded literature that favors one thing at a time. But I have no feud with the inmates of duplexes, and I do not quarrel with Mr. James's "Tragic Muse," which doubles the illustration of its problem, or with Miss Austen's "Sense and

Sensibility," which dramatizes an antithesis. To this tolerance there is one obvious reservation: the story must be born double; the fable must be twofold in the germ. Too many of Mr. Howells's larger works remind one of houses single in design, but hastily remodelled as duplexes in compliance with an impulsive afterthought.

An illustration is afforded by "A Modern Instance." That vigorous novel unfolds a psychic process, a process of alienation between two persons, lovers at first, later husband and wife, which ends in the shame and bitterness of divorce. The progressive mutual attitude of these two persons is the substance and law of the story. Anything that aids that process is legitimate, and we have no right to insist that any point shall aid the process more than once, or that any two such points shall be otherwise related to each other. Sometimes, in fact, they *are* otherwise related to each other. At measured intervals a grim father thrusts his hawk-nose into the shuddering narrative. A backwoods philosopher, who had entertained the husband in his prenuptial days, becomes long after the blameless occasion for a peculiar refinement of infamy on the part of his sometime guest. A Canadian woman, with whom the young man, still unmarried, had joined in a casual flirtation, reappears for a few hours in the sequel, to inflame the discord between husband and wife. Very much the same office is served by a country girl who had attracted the young man's fitful notice in the initial chapter, and whose reappearance in Boston after a long effacement precipitates the delaying crisis. Now, in this type of story, all these recurrences are unessential. They are gratuities, or, if you prefer, they are economies, since the use of a new piece for each new move would constitute a heavy outlay for the most affluent invention. The structural principle of such a tale would remain inviolate if — apart from the married pair themselves — no character and no action were suffered to count twice in the succession of agencies which dissolve their relation.

But every privilege has its tax. It is clear that a story of this frame is bound to be strict — even stern — in its adhesion to this central process, in the measure in which it has made that process a ground for the admission of diverse material. The novel obeys this law for a long time and prospers in its obedience, but in the latter part Mr. Howells succumbs to a tempting irrelevance. There is another young man who loves the wife. In Paris this would be relevant, surpassingly relevant; the young man would at once take a part, a very active part, in the disintegrative process. But we are not in Paris, we are in Boston; and the young man who loves the woman as girl, wife, and widow is Bostonian in his delicacy of conscience. This delicacy is active not only after the marriage, which converts his passion into nominal guilt, but after the divorce, which recalls it to the plane of technical innocence. He is no factor in the separation. He absents himself in Spanish America or other regions, from which he returns at intervals to have his wound dressed — if the phrase be permissible — by a friend who does not spare the caustics in the process of his ministrations. The condemnation of this deedless and wordless passion is a point near to Mr. Howells's heart, and he suspends his story to provide the legal friend with a wife, apparently for no other end than to ensure that fullness and frankness of discussion which domestic leisures and candors invite. The ethics may be salutary, but the momentum of a powerful story has suffered an irremediable check.

The same comment applies, with the natural variations of degree, to the other novels of the class. In "The Rise of Silas Lapham," the injury is less marked. We have here two plots, a love-affair and a bankruptcy. They do not concern each other, but they concern the same persons, and their domiciliation within the same covers would have been entirely pardonable if they had been so domiciled from the outset. As it happens, the bankruptcy story is late; it is so much of a laggard that it has almost the look of a trespasser. "The Minister's Charge" is sufficiently effective up to the night of the fire; from the nervous shock of that conflagration the book never fully recovers. The bold and stirring conception of "The Quality of Mercy," namely, an extended and varied picture of the lines of pressure and fissure which penetrate society in all directions from their point of nascence in a defalcation, authorizes a great latitude of treatment. This latitude the author artlessly or recklessly extends to the insertion of so obvious an irrelevance as the love-affair between Louise and Maxwell. In Mr. Howells's work, stories of any complexity are very likely, somewhere in the last third or quarter of their course, to find themselves either adrift or aground; their hope lies in signalling some tug of circumstance to tow them to the nearest port of safety. "April Hopes" and "Annie Kilburn" owe their completion to this seasonable aid. I may add that "The World of Chance" does not belie its title by any virtuosity of design, and that the excellent story of "The Landlord at Lion's Head" amounts to little more than the trial of the effect of successive poses on the muscular figure of Jeff Durgin.

What is the source of this recurrent error? Any theory that taxes Mr. Howells with incapacity will demand capacity in its defenders, and the safer course is to impute these shortcomings to reluctance or unconcern. In his maturity, Mr. Howells became more and more impatient of conscious style and conscious art; under the ascendency of Tolstoi, he even began to suspect artifice in his beloved Turgénieff. He united a growing toleration for the inconsequence of nature with a declining respect for the ingenuity of man. To be artistic at the expense of labor and also at the expense of verisimilitude affected him as a form of unthrift. This view is defensible if it is thoroughgoing. If a realist forsakes art and undertakes to reproduce literally the anarchy of nature, he is, in a sense, within his rights; the reader is powerless to obtain an injunction. The reader's defence, on the contrary, lies in the exercise of a right quite as primitive and inalienable as that of the intrepid novelist — the right to leave the book unread. But it is also quite clear that a novelist cannot find in the *general* confusion of nature an indorsement for any *particular* confusions in his own work. The fact that nature leaves many things unexplained will not justify you in leaving any particular fact unexplained in a work in which you undertake to furnish explanations. If a writer alters reality at all, he must alter it on principle, and he must be faithful to his principle. Now Mr. Howells's simpler and shorter works are virtual admissions of the righteousness of that process by which the artist clarifies and simplifies the turbid promiscuity of nature. Even in his maturity the briefer works are shapely. He is therefore scarcely justified, in works like "The Quality of Mercy" and "The World of Chance," in playing the recreant to principles to which at almost the same epoch he is avowing his liegemanship in "An Imperative Duty," "An Open-Eyed Conspiracy," and "The Story of a Play."

There is a secondary but important point in which Mr. Howells's relinquishment of art in the interest of truth invites question by its want of thoroughness. Careful artists have usually deprecated — even where they have not renounced — the accidental encounter of persons on occasions favorable to the plot. Mr. Howells has ignored this artistic canon: the motto for his practice might be found in old Chaucer's specious excuse for a similar encounter:

> For alday meteth men at unset stevene [by unforeseen meeting].

Chaucer is perfectly correct, but it must be remarked that, while nature is liberal of coincidence, she is not liberal of tactful coincidence, and the meetings in Chaucer and Mr. Howells are prevailingly opportune. If accident is normally stupid in life, a realist cannot uphold the proposition that it should be normally clever in fiction. The properties of art are transferred to chance; it becomes provident and plastic. Moreover, art is design, and I have an old-fashioned feeling that its obligations to chance are unseemly; I am pained that it should live on the alms of its enemy.

We have noted Mr. Howells's structural success in the short novel and his relative inadequacy in the larger work. The facile inference would be that his short stories would be impeccable. Let us look into the record. His early career was enlivened by one simple but masterly tale, "At the Sign of the Savage." After a long intermission, in his old age he published three volumes of short stories, "A Pair of Patient Lovers," "Questionable Shapes," and "Between the Dark and the Daylight," none of which was remarkable for dexterity of technique. They rested, as it were, on placid levels, or waited with exemplary patience for a noiseless culmination which hardly merited any fever of expectancy. The fact is a little curious. The success of Maupassant and O. Henry in the short story might have seemed indeed to slam the gate in Mr. Howells's face; but the successful passage of Mr. James and Mrs. Wharton through its hospitable opening should have flung the entrance wide to a pilgrim of their own fraternity. The theory of native incompetence may be put aside. The short story is a wide terrene, and its citizenship includes the most diverse talents. Mr. Howells may have some apparent handicaps: he is quiet, for example, and he is subtle; but he is not so quiet as Sarah Orne Jewett and he is certainly no subtler than Henry James. The defect is probably explicable by preoccupation with other interests up to a date when time had robbed his fingers of plasticity.

The connection of novels by the repetition of characters is a practice in which Mr. Howells is surpassed only by Balzac, who is, in this form of conjunction, unsurpassable. The Marches — who should have been named the Aprils — palpitate and vacillate more or less through six novels and two short stories. "A Fearful Responsibility" is faintly odorous of "The Lady of the Aroostook," and, still more faintly, of "A Foregone Conclusion." "The Rise of Silas Lapham" reaches a hand through time to catch the far-off interest of the deceased Bartley Hubbard in "A Modern Instance," and transfers its Boston gentlefolk, its Coreys and Sewells and Bellinghams, from its own odd associations to a still ruder setting in "The Minister's Charge." Clara Kingsbury dashes through three or four novels, even attaching such remote suburbs as "A Woman's Reason" and "An Imperative Duty" to the briskness of the metropolitan centre. "Annie Kilburn" is ancestral in function; its immediate offshoot, "The Quality of Mercy," generates a quieter and remoter scion, "The Story of a Play," and, in the person of the Brandreths, extends the *patria potestas* to "The World of Chance." The fable of Tithonus is heartbreakingly repeated in the successive reappearance, in book after book, in lower stages of senile decay, of the delightful Bromfield Corey. "A Traveller from Altruria" passes its slender thread eventually "Through the Eye of the Needle." The spray of Ponkwasset Falls is dashed in the face of two plays and three or four novels.

III

LOVE AFLOAT AND ASHORE

I shall now pass in review five early novels, "Their Wedding Journey," "A Chance Acquaintance," "A Foregone Conclusion," "The Lady of the Aroostook," and "A Fearful Responsibility," which form a marked group, to which, in certain aspects, "The Undiscovered Country" is loosely attachable. They are short, they are simple, they are linear. They present a few characters strongly segregated, and intensified in their mutual impact by segregation. They abound in realistic detail, but they consist of plats of realism, abstracted from the general field by a choice of material that is curious and half-exotic. They deal with love — that is plain and natural enough; but this love is associated, first with travel, and secondly with the more special peculiarity of a difference, either in social rank or in nationality, between the man and woman. The books smile often, but between the smiles or beneath the smiles they are grave. They have the festal air suited to a young author's honeymoon with the Muses, but they are shot with passages which foreshadow, if they do not forestall, the solemnity which so often clouds the later books. "Their Wedding Journey" is vivacious, but it contains one episode — a nothing, an aimless and fruitless quarrel — which the memory recalls with terror. The catastrophe in "A Chance Acquaintance" is really the mask of a deliverance, and is touched with a merciful lightness; yet somehow it pierces the heart. "The Lady of the Aroostook" is comedy in the actual presentation, but its final curtain is a welcome screen. "A Fearful Responsibility" affects insouciance only to succumb — with the laugh still on its lips — to a haunting sense of the irrecoverable. In "A Foregone Conclusion" two characters out of four die — a high percentage of mortality — and wrath and sorrow wring the souls of Ferris and Florida before they are released — half sadly — to each other's arms.

"Their Wedding Journey" is the plotless and actionless recital of the mild experiences and pungent observations of a newly married couple, Basil and Isabel March, on a trip including Niagara, the St. Lawrence, Montreal, Quebec, and other places. The touch on the love-motive is discreet, though not gingerly; the affection is salted with comedy; and the reader profits by the self-denial of the lovers in hiding their mutual interest resolutely from the fellow pilgrims. The materials are not profuse. Mr. Howells seems to inquire with Milton, —

> What neat repast shall feast us, light and choice?

and it is only the perfection of the housekeeping that gives to these simple viands the reassuring semblance of plenty. This thriftiness may explain the inclusion of certain comicalities in which the habits, if not the standards, of the author seem to have bent to his needs. A fine or a satiric ear might detect a far-off vibration of Smollett in that hotel scene in which a confusion of destinations permits Mr. March and Colonel Ellison to stumble upon a young lady in dishabille.

The book offers us the earliest glimpse of the Marches, Youth is becoming to Isabel—not quite so evidently to Basil, whose figure, in the corporal and the moral sense, is not yet rounded out. The supply of nature in Isabel, even in these immature days, is ample; in her later years she is almost encumbered with it. Basil, at this period, has less the air of a reality. I find both over-tense; their consumption of scenery and fellow passengers is avid, not to say relentless, as if Mr. Howells had doubled their alertness to balance an insipidity in the matter they consume. Their reserves of probity, kindness, and affection are large and sterling, but there is a difference between their reserves and what I shall venture to call their pocket money; the latter is an airier, gayer, more fantastic, and less stable currency. Their dispositions, in a word, are an elfish and wayward burlesque of their characters.

"A Chance Acquaintance" is far more attractive than "Their Wedding Journey." In our present unripe civilization, story is still useful to a novelist. It broaches a theme which was to endear itself to Mr. Howells — the rise of love between persons of disparate social castes. His humor and even his pathos nest and flutter in the hedge that divides the social park from the social wilderness, and affords an impartial outlook into the garden and the copse. He prefers to depict these maladjustments in America, where his subtlety finds them more impressive in the degree in which they are less obvious. In this case a young Bostonian of ineffable gentility woos, wins, and, through a quite final and fatal exhibition of that vulgarity which lies in wait for the exaggeration of refinement, eventually loses, a spirited and lovable girl from western New York. Snobbishness dies hard in a democracy, and both author and reader, who would not like to be called flunkies, rejoice cringingly in Kitty Ellison's bootless conquest of her insipid prize. The man, thus won, hesitates to introduce his betrothed to some fashionable acquaintance, and the girl with equal spirit and good sense rescinds the engagement. This apt catastrophe, so tiny, yet so piercing, which shatters the bright illusion, is of a finished and flawless art; nothing is overdone or oversaid, and the reader cannot vanquish his surprise that a word so severe should be uttered in a voice so gentle. Indeed, the art of this simple tale is almost everywhere impeccable; the passion never quite expands, and the whole idyl has the succinctness, the neatness, and the delicacy of a bud.

Kitty Ellison is one of the most lovable of the author's young women, possibly because she is in some ways a truant from the sisterhood. She might be a Louisa Alcott or a Sophie May girl with the corrective Howells infusion. She justifies even a Bostonian in a passing forgetfulness of his longitude.

The Bostonian himself is far more questionable. Our wavering faith in his reality is hardly confirmed by our surmise that something of his breed or brand might be credible and original. Both Kitty and Mr. Howells treat him with a certain shyness which suggests a fear that he is rather unmanageable; they both call him Mr. Arbuton. Even his courage barely saves him from fatuity. There is something gelid in his constitution, as if his hauteur were a numbness in both heart and frame. He keeps even his creator at a distance.

The chaperonage of the young girl is intrusted to a married couple, Colonel and Mrs. Ellison, in whom unending dispute is the guaranty of substantial concord. They are successfully drawn, if we allow for a kind of laxity, a *lounge*, as it were, in both characters, which becomes, in duplicate, a little wearing.

The book is realistic with a species of cabinet realism, a realism painted on a panel, so to speak. Its style is of that exquisite temper which arrests finish at the exact point where finish becomes a threat to spontaneity.

"The Lady of the Aroostook," which I treat in this place with a slight displacement of chronology, presents the theme of "A Chance Acquaintance" — the opposition between passion and class — with an original setting and a reversed outcome. It is a very singular book. It affects modest limitation and homely candor; it purports to tell us how a young country girl, finding herself the only woman on board a small ocean ship, weathered the social perils and inclemencies to which she was exposed by this trying situation. Here we have apparently the confinement, the slightness, and the salience — the salience in minuteness — which are Mr. Howells's desiderata at this stage of his authorship. But in other regards the book confounds us by its breadth and intrepidity.

To begin with, it starts in South Bradford, Massachusetts, and ends in Venice. I am not aware that literature has ever before sanctioned the vagary of geographers to the effect that Venice and South Bradford are denizens of the same world, and the assertion is one which no verification can rob of its audacity. The countenancing of this scientific crotchet by a responsible novelist was hardly to have been foreseen. From this draught of miracle the author naturally imbibed the hardihood to include among the possibilities the engagement and marriage of a young Bostonian of the straitest inner sect and an uncultivated girl from a rural district. The one anomaly sustains the other. If South Bradford can reach Venice, there are no limits to its adventures; it may even get to Boston.

Between the intemperance of this plot and the Defoe-like gravity and sobriety of the circumstantial and verisimilar narration, the reader is cleft in two; he is equally shocked by the story and by his own skepticism; he is incredulous of his disbelief.

Let us see how the resourcefulness of Mr. Howells alleviates the hardships of the situation. (The point, of course, is to explain the passion of a cultivated man for an uncultivated girl without denying or correcting her want of cultivation.) With that prodigality with which poets and novelists have so often shamed the parsimony of nature, he first provides the girl with rare beauty and a divine voice. He has the fortitude to call her Lydia Blood. She is equipped with a timely reserve which enables Mr. Howells to minimize her conversation. On shipboard, she is mysterious, laconic, and neutral, and the emphasis is adroitly laid on traits of character which are interesting in themselves and do not imply either culture or its absence. Toward the close of the book she commits no social mistake in our hearing except on one or two occasions in which the author recognizes verisimilitude with a parting bow. Though rigid, she is teachable, and the grossness of "wanting to know" is cured by a single experiment of its effect on delicate companions. It is a sign of mastery in Mr. Howells that her character, apart from the ambiguities and temporizings, is firmly and truly drawn. But when all is said, the passion of Staniford remains inexplicable.

James Staniford himself is a gentleman weary of his part, who indulges a whim of ungentlemanliness; and the whim seems more innate, more characteristic, than the conventions which it supersedes. The faithfulness to Lydia, the generosity toward Dunham, his lovable companion, the magnanimity toward Hicks, overlie, but do not quite overpower, the impression of the flippancies, duplicities, and insolencies which marked his early conduct on the voyage. No doubt the sauce in Staniford had to be proportioned to the syrup in Dunham, and the capture of a mocker adds to the glory as well as to the oddness of Lydia's incredible triumph. Staniford's conduct would always be better than his temper, but one hesitates to say which is the truer version of the man.

The seafaring novel has the appearance of being almost literally "*cabined*, cribbed, confined," but this appearance is deceptive; the unfailing, if not unvarying, power of touch shown in characters so diversified as the complex Bostonians, the taciturnly open-hearted sailors, the rough-rinded South Bradfordites, and the Europeanized Americans in Venice, demonstrates a surprising versatility. The velvety Dunham is better as a portrait than the spinous Staniford. Hicks, the reprobate, is drawn with initial sternness and final mercy, the humorist in him pleading not ineffectively with Mr. Howells for a commutation of the sentence on the blackguard.

At Venice an impulse of caricature seizes Mr. Howells; restraint is flung away in the sheer farce of Mr. Erwin's teeming Americanisms, and Mrs. Erwin's snobbishness is hardly more believable. The husband is, however, a real man apart from his crotchet; and at the end Mr. Howells contrives to smuggle a heart and brain somewhere into the loose texture of that moral dishabille which is known in Venetian circles as Mrs. Erwin.

The following extract from the novel is less intimate and winning than some others, but it shows the author's eye for physique, and illustrates in fairly various scenes that delicate emphasis, that penetrating undertone, which distinguishes the work of Mr. Howells. It also brings out that refinement which, by shutting the heart against the unrefined, might almost have vulgarized its possessors, had hearts like theirs not found defences in their charity and warmth.

There was a sixth plate laid, but the captain made no further mention of the person who was not out yet till shortly after the coffee was poured, when the absentee appeared, hastily closing his state-room door behind him, and then waiting on foot, with a half-impudent, half-intimidated air, while Captain Jenness, with a sort of elaborate repressiveness, presented him as Mr. Hicks. He was a short and slight young man, with a small sandy moustache curling tightly in over his lip, floating reddish-blue eyes, and a deep dimple in his weak, slightly retreating chin. He had an air at once amiable and baddish, with an expression, curiously blended, of monkey-like humor and spaniel-like apprehensiveness. He did not look well, and till he had swallowed two cups of coffee his hand shook. The captain watched him furtively from under his bushy eyebrows, and was evidently troubled and preoccupied, addressing a word now and then to Mr. Watterson, who, by virtue of what was apparently the ship's discipline, spoke only when he was spoken to, and then answered with prompt acquiescence. Dunham and Staniford exchanged not so much a glance as a consciousness in regard to him, which seemed to recognize and class him. They talked to each other, and sometimes to the captain. Once they spoke to Lydia. Mr. Dunham, for example, said, "Miss — ah — Blood, don't you think we are uncommonly fortunate in having such lovely weather for a start-off?"

"I don't know," said Lydia.

Mr. Dunham arrested himself in the use of his fork. "I beg your pardon?" he smiled.

It seemed to be a question, and after a moment's doubt Lydia answered, "I did n't know it was strange to have fine weather at the start."

"Oh, but I can assure you it is," said Dunham, with a certain lady-like sweetness of manner which he had. "According to precedent, we ought to be all deathly seasick."

"Not at *this* time of year," said Captain Jenness.

"Not at this time of *year*," repeated Mr. Watterson, as if the remark were an order to the crew.

Dunham referred the matter with a look to his friend, who refused to take part in it, and then he let it drop. But presently Staniford himself attempted the civility of some conversation with Lydia. He asked her gravely, and somewhat severely, if she had suffered much from the heat of the day before.

"Yes," said Lydia, "it was very hot."

"I 'm told it was the hottest day of the summer, so far," continued Staniford, with the same severity.

"I want to know!" cried Lydia.

The young man did not say anything more.

As Dunham lit his cigar at Staniford's on deck, the former said significantly, "What a very American thing!"

"What a bore!" answered the other.

Dunham had never been abroad, as one might imagine from his calling Lydia's presence a very American thing, but he had always consorted with people who had lived in Europe; he read the "Revue des Deux Mondes" habitually, and the London weekly newspapers, and this gave him the foreign stand-point from which he was fond of viewing his native world. "It 's incredible," he added. "Who in the world can she be?"

"Oh, *I* don't know," returned Staniford, with a cold disgust. "I should object to the society of such a young person for a month or six weeks under the most favorable circumstances, and with frequent respites; but to be imprisoned on the same ship with her, and to have her on one's mind and in one's way the whole time, is more than I bargained for. Captain Jenness should have told us; though I suppose he thought that if *she* could stand it, *we* might. There 's that point of view. But it takes all ease and comfort out of the prospect. Here comes that blackguard." Staniford turned his back towards Mr. Hicks, who was approaching; but Dunham could not quite do this, though he waited for the other to speak first.

"Will you — would you oblige me with a light?" Mr. Hicks asked, taking a cigar from his case.

"Certainly," said Dunham, with the comradery of the smoker.

Mr. Hicks seemed to gather courage from his cigar. "You did n't expect to find a lady passenger on board, did you?" His poor disagreeable little face was lit up with unpleasant enjoyment of the anomaly. Dunham hesitated for an answer.

"One never can know what one's fellow passengers are going to be," said Staniford, turning about, and looking not at Mr. Hicks's face, but his feet, with an effect of being, upon the whole, disappointed not to find them cloven. He added, to put the man down rather than from an exact belief in his own suggestion, "She 's probably some relation of the captain's."

"Why, that 's the joke of it," said Hicks, fluttered with his superior knowledge. "I 've been pumping the cabin-boy, and he says the captain never saw her till yesterday. She 's an up-country school-ma'am, and she came down here with her grandfather yesterday. She 's going out to meet friends of hers in Venice." The little man pulled at his cigar, and coughed and chuckled, and waited confidently for the impression.

"Dunham," said Staniford, "did I hand you that sketch-block of mine to put in your bag, when we were packing last night?"

"Yes, I 've got it."

"I 'm glad of that. Did you see Murray yesterday?"

"No; he was at Cambridge."

"I thought he was to have met you at Parker's." The conversation no longer included Mr. Hicks or the subject he had introduced; after a moment's hesitation, he walked away to another part of the ship. As soon as he was beyond ear-shot, Staniford again spoke: "Dunham, this girl is plainly one of those cases of supernatural innocence, on the part of herself and her friends, which, as you suggested, would n't occur among any other people in the world but ours."

"You 're a good fellow, Staniford!" cried Dunham.

"Not at all. I call myself simply a human being, with the elemental instincts of a gentleman, as far as concerns this matter. The girl has been placed in a position which could be made very painful to her. It seems to me it 's our part to prevent it from being so. I doubt if she finds it at all anomalous, and if we choose she need never do so till after we 've parted with her. I fancy we can preserve her unconsciousness intact."

"Staniford, this is like you," said his friend, with glistening eyes. "I had some wild notion of the kind myself, but I 'm so glad you spoke of it first."

"Well, never mind," responded Staniford. "We must make her feel that there is nothing irregular or uncommon in her being here as she is. I don't know how the matter 's to be managed, exactly; it must be a negative benevolence for the most part; but it can be done. The first thing is to cow that nuisance yonder. Pumping the cabin-boy! The little sot! Look here, Dunham; it 's such a satisfaction to me to think of putting that fellow under foot that I 'll leave you all the credit of saving the young lady's feelings. I should like to begin stamping on him at once."

"I think you have made a beginning already. I confess I wish you had n't such heavy nails in your boots!"

"Oh, they 'll do him good, confound him!" said Staniford.

"I should have liked it better if her name had n't been Blood," remarked Dunham, presently.

"It does n't matter what a girl's surname is. Besides, Blood is very frequent in some parts of the State."

"She 's very pretty, is n't she?" Dunham suggested.

"Oh, pretty enough, yes," replied Staniford. "Nothing is so common as the pretty girl of our nation. Her beauty is part of the general tiresomeness of the whole situation."

"Don't you think," ventured his friend, further, "that she has rather a lady-like air?"

"She wanted to know," said Staniford, with a laugh.

Dunham was silent a while before he asked, "What do you suppose her first name is?"

"Jerusha, probably."

"Oh, impossible!"

"Well, then, — Lurella. You have no idea of the grotesqueness of these people's minds. I used to see a great deal of their intimate life when I went on my tramps, and chanced it among them, for bed and board, wherever I happened to be. We cultivated Yankees and the raw material seem hardly of the same race. Where the Puritanism has gone out of the people in spots, there 's the rankest growth of all sorts of crazy heresies, and the old scriptural nomenclature has given place to something compounded of the fancifulness of story-paper romance and the gibberish of spiritualism. They make up their names, sometimes, and call a child by what sounds pretty to them. I wonder how the captain picked up that scoundrel."

"A Foregone Conclusion" is a novel of two hundred and sixty-five pages; but it is all marrow. Its scene is Venice; its characters are a consul who paints, an Italian priest who is technician and freethinker, and two half-expatriated American women, mother and daughter; it has, in short, every right to be arabesque and grotesque; but it is eminent, if not solitary, among the tales in the straightforwardness of its clear appeal to the unsophisticated human heart. By a not too frequent chance — for contrivance in Mr. Howells seems always the offshoot of fortuity — its exhibits those self-enclosed and self-sustained reciprocities of act and motive which are technically known as plot; and the conduct of this plot is excellent. The motives satisfy, and a delicate progressiveness finds room and freedom within straitened limits. The story is grave almost in self-despite. The Venetian setting, the opening key, and the temper of Ferris all make for elasticity; but the situation masters these antagonisms, and the two deaths which finally occur merge into a gloom which they scarcely deepen.

The priest who doubts his faith and loves a woman passionately is a figure of tragic proportions beyond the scale of the author's canvas if not beyond the power of his brush. The problem, therefore, is to temper the effect of the passion without tempering the passion itself, and this difficulty is admirably solved. Don Ippolito walks from the first in illusions which at last engulf even his actuality; compassion is substituted for realization, and we read of his anguish as of a tale within a tale. The unreality of the tragedy is felt by Mr. Howells to be not least among its tragic elements. The priest is very Italian, but very human, too; and his unswerving gentlemanliness is not the less genuine for being racial, though in the race itself the genuineness is so often doubtful. It is noteworthy that, with all Mr. Howells's predilection for a European setting, Don Ippolito is the only instance in his works of a full-length or full-dress portrait of a foreigner other than an Englishman.

Florida Vervain has an inept name, but the rest of her is priceless. There is something primal (or ultimate) about her, in happy contrast with many of her sisters in other books, who seem to be always in breathless pursuit of their fugitive selves through the windings of their labyrinthine consciousness. She is portrayed with a subtle art which emphasizes her goodness under cover of a thin pretense of candor in the exposure of her faults. Her fierceness is endearing; indeed, she wakes in the reader the rebellious and defiant love which marks her own relation to the objects of her tenderness. Perhaps her love for Ferris, who is hardly of her tribe, requires a little more explanation than it obtains; but Mr. Howells felt rightly that her character must be viewed exclusively from the outside.

Mrs. Vervain is one of those silly mature women, in whom silliness profits more by the alleviation of sex than it suffers by the aggravation of maturity. Her mixture of egotism and kindness, of querulousness and gayety, is humanized by some impenetrable magic. She is one of those persons for whom sickness seems an inadvertence and death an oversight, and the story gathers a pathetic brightness from the smile of this fading invalid.

Our liking for Henry Ferris is indisputably robust, since it outlives much hard usage from that young gentleman himself. His temper is underbred, while his character is delicate; or, to put the matter a little more harshly, his breeding is impersonal, and imposes its law on the chafing individual. "The inexorable delicacy of his position made him laugh" is a phrase that embodies equally his submission and his revolt.

"A Fearful Responsibility," which supplies, not a mock-serious, but a mock-comic, title to the brief Venetian story which fills the next place in the list, narrates the quietus given by a young American professor domiciled in Venice to an incipient love-affair, in which an Austrian officer and a young American girl in the professor's care are the protagonists. The main story, which is really the minor story, is very sketchy, and touches comic opera on one side and tragedy on the other, without any occupation of that mid-zone of romance which would seem its proper habitat. In two points its deviation from the usage of romance is profoundly significant of its author's temper. Traditionally, the happiness lost to the young girl would have been indisputable, and the girl's attitude would have been hostile or constrained. In this story the happiness is questionable, and the girl is amiably, though misgivingly, acquiescent. It is part of that fine consentience with the spirit of things which classes Mr. Howells with the nobler realists, that he should allow this girl, after a time, to marry happily in America and to allay the compunction which had loaded her friends for years with the guilt of her imagined heart-break. He has learned even at this date to combine a deep reverence for the actuality of the love-passion with a profound contempt for its romantic simulacra.

The heroine herself hardly rises to her opportunities; not much pains are taken with her; her girlhood and her Americanism answer or avert all questions. The real drama lies in the repercussions which her story excites in the mind of the

American and his wife, and the book marks Mr. Howells's earliest use, in its complete form, of a favorite and a characteristic expedient, which is separable into distinct phases. First, we install an observer and commentator. Second, we make him dual for diversity of outlook and piquancy of dialogue. Third, we make this dual observer a married couple with the opportunities and the dispositions for combat which bring matrimony so obviously within the scope of the Brunetière interpretation of drama. Fourth, we give each of these persons a double or multiple attitude toward the case, and this variation in their individual views is naturally the source of still greater complications in their reciprocities. The question as to whether these planets are in conjunction or opposition, or trine or quadrate has, of course, everything to do with the fortunes of the body on which they shed their concurring or contending influence. Such, at least, is the decorum of the case. In practice it sometimes happens that the young people pursue their love-affair with a mature steadiness and gravity, while their advisers and superiors gyrate and eddy round them in all the volatility of youthful impulse. The device has both felicity and peril. Mr. Howells can cope with its obvious difficulties, but, if his conduct should form a precedent, I doubt if his success would prove an augury.

The best portrait in the novel is the consul, Captain Hoskins, whose mere name is half a portrait. He is one of the company of bachelors who are sent up at intervals for rejection at the hands of Lily Mayhew, for reasons inscrutable to criticism. There is much pleasing local color, and the concussions of the American Civil War rock the gondolas of Venice.

In 1875 and 1876, Mr. Howells published in the "Atlantic Monthly" a novel called "Private Theatricals," which, after a sleep of nearly half a century in the columns of the periodical, was republished in 1921, after his death, under the new title, "Mrs. Farrell." In making this book an exception to his nearly unbroken practice of reprinting his serials in book form, he wa probably not unwise, though the book contains nothing that could imperil or impair his fame. The setting, local and personal, is handled with mastery, and it is odd that two books so close in date of publication and so far apart in time of authorship as "Mrs. Farrell" and "The Vacation of the Kelwyns" should both deal with the never-blunted theme of the summer boarding-house for city people. For once, however, the characterization is weak; the farm-folk in their minor parts are excellent, but the two heroes are neutral, and the heroine, though subtly conceived, is imperfectly imagined. I once went so far as to say that Mrs. Farrell, who gives the book its second name, held among Mr. Howells's characters the double disgrace of being the only bad woman and the only woman badly drawn. On rereading the work, it is impossible for me to put the matter quite so trenchantly.

"Bad woman" still seems to me an accurate account of Mrs. Farrell, but "bad drawing" is too severe a censure for the workmanship. Mrs. Farrell is a flirt. Among Mr. Howells's leading women, I recall no other flirt but Bessie Lynde, and Bessie Lynde, though reckless and unwomanly, is not bad. But Mrs. Farrell is a heartless and unscrupulous woman, who is under the necessity of deluding herself and others into the belief that she is possessed of heart and scruple. That means much jugglery, but very little basic complication. She differs from the vulgar coquette only in the fact that she coquettes, not with men merely, but with virtue. Like that French aristocrat who believed that God would think twice before damning a scion of the old noblesse, Mrs. Farrell thinks that the moral law will not be ruthless to a pretty woman. It must be handled tactfully, like a man. It must be flattered and caressed and respectfully lauded and demurely courtesied to, until it is wheedled into forgiving one for disobedience. There is, again, one point in which Mrs. Farrell is distinctly worse than a vulgar coquette. The two men whom she befools are firm friends, officers of the Civil War, whose relation is barely shadowed by the fact that the one had, at the other's urgency, accepted a promotion which the other had merited and failed to win. The wedge which the woman's tongue drives between hearts so solidly knit and so impalpably divided is more awful, more impious, than the shaft which her coquetry drives into either heart. This moral turpitude is not of course a literary blemish, but the literature, though excellent in many ways, has its point of weakness. Mr. Howells, like most other novelists of his time, observes and imagines; and he is probably not alone in the fact that when, having observed all he can, he proceeds to imagine, he imagines *observations*. He *watches*, or subtly feigns to watch, even when he invents. Now in the portraits of these men, and more conspicuously in the larger and more solicitous portrait of Mrs. Farrell, this effect of *ascertainment* is much less noticeable than elsewhere. All three, in a word, seem somewhat conjectural, though never was conjecture more delicate or wakeful. All three are too discerning, too felicitous; in a stupid world which one proposes to draw faithfully, one should not seek in every thought and every phrase a bludgeon for the commonplace. Mr. Howells was, in later days at least, to become the defender of the commonplace, but it never quite outgrew its trick of fleeing from his presence.

"Mrs. Farrell," or "Private Theatricals," belongs in time rather than quality to the first group. It has been reviewed in this place because its claim to a place under our second heading, "Widenings and Deepenings," could scarcely be defended with success.

IV

WIDENINGS AND DEEPENINGS

"A Fearful Responsibility" terminates the early group of novels. "The Undiscovered Country," which comes next in order, might be drawn by a kind of conscription into their company, since it deals with wandering if not travel, and records a love-story which has some aspects of *mésalliance*. But its handling of spiritualism and Shakerism affirms its place in a new order of experiment — the exposition of social movements.

The story of "The Undiscovered Country" is concerned primarily with two spiritualists, a father and a daughter. The father, Dr. Boynton, is a generous and upright dupe, and the girl Egeria, whom he mesmerizes and controls, is his passive and suffering instrument. They are drawn by charlatans into a fraudulent séance, and the father engages in bitter conflict with a rough-mannered but large-hearted young skeptic named Ford, who is finally induced by compassion for the girl to give up his half-framed purpose of antagonizing and exposing the father. The doctor becomes convinced that Ford has cast an evil spell upon his daughter, while the girl, in a touching note, thanks the young man for his consideration. The Boyntons, leaving Boston to return to disapproving kinsfolk, become the prey to every sort of cruel and degrading misadventure. They take the wrong train; they lose their money; they eat the bread of charity in a schoolhouse; and they are detained in a sordid inn by ignominious suspicions. At last, between chance and design, they find themselves in a colony of Shakers, to whom the doctor looks, a little too hopefully, for sympathy and aid in his experiments. The girl falls ill, is delicately nursed, recovers; she recoils more and more from her task as medium. The crushing, though not abject, failure of an attempted demonstration of her powers under the kind but wary scrutiny of the assembled Shakers intensifies her revolt, and disheartens the imperious doctor. Worn out with overstrain and disappointment, he sinks into the grave, but not before he has had one hostile, and many friendly, encounters with his old adversary whom chance, the age-long friend of novelists, has led to the Shaker's always open door. The shy and quiet love between the young man and the girl ripens oddly but pleasingly in the shadow of impending death and the demureness of the Shaker domicile. In the final scene of trembling explanation, the girl admits that she had half assented to her father's earlier belief that Ford had cast an evil spell upon her, and confesses in his arms that the real spell had been, not sorcery, but love.

"The Undiscovered Country" is interesting, — a quality insured by its authorship, — and its teaching is sound and wise. But the 'prentice hand is betrayed in the new experiment: at the close one hesitates to say just what has been accomplished in the four hundred and nineteen pages which its formless diligence has amassed. There is no plot; there is no organic process, though the love-affair between the laconic Ford and the spellbound Egeria now and then blinks lazily under a half-raised eyelash from the cushion on which it comfortably naps. But in the main the novel is symptomatic, that is, it embraces a social fact by successive sides or aspects; and, when the movement is twofold, including such diversities as spiritualism and Shakerism, and when a loose thread of mild wayside adventure is employed to connect these inadhesive parts, the aggregate is doomed to incoherence. Where neither logic nor process obtains, only compactness can avert promiscuity. The motivation is exceptionally weak; my notes record seven instances of inadequately grounded acts, which I forbear to transcribe on the supposition that readers prefer to have their faith taxed rather than their patience. Coincidence also dispenses its benefactions. When Ford's presence is wanted at the Shaker colony where Egeria is already established, he knocks at the door one evening, and is let in; art reverts to its cradle.

One opening for drama is indeed presented by the story. That a spiritualist and his opponent should have their relations vivified by the opponent's love for the spiritualist's daughter, who is likewise his medium, is a not unexciting or unfruitful idea. But this carnal and worldly expedient, so attractive to our fallen nature, is inchoate from the start and is afterwards unreservedly abandoned; the realist in Mr. Howells is an anchorite.

The main characters are not masterly. Egeria, always colorless, discloses in the sequel a tenuous charm which is largely the reflex of spring and convalescence. Ford, whose bearishness would be indistinguishable from boorishness in a character whose breeding was not supervised by Mr. Howells, succeeds in winning our regard; but, later on, he suffers that abatement of vitality by which surly characters pay for the appeasement of their surliness; the extracted teeth leave nothing but the gums. Boynton muffles himself in verbiage without really cloaking himself in it. We can hardly forgive his not being a mountebank: a mountebank might have been interesting. The other characters tend to irrelevance. Hatch, who is thoroughly human, now and then struggles briefly to the foreground; Phillips has an effect of being always in the doorway and Mrs. Perham of being always at the keyhole. The dupes and frauds are handled with a mixture of tolerance and shrinking. Mr. Howells is consciously lenient toward such persons: the impalement they suffer on his pen is involuntary. He treats them with an inhuman fairness, a formidable moderation. They are not so very bad; they are simply — *another species*.

The doctrine of this book — that spiritualism is unspiritual — is instilled without severity and without derision. The Shakers, on whom so many chapters are lavished, are meant to illustrate the opposite condition of true spirituality. The difficulty is that these worthy Shakers are not spiritual; they are mild, kind, dull persons, conventional in their very refusal of custom. They were meant to be winning, and a tender and touching irony was to enfold the birth of a love-idyl in their house. But they are too phlegmatic for this dainty office, and they evoke in the reader only that ghost of sympathy which consists in remorse for the failure to sympathize.

The relation of Mr. Howells to the Shakers is almost an exposition of his character. Their life has moved him more profoundly than that of any other religious or communistic body; they have been to him a lure, a torment, a solace, and a reproach. They have defied one of his foremost instincts, the instinct of sex, and have fulfilled another equally powerful, the longing for fellowship in endeavor and equality in goods.

Many people would blame Mr. Howells for aloofness from life; aloofness from life is undoubtedly the mark of the Shakers; it is therefore very curious that in two distinct cases in which Mr. Howells has transcended his supposed limitations by acting with powerful directness on the normal or average heart, he has found his theme in this lonely and peculiar sect. The two novelettes which I shall mention here in violation of chronology are called "A Parting and a Meeting" and "The Day of the Wedding"; they are brief, homely, unpretending, and little known.

In "A Parting and a Meeting," a young man and woman, in the elation of betrothal, visit a community of Shakers; the young man is austere and visionary; and the girl returns to her father's house alone. The matter is humble, but the reader's heart is cleft.

They meet again in advanced age when the woman revisits the settlement with her granddaughter. I am not sure but that the encounter, which is superficially gay with the gossip of the voluble old woman, does not embody the bitterest moment in the works of an author who has not been niggardly of disenchantments. The vanity of both choices, the worldly and the ascetic, seems intimated in the impartial ravage which has made the man a dotard and the woman a featherbrain. The art of this homespun book is of distinguished quality.

"The Day of the Wedding" is a small affair, but a heart-break is not clamorous for space. It deals with two Shakers who resolve to leave the community and marry, and the slight book depicts the few hours of their planless wedding-day in Saratoga, at the close of which they resign each other and return unsolicited to the brotherhood.

I do not admire the general conduct of this ungroomed and formless story. The day's events seem to emulate the shuffle one can so readily imagine in the gait and mental process of the characters. The buzz of worldly incident, the florid purchases, the cabman's troubling recrudescence, the tawdry acquaintance of the hotel, affect one with a dissonance which the talks with the gracious minister in the rest and coolness of the shuttered house cannot wholly countervail. The style has an untidiness which in a point-device writer like Mr. Howells reminds one of the studied disarray of an Elizabethan lover. But the culmination satisfies. The hold of that inexorable past, which reasserts itself in the hour of love's triumph, and draws the couple back to the life which has become imbedded in instincts deeper than their mutual attraction, — this is drama — this is tragedy. The kiss which seals the parting, not the union, is delicately imagined, and the sorriness and rustiness of it all is taken up into the mastering pathos. The book recalls Mrs. Wharton's "Ethan Frome" in the circumstance that the high-bred writer has here, by some lucky chance, felt deeply and felt with other men. The reader instantly responds. Hector has taken off his casque and plume, and Astyanax runs into his arms.

I have ventured out of my course in order to embrace in one

view Mr. Howells's portrayals of an institution which, as I have said, has had the singular fortune to relate itself in opposite ways to two of the dominant incentives of his life. I return to the beaten path of criticism.

"Dr. Breen's Practice" is a book remarkable for extent of performance, within scant limits, without apparent haste, and without parade of succinctness. It expounds a thesis and it evolves a love-story; it even luxuriates in a plot. Again, the flimsiness of summer-hotel life is effectively sketched in relation to the ancestral sturdiness and stolidness of the surrounding rusticity in which it has been whimsically set down like egg-shell china in an earthen jar. Furthermore, the book is a treasury of characterization, and it is noteworthy that this excellence is almost exclusive of the two nominal protagonists, one of whom, the girl, harasses us with doubts, while her male counterpart, though attractive enough in his way, almost surfeits us with securities. The space they naturally absorb increases our wonder at the freedom and fullness with which the secondary characters unfold their possibilities in this doubly straitened area.

The thesis, which is a polite, almost a reverent, suggestion of the incompetence of the woman physician, is the least successful aspect of the work. Mr. Howells has no trouble in disproving the competence of Grace Breen, but the blame in the case is so clearly referable to the individual that she becomes the shield rather than the accuser of her sex. She is tested by her first case, a test unfair even to a male; she has no inbred love for her vocation — a limitation that would cripple a man. She has not even the superficial self-command which successful training would bestow on a nature ultimately incompetent. She is a society woman; she allows her nerves to govern her practice, and the vacillations of the drawing-room confuse the precepts of the laboratory. A higher sanity than that of the average male is presumed to exist in the male physician; the woman-doctor is entitled to the benefit of the same presumption; yet the sex's competence is tested by a representative who would seem morbid or half distraught to the average woman.

Grace is not wholly unlovable in spite of the unloveliness of her behavior; but, compared with her sisters in other books and her associates in this book, she is little better than a failure. Libby, the hero, is sparsely drawn, but a sweetness which his efficiency has not sapped links him with Dunham and Tom Corey in a triad of chivalrously modest spirits. Mrs. Breen is masterly. Mr. Howells spares hardly a dozen pages to the informing of George Maynard with a vitality which might have made the fortune of a book. Dr. Mulbridge is richly effective, in spite of the trace of artifice which masterful characters are prone to exhibit in fiction, and which makes them possibly as difficult to paint as they are readily and effectively sketchable. The doctor is too large for the book, which shudders and creaks, like an infirm veranda, under the violence of his imperious tread. Mrs. Mulbridge abundantly proves that her son's lifelikeness is hereditary, and the dialogue over the morning coffee-pot is fairly resinous with vigor and pugnacity. Mrs. Maynard, if less cunning as picture, is hardly less pregnant as document. The opulence of vivid portraiture does not overlook even the hired man, Barlow, in its largess of vitality, and the novel, whose minutes are priceless, cannot pass the rural grocery without looking in to leave its vivifying touch on the sodden loafers in their sluggish drawls and chucklings.

I quote, with omission, the morning scene at the Mulbridges', in which the refined strength of Mr. Howells's portrayal of unrefined strength is put beyond question.

". . . You must n't believe too much in doctors, mother. Mrs. Maynard is pretty tough. And she 's had wonderfully good nursing. You 've only heard the Barlow side of the matter," said her son, betraying now for the first time that he had been aware of any knowledge of it on her part.

That was their way: though they seldom told each other anything, and went on as if they knew nothing of each other's affairs, yet when they recognized this knowledge, it was without surprise on either side. "I could tell you a different story. She 's a very fine girl, mother; cool and careful under instruction, and perfectly tractable and intelligent. She 's as different from those other women you 've seen as — you are. You would like her!" He had suddenly grown earnest, and crushing the crust of a biscuit in the strong left hand which he rested on the table, he gazed keenly at her undemonstrative face. "She 's no baby, either. She 's got a will and a temper of her own. She 's the only one of them I ever saw that was worth her salt."

"I thought you did n't like self-willed women," said his mother impassively.

"She knows when to give up," he answered, with unrelaxed scrutiny.

His mother did not lift her eyes, yet. "How long shall you have to visit over there?"

"I 've made my last professional visit."

"Where are you going this morning?"

"To Jocelyn's."

Mrs. Mulbridge now looked up, and met her son's eye. "What makes you think she 'll have you?"

He did not shrink at her coming straight to the point the moment the way was clear. He had intended it, and he liked it. But he frowned a little as he said, "Because I want her to have me, for one thing." His jaw closed heavily, but his face lost a certain brutal look almost as quickly as it had assumed it. "I guess," he said, with a smile, "that it 's the only reason I 've got."

"You 've no need to say that," said his mother, resenting the implication that any woman would not have him.

"Oh, I 'm not pretty to look at, mother, and I 'm not particularly young; and for a while I thought there might be someone else."

"Who?"

"The young fellow that came with her, that day."

"That whipper-snapper?"

Dr. Mulbridge assented by his silence. "But I guess I was mistaken. I guess he 's tried and missed it. The field is clear, for all I can see. And she 's made a failure in one way, and then you know a woman is in the humor to try it in another. She wants a good excuse for giving up. That 's what I think."

"Well," said his mother, "I presume you know what you 're about, Rufus."

She took up the coffee-pot, on the lid of which she had been keeping her hand, and went into the kitchen with it. She removed the dishes, and left him sitting before the empty table-cloth. When she came for that, he took hold of her hand, and looked up into her face, over which a scarcely discernible tremor passed. "Well, mother?"

"It 's what I always knew I had got to come to, first or last. And I suppose I ought to feel glad enough I did n't have to come to it at first."

"No," said her son. "I 'm not a stripling any longer." He laughed, keeping his mother's hand.

She freed it and, taking up the table-cloth, folded it lengthwise and then across, and laid it neatly away in the cupboard. "I shan't interfere with you, nor any woman that you bring here to be your wife. I 've had my day, and I 'm not one of the old fools that think they 're going to have and to hold forever. You 've always been a good boy to me, and I guess you hain't ever had to complain of your mother stan'in' in your way. I shan't now. But I *did* think —"

She stopped, and shut her lips firmly. . . .

"If she were like the rest of them, I 'd never have her. But she is n't. As far as I 'm concerned, it 's nothing against her that she 's studied medicine. She did n't do it from vanity, or ambition, or any abnormal love of it. She did it, so far as I can find out, because she wished to do good that way. She 's been a little notional, she 's had her head addled by women's talk, and she 's in a queer freak; but it 's only a girl's freak after all: you can't say anything worse of her. She 's a splendid woman, and her property 's neither here nor there. I could support her."

"I presume," replied his mother, "that she 's been used to ways that ain't like our ways. I 've always stuck up for you, Rufus, stiff enough, I guess; but I ain't agoin' to deny that you 're country born and bred. I can see that, and she can see it, too. It makes a great difference with girls. I don't know as she 'd call you what they call a gentleman."

Dr. Mulbridge flushed angrily. Every American, of whatever standing or breeding, thinks of himself as a gentleman, and nothing can gall him more than the insinuation that he is less. "What do you mean, mother?"

"You hain't ever been in such ladies' society as hers in the same way. I know that they all think the world of you, and flatter you up, and they 're as biddable as you please when you 're doctorin' 'em; but I guess it would be different if you was to set up for one of their own kind amongst 'em."

"There is n't one of them," he retorted, "that I don't believe I could have for the turn of my hand, especially if it was doubled into a fist. They like force."

"Oh, you 've only seen the sick married ones. I guess you 'll find a well *girl* is another thing."

"They 're all alike. And I think I should be something of a relief if I was n't like what she 's been used to hearing called a gentleman; she 'd prefer me on that account. But if you come to blood, I guess the Mulbridges and Gardiners can hold up their heads with the best, *any*where."

"Yes, like the Camfers and Rafflins." These were people of ancestral consequence and local history, who had gone up to Boston from Corbitant, and had succeeded severally as green-grocers and retail dry-goods men, with the naturally attendant social distinction.

"Pshaw!" cried her son. "If she cares for me at all, she won't care for the cut of my clothes, or my table manners."

"Yes, that 's so. 'T ain't on my account that I want you should make sure she *doos* care."

He looked hard at her immovable face, with its fallen eyes, and then went out of the room. He never quarrelled with his mother, because his anger, like her own, was dumb, and silenced him as it mounted. Her misgivings had stung him deeply, and at the bottom of his indolence and indifference was a fiery pride, not easily kindled, but unquenchable. He flung the harness upon his old unkempt horse, and tackled him to the mud-encrusted buggy, for whose shabbiness he had never cared before. He was tempted to go back into the house, and change his uncouth Canada homespun coat for the broadcloth frock which he wore when he went to Boston; but he scornfully resisted it, and drove off in his accustomed figure.

The story is very well handled. The plot is a real aid, though it is not rashly emphasized, and bears itself, among the portraits and the propaganda, with the modesty proper to doubtful characters admitted on sufferance to the society of their betters. The novelette is packed with quiet action, yet the incidents move forward in fluid, unembarrassed sequence. Room is made for elaborations and parentheses, in virtue of the same law that makes busy people tolerant of interruption.

"Dr. Breen's Practice" was the last novel which Mr. Howells published in the "Atlantic Monthly"; "A Modern Instance" marked his earliest contribution to the "Century Magazine." The passage from the "Atlantic" to the "Century" is a change from the park to the square; and, while the close of his editorship no doubt influenced his choice of vehicle, it is certain that his work passed at the same period from the by-way to the avenue. Mr. Howells's journeyings in the earlier tales are half-retirement, as his aristocracy — being Bostonian — is half-recluse. In "A Modern Instance" the main characters are for the first time of relatively coarse fibre, and their little bark steers its devious course in the swift mid-current of metropolitan activity.

The book is almost a popular novel. That rapid succession of clear and crisp incident which creates a public for Mr. Churchill and Mr. Dreiser, as it has broadened and varied the public of abler writers like Flaubert and Daudet, appears in Mr. Howells's work for the first time. This imperfect but vigorous fiction has a rare momentum, a rich abundance, on planes accessible to normal capacity. I doubt if, in subsequent work, Mr. Howells ever quite recaptured this impetus or this material.

The book contains some perfect narrative. The love-affair is good, and the record of the early married life is a model of clear, swift, interesting, richly incidental and sparingly eventful, story-telling. The style recedes — I do not say declines, but simply recedes — and I attribute the beautiful expertness of the story-telling in part to this recession.

I have spoken before of the unfortunate decentralization which this book suffers when in the last part the Halleck-Atherton interest opens business on its own account, and becomes, according to the wont of commerce, the competitor of its former chief. A story — or rather a mere state — of inactive and inarticulate love presented by discussion should clearly not have been allowed to interpose its non-conducting tissue between the successive phases of a rapid tale of collapsing character and dissolving marriage. Partly through this error, the book rejects the offer of dramatic climax which the plot involves, and the crisis, on its delayed arrival, instead of claiming the leadership, ranges itself quietly in the line of common incidents.

The ethical purpose of "A Modern Instance" is clearest in the secondary drama. Ben Halleck silences his love for the wife of Bartley Hubbard, but this silence is no arrest to the flow of condemnation from his friend Atherton, who, a lawyer by trade, acts in this point as attorney for Mr. Howells. Even after Bartley Hubbard's death, the struggle is prolonged by the question whether an act otherwise innocent can be compromised by its source in an emotion which was once the unheeded prompter to acts of guilt. This scruple is fine in Halleck but finical in Atherton, whose moral arrogance is finally punctured by the discovery that life is a rude and hardy business in which the refinements of abnegation may be sought for one's self but cannot decently be imposed upon other people.

So far the teaching, to wit, the horror and shame of any love that overrides marriage, is entirely clear. But it is not quite so easy to see the relation of this secondary theme to the vivid and strenuous picture of unlovely and ill-starred marriage which occupies the larger portion of the book. The picture might be viewed as a lofty paradox or hyperbole, asserting the faith that marriage is august even in its meanness, that its very profanation is inviolable. Such is Mr. Howells's conviction, without doubt, but I question if it be the animus of the Bartley–Marcia chronicle, or if the story could convey such a lesson to the normal reader. That personage would no doubt find the sanctity of marriage in its beneficence, and the failure of that beneficence in the Hubbard case would seem the last material from which to derive a confirmation of its sanctity.

The shattering of marriage against the undisciplined wills of the participants — the demand for character in marriage — is the version of the theme which agrees best with the offered data. The proposition, though sound, is unexciting, and its value is mainly intellectual, since the specification of a necessity which cannot be imported or improvised, whose absence is for the time being unchangeable, is more useful to philosophy than to reform. I am not much concerned with this shortcoming, — a novel's inadequacy in its thesis is after all only a shortage in a superfluity, — but I think it fitting to suggest that, as demonstration, the main narrative of "A Modern Instance" is far from unassailable. The author purposes to tell us why Bartley Hubbard's character falls to pieces, why his marriage issues in dissension and divorce. I doubt if either of these issues is made highly probable.

I could make shift to specify the point in Bartley Hubbard's career when he becomes a bad man. It is at the close of section XXIII. Other readers would probably dissent, but I think a perfect art should make it impossible for any attentive reader to find a sharp angle in what purports to be a mellow curve. Moreover, his deterioration is not explained by his circumstances. The circumstances do not favor depravation; they favor uprightness. He is doubly fortunate in a prosperity which provides revenue without dishonesty and in a marriage which appeases sexuality without license. The goodness — or, let us say, the harmlessness — of many men is contingent; but where, as in this case, the contingencies are auspicious, ruin is inevitable only to men much worse than the original Bartley Hubbard. We have to presume a latent wickedness which events successively uncover rather than a nascent wickedness which they successively induce. The conclusion infers an original badness which is not declared or fairly implied in the premises.

Mr. Howells is at once very lenient and very severe toward Bartley Hubbard. He is lenient in his indictments; he is merciless in the final — perhaps I should rather say the initial — estimate. He often mocks the Puritan conscience; but the Alleghanies form a slender barrier to the enterprise of that adventurous faculty, and the Ohio lad drew in much of its attitude toward evil. His mercy, indeed, is unfailing, but his horror in the presence of wickedness is Puritanic or mediæval. He surveys it with the awe, the terror, and the charm with which a child rivets its reluctant but devouring eyes upon some gilded and venomous thing. The spell, the enthrallment, which Balzac found in Père Grandet, even that which Hawthorne found in Judge Pyncheon, is reproduced, of course with the proper differentia, in the sober record of this faithful realist. His convictions — like Hawthorne's, in all probability — were the reverse of Puritanical. In "Imaginary Interviews" he could suggest that "there is n't any purely voluntary evil among the sane"; but before an act of meanness or perfidy or cruelty a shudder traverses his frame, and that shudder is Draconic. He is always forbearing and open-minded, but in his scrupulous attenuations and reservations he has an effect of carrying water to the damned.

Of this form of badness Bartley Hubbard supplies a clear illustration; it is a pervasive, inherent, original badness, like Calvinistic sin, separable in a sense from all the man's definable transgressions, as it is in a kindred sense inseparable from his virtues and benefactions. Accordingly, a great indifference, a great easiness, in the particularization of misdeeds. What does it matter whether Bartley Hubbard be a brute, a sot, a cheat, or a libertine? It is enough that he is Bartley. In another still better picture, that of Jeff Durgin, in "The Landlord at Lion's Head," the establishment of any particular charge seems to be rendered once for all unnecessary by the damning certainty that he is Jeff. Mr. Howells draws such beings superlatively, because they are vivified, and they are not distorted, by his horror; he refuses to darken their contours, not because he lacks bias, but because his bias is so profound and secure that it finds a chivalrous or disdainful pleasure in wresting the facts to the profit of its enemies.

It may seem a strange postscript to the above remarks to

add that Mr. Howells is fond of this very Bartley Hubbard whom he abhors. Bartley has a bright tongue, which propitiates the author and even the virtuous reader, and the rogue is accepted as a faint extenuation of the scoundrel.

The demonstration of the necessity of disaster in the marriage is again incomplete. The defences in this marriage are the wife's devotion, the husband's sincere though cooling passion, domesticity on both sides, a child loved by both, no proved unchastity, cruelty only in speech. The disruptive forces are the wife's passionate and jealous temper, the husband's accesses of wrath breaking forth in brutal speech, and his crookedness within the rim of legal safety. Now, hot temper that is mere hot temper does not *strain* the fabric of marriage to anything like the degree in which it makes it sway and heave; and the wife's conscience has had to overlook or overcome its objections to the business ethics of the husband in supposably a fairly large proportion of happy unions. The hardiness of marriage is as amazing as its frailty, and it seems fairly certain that crafts no better manned than "The Hubbard" have steered successfully into port.

I would not say for a moment that in the points of Bartley's degeneracy and the ruin of his marriage Mr. Howells has not made the recorded issues conceivable. But, after all his pains, the opposite issues are also conceivable, and I am not sure that this was the outcome he intended.

The demonstration of necessity is hardly the function of literature; its field is the exposition of the possible. I doubt if processes analogous to those of growth and decay in the organic world, processes at once extended and traceable, the cessation or reversal of which it would be difficult to imagine, occur largely in the fields from which literature draws its nutriment. Indeed, an actuality excites our interest mainly as a defeat to an alternate possibility. Let us put the merit of "A Modern Instance" uncompromisingly where it belongs, not in its geometrical exactness, but in the range and minuteness, the rapidity and variety, of its picture of current life on sordid levels.

The characterization of this book as a whole is below that of "Dr. Breen's Practice," though neither "Dr. Breen's Practice" nor any preceding novel contains a portrait comparable to that of Bartley Hubbard for curious and various particularity, for the mixture of fondness and recoil with which touch upon touch is patiently accumulated. Marcia, the wife, is a far less interesting figure, in spite of the pointed contrast which her apathies offer to her passions, her sagacity to her dullness, her grovellings to her rebellions. Her mother, Mrs. Gaylord, is a tiny masterpiece. That self-infolding, self-screening nature discloses only a line of its physiognomy through the slit in its apparel, but that line is a portrait. The squire, who diffuses bleakness through the novel like an east wind, is better to my mind in individual moments than in the sum and concourse of his divergent, not to say discrepant, traits. The Hallecks are an amiable group. The son Ben is unfortunate in the self-belying, self-calumnious rôle which the story bids him undertake. Olive is readily effective at the trifling expense of a little causticity. The mild parents are drawn with a discreet tenderness; they remind us a little of two characters of later date, the Vockerats in Hauptmann's "Lonely Lives," whose relation to their son is dimly prefigured in the New England family. Atherton is tryingly wise, and Clara Kingsbury, whom he anomalously marries, is agreeably foolish. Kinney, the cook of the logging camp, is effective, except that he has the air — not uncommon in Mr. Howells's rustics — of having been rather too sedulously observed.

"A Modern Instance" is clearly an emphatic departure. The previous works had been marked by guarded or demure subjects, leisurely narration, and select characters; in this book the subjects are bold, the narrative is rapid and varied, and the characters are under-bred or half-bred. The author seemed to have relinquished the delicate tête-à-têtes in the secluded bow-window commanding the rich terrace and the view of manors and steeples in the distance, and to have taken a turn that looked toward passion and power, and even — one might cautiously surmise — toward popularity. The subjects — in particular, divorce and the passion for the neighbor's wife — seemed falling into step with the moving and daring themes which had assured to so many of the European novels of the century their resonance, if not their fame. But Mr. Howells, in his later work, neither returned to his dainty idyls nor pursued with any steadiness or hardihood the path broken by "A Modern Instance." He never reverted to the themes of dissolving marriage and an unhallowed love; and while he did revert to crisp, elastic, straightforward narrative and to plebeian or pedestrian characters, he never again lent himself so absolutely and trustingly to these means of interest as in the remarkable and isolated "Modern Instance." Not ready either to retreat or to advance, he preferred a diagonal course, which we must now follow through "A Woman's Reason," "The Rise of Silas Lapham," and "The Minister's Charge."

V

SOCIETY AND SOCIALISM

"A Woman's Reason" is a summer cottage in which Mr. Howells recovers from the wrestle with "A Modern Instance." In spite of its surfeit of troubles and worries, it gives in its entirety a rebellious effect of cosiness and sunshine. People take the most delightful comfort in the intervals of their distresses. Helen Harkness loses her father, loses her fortune, loses the salvage from her fortune, quarrels with her lover, loses — as she believes — her lover by death, is pestered by an aging widower with shabby claims and shabbier proffers, fails in half-a-dozen callings, and falls sick. The list, as a list, is appalling; but in life itself ills are not listed, and the book is cheery and sportive, with Ray and Marian, with the delayed betrothal, with the delicious trustfulness of the tie with the Butlers, with Lord Rainford's oddities and Miss Kingsbury's expansiveness, with the irresistible fun that Mr. Evans makes of the irresistible appeal made by Helen's distress to the latent snobbishness in Cornelia Root, with Robert's return, with something that cannot be specified, or is specifiable only as a laughing nonchalance. The trouble is so desultory that it seems only a whim of gayety.

A young lady is left orphaned and penniless; she is without special training, and the failure of her successive experiments in self-support constitutes the kernel, and conveys the lesson, of the story. Some of this makes, or should make, rather painful reading; but the reader, who is a snob himself, is solaced by his belief that Fortune is a snob, too, and may tease, but will not really hurt, a young lady of the pure noblesse of Boston. As in "St. Ronan's Well," the silk petticoat makes all the difference. I do not mean that Mr. Howells trims the facts; I mean only that we confide in the issue.

The art of the book is less than irreproachable. There is a legitimate promiscuity behind which we discern another promiscuity whose lawfulness is not so obvious. Mere likeness, generic likeness, is a form of coherence; and Helen's attempts at self-support, though all separable, possess unity. But the love-making and the bread-winning are distinct in kind, and the shuttle of logic which plays rather loosely and casually between the two evolves a web that is not wholly flawless. It is a case of that unguarded, that unwary, mixture of types which no rightness in the types themselves can justify. The novel, like actual business, is shredded into tiny incidents, and involves the semi-casual coming and going of many loosely assorted persons, with an effect of nimbleness which hardly amounts to vivacity. The grace of Mr. Howells aërates even his pursuit of business; the touch is graceful perhaps because it is slight; but one is thankful for slightness and grace alike, when one imagines how a sumpter like Balzac would have stooped and strained under the panniers of his overflowing knowledge.

The young woman whose attempts at self-support provide sustenance only for Mr. Howells has a lover in the American navy, from whose station in the Pacific a false rumor of his death reaches her at a turning-point in her destiny. In the process of supplying a basis for this rumor, Mr. Howells finds himself on a wrecked ship, and later, helpless, on a coral island. There is something Gilbertian in the image of Mr. Howells on a coral island. As Emerson said of Webster's Seventh of March speech, "How came he there?" These episodes are related with an extraordinary swiftness, almost like the swiftness of fear, and with an exceptional gravity, possibly the gravity of one who swallows a laugh. They are interesting, but very light, and they excite no displeasure in the wondering reader. Perhaps Mr. Howells in the deprecatory attitude of a purveyor of adventure evokes an indulgence proportionate to his distress.

The coincidences in this book are of a bold, not to say daredevil, character. There is a policeman who comes up unexpectedly four times, exactly when he is wanted. It is needless to remind Mr. Howells that such behavior is unprofessional. Helen Harkness, in a Boston restaurant, overhears a California woman relate an episode in which she had figured as *vis-à-vis* to Helen's own lover, Robert Fenton, on a Pacific steamer returning to San Francisco. This incident is not useful to the author, and the reader hardly knows whether the sin is excused by its disinterestedness or aggravated by its impertinence. In another place, Helen leaves her friends, the Butlers, to avoid a meeting with an English lord, and finds the lord preëstablished in the very dwelling in which she had sought an asylum from his courtship. Things like this do happen, undoubtedly, but their appearance in sober literature is almost the quixotry of realism.

The characterization is good, but not superlative. Helen is individual and lovable; but just as her character is simple under all its complication of acquired subtleties, so it remains light in the presence of sorrows, endeavors, and sacrifices that are tragically real. Her personality hardly bears up her character. Fenton is likable, but elementary: he might almost have been borrowed from Walter Scott. The Butlers, vivid as a group, hardly live as individuals except intermittently when they flash into life in the person of the palpitating Jessie. Lord Rainford, a little nebulous at the start, grows more distinct with successive chapters and successive readings. Mr. Howells draws few Englishmen, but his Rainford, his Westgate, his Crayburne, fairly rehabilitate their nation. I should call them exquisite, only Mr. Howells thinks Mark Twain exquisite and these Englishmen are not like Mark Twain. Mr. Evans's satire is pushed beyond nature, but in a fashion that would have made adhesion to nature at the expense of comedy unforgivable. Mrs. Evans and Mrs. Hewett are very happy examples of the creative efficiency of a very few discriminating touches; they suggest creation by fiat. Clara Atherton appears as Clara Kingsbury, restored to virginity and exuberance; a chivalrous retreat of the calendar has allowed the rose to shut and be a bud again. Cornelia Root, whom Miss Kingsbury penetratingly describes as rectangular, is perhaps the most effective person in the book, and the breadth of Mr. Howells's sympathy aids the dexterity of his hand in the admirable picture of the old cook Margaret.

The book shows some trenchant discriminations. Once more the actuality of love is handled with a reverence which unbelievers would reject as sentimental, while the humbug in which fiction has disguised the passion is cast aside with a decision that seems cynical to romanticists. Similarly, America is censured as an undemocratic democracy, but the republicanism of English aristocrats is pictured as a whim.

"The Rise of Silas Lapham" is a Bostonian novel. A Boston family of the strict Brahminical type, the Coreys, finds itself under obligations for help in a painful emergency to the Laphams, a family of crude manners, mushroom wealth, and sterling virtue. The Laphams, pricked to social ambition by the new acquaintance, build a house on the Back Bay. The contrast of the two social worlds is amusingly depicted in the chapters that record their intercourse; and the elder Lapham allows himself to become intoxicated at a dinner to which he and his family have been self-sacrificingly invited by the Coreys. Meanwhile, Tom Corey, only son of the distinguished family, has obtained a place in the mineral-paint establishment of Silas Lapham, and has seen something informally of the two Lapham girls, the elder of whom, Penelope, is interesting, while her younger sister Irene is dazzlingly beautiful. The young man makes love to the elder girl, but so unobtrusively that he is supposed by both families and both girls to be making love to the other. He proposes to Penelope; she refuses in remorse and dismay; Irene is momentarily furious; the Lapham family is thrown into consternation, and the Corey family, recoiling from any bond with the Laphams, is still further distressed by the discovery that the choice has fallen on the plainer and less valued girl. The question whether a girl may decently marry the man she loves if the joint anticipations of two families have previously bestowed him on a consenting sister seems to be too easy to be worth putting or answering when you have removed it from the texture of the novel; but it is argued extendedly and gravely and dejectedly by the lover and the girl and the girl's parents and the Unitarian minister and the Unitarian minister's wife. The end is marriage, and the flight of the mésalliance into Mexico. Meanwhile, the new Lapham house burns to the ground, while the Lapham fortune, of which it was the bright particular sign, crumbles to nothingness. Safety is offered through dishonesty; but character finally triumphs over interest, and Silas Lapham carries his poverty and his self-respect to a last asylum in his country home.

In the "Rise of Silas Lapham" we find Mr. Howells retightening the cords the tension of which in "A Woman's Reason" had perceptibly relaxed. In "Silas Lapham" there is a story; persons interact; events are procreative; a natural and simple misunderstanding as to a young man's object in his intercourse with two sisters offers a piquancy not quite usual in Mr. Howells, and evokes a surprisingly large amount of subdued and leisurely but interesting drama. The story of the business difficulties of the father is united to this love-tale by ties which a logician might blame as inadequate, but which, in an age in which art measures its prosperity by its indifference to logic, criticism must not hasten to condemn. Structurally perhaps it is the shapeliest of the novels; the broad, clean-cut reaches of the two main elements in the fable make the book notable for *prospect* in comparison with its congested predecessor, "A Woman's Reason," and its unexpected successor, "The Minister's Charge." The detail is naturally copious, but mere detail is not inimical to breadth; a half-dozen shrubs or saplings will interrupt the simple lines and large continuity of a prairie more effectually than a million grass-blades. The story, which is cheerful and demurely sportive through the greater part of its course, becomes subject, at one point, to an infirmity which is prone to attack Mr. Howells's novels in what I shall call their later middle-age — an ataxia or paralysis of the limbs, which arrests motion and slackens enterprise. In the penultimate chapters the story and Penelope mope together, and the vanishing gleam of Lapham's dollars, which have scattered a Philistine sunshine through the book, plunges the reader into a melancholy from which he is only half redeemed by the technically happy ending.

The appeal of "Silas Lapham" was relatively popular. An interest in King Cophetua's love for the beggar maid is a feeling which the masses share with Mr. Howells; and when a resigned court and a jubilant proletariat are mistakenly convinced that the object of Cophetua's regard is the beggar maid's sister, the misunderstanding has savor even for the untaught palate. Not that Mr. Howells has not secreted a few choicer vintages to be sipped in elect privacy by his discerning guests, while the lighter distillations are freely offered to the cheaper public. The delicacies of the encounter between the Bostonian aristocracy and the rusticities of the province have not escaped so shrewd an observer, and the ethics of marrying a man whom family expectation has assigned to a receptive sister is settled by a stout affirmative. The point is so obvious that we are apt to do no justice to its originality, or to the interest of the spectacle of literature recanting its own tenets to align itself with the robust sanities of life.

The leisurely pace at which the story moves may be inferred from the fact that thirty-one pages are allotted to a dinner at which nothing decisive occurs, to say nothing of the assignment of from twenty to twenty-five pages to the elaboration of pre-prandial arrangements. The artist in Mr. Howells reasserts his distinction in the beauty of the succession of unobtrusive motives which lead up to Tom Corey's proposal to Penelope.

The Laphams stand for plain worth, but they are placed in a situation that is libellous. They are vulgar, but they are also honest, loving, and intelligent, and their situation is such that the accent falls relentlessly upon their vulgarity. Virtues which outweigh, if they do not outshine, the refinements, wear in the presence of the Coreys the cringing and hangdog look of insufficient compensations for the lack of breeding. One hardly knows whether they are worse used in having Mr. Howells for their photographer or in having the Coreys for their fellow sitters. Both families are, in some sort, exhibits to each other, but the Laphams have a shamefaced sense that they hold the first rank as curiosities. The Coreys, who invite them to dinner, have an unmistakable air of "feeding the elephant."

Silas Lapham is an excellent portrait. If he does not rank with the superlative drawings in the Howells collection, with Fulkerson and Jeff Durgin, for example, he misses that level by a margin of honorable narrowness. What is wanting? Body, I think, bottom or constitution. There is not quite enough of him; he does not wholly fill out his clothes, and the resulting bagginess and limpness is prejudicial to his figure. He fidgets unduly in a moral sense and his vacillations checker his stubbornness. He is loud, he is boastful, he gets drunk at a dinner-party, but he is generous, affectionate, and ultimately honest. The precariousness of this honesty, its liability to great temptations and slight reverses, admirably reflects the battle between tradition and practice in the minds of many vigorous and successful Americans. It is characteristic of realism that his probity should win and yet should hardly triumph; its victory is wingless. I am sorry to see his business faculty discredited; his personality needed that clamp.

Mrs. Lapham is equally good. She is absolutely much less vulgar than her husband, but what vulgarity she has is accentuated by her sex. Her self-assertion is an excellent correlative to her husband's, equal in degree but different in kind. In both, the swelling and shrinking of self-confidence is noteworthy; in fact, the actual quantity and variety of experience through which Mr. Howells causes these two simple-minded persons to pass is a symptom of the fullness and delicacy of his comprehension of life.

Penelope, in her cheerful days, is excellent. But she is so simply made that her humor is more than half her being, and the cloud which suppresses this humor obscures her individuality. The reader who misses her gayety is inclined to cry with stout Capulet:

> How now! a conduit, girl? what, still in tears?
> Evermore showering?

A consummate tact leaves the question of her refinement in lasting abeyance; she is never shown in circumstances where the author might have to choose between the sacrifice of her charm and the suspension of his realism. In the end her lover is vouchsafed to her, but the sensibilities of Boston are spared by the prompt deportation of the offending couple to Mexico. Mexico is a country in which the irruption of primitive elements into a ripened social organism is too common to excite surprise.

Irene's early vacuity is rather suddenly converted into energy and resolution. The two parts are both distinct; the indistinctness lies in the copula.

Bromfield Corey has the effect of long ripening in sunny leisure, both in his own person and in the fond image of him in the mind of the novelist. New England could not have bred that varied and sensitive culture, but New England has safeguarded the purity which stamps that culture with an original grace. He was fated to be impossibly clever from the moment that Mr. Howells took him in hand, but he *lives* in contempt of possibility. The joy the author takes in him is quite separable from approbation. Mr. Howells is quite alive to the incivism, as he would say, of an idler who makes idleness lovable. To convict aristocracy of unsoundness in the person of its most delightful representative is an artistic victory of the first order.

Mrs. Corey is a good woman in an ungracious part; Mr. Howells has treated her with a subtle justice.

Tom Corey is — is an aroma endowed with a faculty for business. Mr. Howells has made the most impalpable of his young men at once the most winning and the most practical. Walker is good realism, and Rogers, a being of small initial promise, develops into a specimen of the grotesque admirable enough to suggest a profane comparison with Dickens.

A few pages from the dinner scene may be quoted; it requires fortitude not to print the whole.

These names, unknown to Lapham, went to his head like the wine he was drinking; they seemed to carry light for the moment, but a film of deeper darkness followed. He heard Charles Bellingham telling funny stories to Irene and trying to amuse the girl; she was laughing, and seemed very happy. From time to time Bellingham took part in the general talk between the host and James Bellingham and Miss Kingsbury and that minister, Mr. Sewell. They talked of people mostly; it astonished Lapham to hear with what freedom they talked. They discussed these persons unsparingly; James Bellingham spoke of a man known to Lapham for his business success and great wealth as not a gentleman; his cousin Charles said he was surprised that the fellow had kept from being governor so long.

When the latter turned from Irene to make one of these excursions into the general talk, young Corey talked to her; and Lapham caught some words from which it seemed that they were speaking of Penelope. It vexed him to think she had not come; she could have talked as well as any of them; she was just as bright; and Lapham was aware that Irene was not as bright, though when he looked at her face, triumphant in its young beauty and fondness, he said to himself that it did not make any difference. He felt that he was not holding up his end of the line, however. When some one spoke to him he could only summon a few words in reply, that seemed to lead to nothing; things often came into his mind appropriate to what they were saying, but before he could get them out they were off on something else; they jumped about so, he could not keep up; but he felt, all the same, that he was not doing himself justice.

At one time the talk ran off upon a subject that Lapham had never heard talked of before; but again he was vexed that Penelope was not there, to have her say; he believed that her say would have been worth hearing.

Miss Kingsbury leaned forward and asked Charles Bellingham if he had read "Tears, Idle Tears," the novel that was making such a sensation; and when he said no, she said she wondered at him. "It 's perfectly heart-breaking, as you 'll imagine from the name; but there 's such a dear old-fashioned hero and heroine in it, who keep dying for each other all the way through, and making the most wildly satisfactory and unnecessary sacrifices for each other. You feel as if you 'd done them yourself."

"Ah, that 's the secret of its success," said Bromfield Corey. "It flatters the reader by painting the characters colossal, but with his limp and stoop, so that he feels himself of their supernatural proportions. You 've read it, Nanny?"

"Yes," said his daughter. "It ought to have been called 'Slop, Silly Slop.'"

"Oh, not quite *slop*, Nanny," pleaded Miss Kingsbury.

"It 's astonishing," said Charles Bellingham, "how we do like the books that go for our heart-strings. And I really suppose that you can't put a more popular thing than self-sacrifice into a novel. We do like to see people suffering sublimely."

"There was talk some years ago," said James Bellingham, "about novels going out."

"They 're just coming in!" cried Miss Kingsbury.

"Yes," said Mr. Sewell, the minister. "And I don't think there ever was a time when they formed the whole intellectual experience of more people. They do greater mischief than ever."

"Don't be envious, parson," said the host.

"No," answered Sewell. "I should be glad of their help. But those novels with old-fashioned heroes and heroines in them — excuse me, Miss Kingsbury — are ruinous!"

"Don't you feel like a moral wreck, Miss Kingsbury?" asked the host.

But Sewell went on: "The novelists might be the greatest possible help to us if they painted life as it is, and human feelings in their true proportion and relation; but for the most part they have been and are altogether noxious."

This seemed sense to Lapham; but Bromfield Corey asked: "But what if life as it is is n't amusing? Aren't we to be amused?"

"Not to our hurt," sturdily answered the minister. "And the self-sacrifice painted in most novels like this —"

"'Slop, Silly Slop'?" suggested the proud father of the inventor of the phrase.

"Yes — is nothing but psychical suicide, and is as wholly immoral as the spectacle of a man falling upon his sword."

"Well, I don't know but you 're right, parson," said the host; and the minister, who had apparently got upon a battle-horse of his, careered onward in spite of some tacit attempts of his wife to seize the bridle.

"Right? To be sure I am right. The whole business of love, and lovemaking and marrying, is painted by the novelists in a monstrous disproportion to the other relations of life. Love is very sweet, very pretty —"

"Oh, *thank* you, Mr. Sewell," said Nanny Corey, in a way that set them all laughing.

"But it 's the affair, commonly, of very young people, who have not yet character and experience enough to make them interesting. In novels it 's treated, not only as if it were the chief interest of life, but the sole interest of the lives of two ridiculous young persons; and it is taught that love is perpetual, that the glow of a true passion lasts for ever; and that it is sacrilege to think or act otherwise."

"Well, but is n't that true, Mr. Sewell?" pleaded Miss Kingsbury.

"I have known some most estimable people who had married a second time," said the minister; and then he had the applause with him. Lapham wanted to make some open recognition of his good sense, but could not.

"I suppose the passion itself has been a good deal changed," said Bromfield Corey, "since the poets began to idealise it in the days of chivalry."

"Yes; and it ought to be changed again," said Mr. Sewell.

"What! Back?"

"I don't say that. But it ought to be recognised as something natural and mortal, and divine honours, which belong to righteousness alone, ought not to be paid it."

"Oh, you ask too much, parson," laughed his host, and the talk wandered away to something else.

It was not an elaborate dinner; but Lapham was used to having everything on the table at once, and this succession of dishes bewildered him; he was afraid perhaps he was eating too much. He now no longer made any pretence of not drinking his wine, for he was thirsty, and there was no more water, and he hated to ask for any. The ice-cream came, and then the fruit. Suddenly Mrs. Corey rose, and said across the table to her husband, "I suppose you will want your coffee here." And he replied, "Yes; we 'll join you at tea."

The ladies all rose, and the gentlemen got up with them. Lapham started to follow Mrs. Corey, but the other men merely stood in their places, except young Corey, who ran and opened the door for his mother. Lapham thought with shame that it was he who ought to have done that; but no one seemed to notice, and he sat down again gladly, after kicking out one of his legs which had gone to sleep.

In "The Rise of Silas Lapham" Mr. Howells struck out a new and interesting type: the love-story, with a subdued and simple but unmistakable plot, with parts for six or eight characters, in which the comedy of social disparities is combined with a grave moral issue. The promise of the departure was great. But Mr. Howells pursued his own course inflexibly; the experiment of "Silas Lapham," like the experiment of "A Modern Instance," was unrepeated in its entirety and fullness. His next novel, "The Minister's Charge," was conducted on another plan.

In this novel, otherwise known as "The Apprenticeship of Lemuel Barker," a country lad comes to Boston and undergoes a miscellany of experiences, in the course of which he relates himself as servant and employee to many phases and many layers of Boston life. This variety of relations, which is prompted by the author's interest in class distinctions, has been purchased by a loss of verisimilitude, not so much in specific passages as in the cast or complexion of the apprenticeship as a whole. A character so massive would have been less at the mercy of vicissitude. There is a nucleus of plot in the trenchant alternative which forces the young man to choose between the serious passion of his riper self and the engagement in which a passing fancy for a foolish girl had involved his rustic ignorance. This organic nucleus is imbedded, like a fossil in the inorganic rock, in a larger mass of what I may loosely call experience. To add to the diversity, the narrative is bifocal, like an ellipse, and surveys the situation partly from the point of view of Lemuel Barker, partly from that of a prevaricating minister, Mr. Sewell. This minister's insincere and incautious praise of the boy's uncouth verse is responsible for Lemuel's journey to Boston and, less directly, for his arraignment on a baseless charge before a police court and his acceptance of a night's lodging in the so-called "Wayfarers' Lodge." The minister, in whom mendacity fraternizes with the noblest virtues and who, in Stevenson's phrase, has domesticated the "Recording Angel" in the person of an immitigable wife, undergoes a severe but salutary penance which issues at last in the championship of a principle known as complicity.

The author pilots Lemuel with deft celerity through the variety of incidents and abundance of characters which congest the book, until, somewhere in the last third of the novel, a fire breaks out in Mrs. Harmon's pinchbeck boarding-house. The story never recovers from the shock of the fire; it wanders, thenceforth, houseless and adrift, uncertain even of its route. The uncertainty of Mr. Howells between the competing love-claims reminds us of Lemuel's, and, like Lemuel, he temporizes and drifts. In the rapid, almost fugitive, close of the narrative, the author seems running away from decisions which he lacks the hardihood to face, and the happiness which he flings in the faces of the unexpectant lovers at the close has almost the quality of a rebuff.

The "complicity" which the volume exposes has two forms: first, the accessory or ancillary responsibility which the audience at a vile play or the bribe-giver in the custom-house cannot disclaim; second, the propagation of joy or sorrow from its primary subject into related lives. As generality this is threadbare; the novelty lies solely in the increased rigor and courage of the applications. Carlyle had put the matter with his usual force as early as 1834: "I say, there is not a red Indian, hunting by Lake Winnipic, can quarrel with his squaw, but the whole world must smart for it; will not the price of beaver rise?" Emerson had added: "You have just dined, and however scrupulously the slaughter-house is concealed in the graceful distance of miles, there is complicity." In spite of these anticipations, which in their turn are replications, I think Mr. Howells merits respect for the early emphasis which he gave to the special forms in which this historic truth has made its appeal to our contemporaries. That respect, however, belongs rather to the philosopher than to the novelist.

"The Minister's Charge" is not, in my judgment, an effective illustration of this principle. It is a much less powerful exposition of the interlacement of human destinies and responsibilities than a later novel from the same hand, "The Quality of Mercy." Sewell's relation to Lemuel Barker implies the original and impressive thought that the wrongs we do to others may bind us everlastingly to their service; but in Sewell's case the sensibility which creates the bond is idiosyncratic, and the sort of peonage in which the clergyman is held in the working-out of his intolerable debt irks the reader to a point which deadens his responsiveness to precept. The other examples of complicity do not satisfy us. The "Wayfarers' Lodge," after the manner of such institutions, offers a little temporary assistance. The Coreys shed their civic responsibilities, and the Harmonites their domestic obligations. In the background, too indistinct to be really efficacious, hovers the idea of the responsibility of the rich and the cultivated for the untaught and suffering masses.

I reserve my treatment of Mr. Howells's economics for a later section. In relation to "The Minister's Charge," two brief observations are in place. This topic of social inequality has its full share in the confusion and uncertainty which mark everywhere the broad lines and larger framework of this novel. Further, while Mr. Howells's proclivities are democratic, it is a singular fact that, in this particular book, there is hardly a sympathetic figure in his plebs, while his patriciate as a group is exceptionally attractive.

Lemuel Barker's career is factitious. That the lad whose effect on Sewell was petrific should in a year or two have become the acceptable reader, almost the favored protégé, of Bromfield Corey is a proof of the ameliorative virtue of the air of Boston. But Lemuel Barker is not living a life: he is pursuing a curriculum which will fit him to pass that examination on the caste system in Boston to which he will eventually be subjected by the inquisitive Mr. Evans. His personal beauty is occasional; it is felt only when it is mentioned. The arctic rigors of his glacial period are excellently done, and his trustworthiness and his taciturnity are both very clear, if we allow for the propensity of both qualities to take recesses. Lemuel lies with a readiness that surprises us in a layman, and his double ways with Statira and Miss Carver are out of character without being out of nature.

Sewell remains not unlikable throughout the book, though he needs all his faults to extenuate his virtues. The relation between him and his wife is delightfully conceived, but the virago in Mrs. Sewell tempers our delight in the execution. Statira Dudley and Manda Grier, the working-girls, are handled with the unpitying, unmalicious, precision of science; Mr. Howells's attitude toward such persons may be defined as officially lenient but instinctively severe. Williams and Berry, the same character on different planes, are happy portraits on whom wit has been lavished with a prodigality unknown to nature. Evans, a little shrunken since "A Woman's Reason," is nevertheless natural enough. The Coreys, with their Dresden-china effect, are almost prettier here than in the Lapham book where their lambencies are shadowed by responsibility. In Charles Bellingham every touch tells. Miss Vane is pleasant, and Sibyl's unreason is entirely credible. Miss Carver is best in the early dimness faintly starred by Lemuel Barker's adoration.

"The Minister's Charge" is emulous of "A Modern Instance" in the singular affluence of rapid, pregnant narrative, dealing with tangibilities in the half-world or even the underworld. The author never quite regained this level of narrative piquancy in later novels. The story walks in unclean ways without staining its apparel and without blackening their uncleanness. In one point his art is conspicuous. To convey the vulgarity of surroundings through the impressions of a mind largely impervious to their vulgarity, to utilize the sharpness with which urban life stamps itself on the receptive plate of rural inexperience, and yet not to restrict too much his own communications with the reader — this was a problem worthy of Mr. Howells's mettle, and the result is usually happy. The value and interest which these excellences confer is undeniable; they do not redeem the faults of an inartistic and confusing novel.

VI

LOVE UNDER LENS AND PROBE

In this section I handle four love-stories: "Indian Summer," "April Hopes," "The Shadow of a Dream," and "An Imperative Duty." In this order I violate chronology to the extent of postponing to a later place and a different group two novels, "Annie Kilburn" and "A Hazard of New Fortunes," which in the time-sequence fall between "April Hopes" and "The Shadow of a Dream."

I have already distinguished "Indian Summer" as the single long fiction which is comparable with the short novels in point of structure. The reason is evident. "Indian Summer" is a short novel amplified. It has, in fact, all the markings of the earlier group; it is a love-story, it has three leading characters, its setting is foreign and select, its process barely attains or barely misses the status of a plot, and it lacks both the weight and the burden of a sociological motive. Its scene is Florence, and its leisure is doubtless reminiscent of the pace at which Mr. Howells has often traversed in person the road from the Ponte Vecchio to the Duomo and the Baptistery. The emphasis, nevertheless, falls on modernities and the ways of foreign residents in Florence, and the story keeps its privacy, like a carriage in the street, in the very act of touching widely and deftly on the bright points supplied by class and city life.

The competence, leisure, and culture which make the atmosphere of this book would almost indicate that Mr. Howells sought in "Indian Summer" an asylum from "The Minister's Charge." Of the three main characters, middle-aged bachelor, middle-aged widow, and young girl, all Americans, the first two love each other from the outset, and the young girl does not love the man. Complication seems precluded by this smoothness of mutual adjustment, but appears abruptly in the young girl's determination to marry the man to compensate him for his bad luck in a youthful passion for a faithless woman. An engagement between the bachelor and the young girl, in which both are victimized by the latter's romantic ideals, is the obvious sequel, and the making and breaking of this irrational engagement constitutes the process of the narrative. This seems the proper stuff of comedy; but, under the strain of this morbid entanglement, the two women (who are both good, in the chivalrous latitude which Mr. Howells concedes to that term in his traffickings with a difficult sex) develop capacities for suffering and even for wrath and cruelty which seem alien alike to the book's temper and their own. The novel does not wholly lose its amenity: it includes, without accepting, these acrid ingredients. Matters end happily, though the bitterness persists to the penultimate chapter, and the reader has the sense of a lawn party arrested by a thundershower and only half reconstructed by a transfer to the house.

The characters are less attractive as individuals than as members of a select class. There is a fine delicacy and intimacy in the work; it offers the reader the luxury of constant relation to subtle insights and high refinements. He may not share these endowments, but that no more bars him from appreciation than the absence of a title prevents the barmaid from following with sympathy the fortunes of Lady Flora Cavendish.

Imogene Graham, the younger woman, is not emphasized; she is allowed the foreground, but not the primacy. The difficulty, of course, is to make the young person in the ampler rôle less interesting than the elder person in the smaller one; and Mr. Howells has attained this object by making her a little dull, a little foolish, a little aggressive, and a little metallic. So much self-abnegation hardly consorts, in average experience, with so much superficiality; but self-abnegation for Mr. Howells is one of the forms of the superficial. At the end she tires out our sympathy, and we are content with the rigor which decrees her union with a vapid clergyman.

The mixture of sharpness and amiability which pervades both women distresses us more in Mrs. Bowen than in Imogene Graham. We decide hastily that she is to be attractive and simple. Frank, of course, she cannot be: her very soul is gloved; but nevertheless that soul expresses itself in a way in the very fineness and softness of the medium that intercepts expression. Simple and attractive — that is our initial formula. Our perplexity, our distress, arises when we discover that she is less attractive and more complex than we foresaw. Her faults, without being extraordinarily grave, are peculiarly unforgivable. She is strict almost to prudery, but she relaxes her strictness by spasms, and by untimely spasms. As often in Mr. Howells's women, a temperament masquerades as a character. She is furious with Colville for accepting the tie with Imogene; her refusal to marry him after his release is a bit of quixotic unreason which unmasks its own triviality by its instant surrender to an insufficient motive.

Colville, in early readings, struck me as very attractive, but, in my latest return to the book, I found myself rather bedeafened and bedazzled by the incessant crackle of his wit and the unremitting splendor of his virtues. He is always wise, always delicate, and his facetiousness is limitless. He is not conceited, not pompous, not snobbish in the vulgar sense; he grudges our inferiority even these meagre consolations. If he would but talk plainly now and then! If he would drop for some reconciling moment into fraternizing and humanizing commonplace! This outburst of mine illustrates the curious faculty he has for inducing childishness in other persons.

The child, Effie, with whom pains have been taken, fluctuates in distinctiveness, but, at her best and her maker's best, is very lifelike and attractive. Possibly it might be said of mother and child alike that they are very attractive without being wholly likable. The aged minister, Mr. Waters, is antipodal to the child, and the scale of life is completed by youth embodied in Imogene and that middle-age, allegorized as Indian Summer, which Colville shares with Mrs. Bowen.

The book follows "The Rise of Silas Lapham" in its gentle suggestion of the folly of the substitution of magnanimity for sanity in affairs of the heart. It is one of the most flawless of its author's works and, to my mind, one of the most winning. I divine a joy in its composition not the less real in that the book may have been in a sense an intermission of his graver purposes.[1] I am reminded of the touching pleasure of Louise Maxwell at the ladies' lunch when she forgot, in a brief return to the delicate and costly leisure of her early life, the graver obligations of her marriage.

I quote a passage illustrative of the shadings which Mr. Howells can find in or behind the few words exchanged by two Americans in a chance encounter on a bridge in Florence.

> Colville had reached this point in that sarcastic study of his own condition of mind for the advantage of his late readers in the *Post-Democrat-Republican*, when he was aware of a polite rustling of draperies, with an ensuing well-bred murmur, which at once ignored him, deprecated intrusion upon him, and asserted a common right to the prospect on which he had been dwelling alone. He looked round with an instinctive expectation of style and poise, in which he was not disappointed. The lady, with a graceful lift of the head and a very erect carriage, almost Bernhardtesque in the backward fling of her shoulders and the strict compression of her elbows to her side, was pointing out the different bridges to the little girl who was with her.

---

[1] Since the above was written I have come upon an express declaration of Mr. Howells that he enjoyed writing "Indian Summer" more than any other of his novels.

"That first one is the Santa Trinità, and the next is the Carraja, and that one quite down by the Cascine is the iron bridge. The Cascine you remember — the park where we were driving — that clump of woods there —."

A vagueness expressive of divided interest had crept into the lady's tone rather than her words. Colville could feel that she was waiting for the right moment to turn her delicate head, sculpturesquely defined by its toque, and steal an imperceptible glance at him: and he involuntarily afforded her the coveted excuse by the slight noise he made in changing his position, in order to be able to go away as soon as he had seen whether she was pretty or not. At forty-one the question is still important to every man with regard to every woman.

"Mr. Colville!"

The gentle surprise conveyed in the exclamation, without time for recognition, convinced Colville, upon a cool review of the facts, that the lady had known him before their eyes met.

"Why, Mrs. Bowen!" he said.

She put out her round, slender arm, and gave him a frank clasp of her gloved hand. The glove wrinkled richly up the sleeve of her dress half-way to her elbow. She bent on his face a demand for just what quality and degree of change he found in hers, and apparently she satisfied herself that his inspection was not to her disadvantage, for she smiled brightly, and devoted the rest of her glance to an electric summary of the facts of Colville's physiognomy; the sufficiently good outline of his visage, with its full, rather close-cut, drabbish-brown beard and moustache, both shaped a little by the ironical self-conscious smile that lurked under them; the non-committal, rather weary-looking eyes; the brown hair, slightly frosted, that showed while he stood with his hat still off. He was a little above the middle height, and if it must be confessed, neither his face nor his figure had quite preserved their youthful lines. They were both much heavier than when Mrs. Bowen saw them last, and the latter here and there swayed beyond the strict bounds of symmetry. She was herself in that moment of life when, to the middle-aged observer, at least, a woman's looks have a charm which is wanting to her earlier bloom. By that time her character has wrought itself more clearly out in her face, and her heart and mind confront you more directly there. It is the youth of her spirit which has come to the surface.

"I should have known you anywhere," she exclaimed, with friendly pleasure in seeing him.

"You are very kind," said Colville. "I did n't know that I had preserved my youthful beauty to that degree. But I can imagine it — if you say so, Mrs. Bowen."

"Oh, I assure you that you have!" she protested; and now she began gently to pursue him with one fine question after another about himself, till she had mastered the main facts of his history since they had last met. He would not have known so well how to possess himself of hers, even if he had felt the same necessity; but in fact it had happened that he had heard of her from time to time at not very long intervals. She had married a leading lawyer of her Western city, who in due time had gone to Congress, and after his term was out had "taken up his residence" in Washington, as the newspapers said, "in his elegant mansion at the corner of & Street and Idaho Avenue." After that he remembered reading that Mrs. Bowen was going abroad for the education of her daughter, from which he made his own inferences concerning her marriage. And "You knew Mr. Bowen was no longer living?" she said, with fit obsequy of tone.

"Yes, I knew," he answered, with decent sympathy.

"This is my little Effie," said Mrs. Bowen after a moment; and now the child, hitherto keeping herself discreetly in the background, came forward and promptly gave her hand to Colville, who perceived that she was not so small as he had thought her at first; an effect of infancy had possibly been studied in the brevity of her skirts and the immaturity of her corsage, but both were in good taste and really to the advantage of her young figure. There was reason and justice in her being dressed as she was, for she really was not so old as she looked by two or three years; and there was reason in Mrs. Bowen's carrying in the hollow of her left arm the India shawl sacque she had taken off and hung there; the deep cherry silk lining gave life to the sombre tints prevailing in her dress, which its removal left free to express all the grace of her extremely lady-like person. Lady-like was the word for Mrs. Bowen throughout — for the turn of her head, the management of her arm from the elbow, the curve of her hand from wrist to finger-tips, the smile, subdued, but sufficiently sweet, playing about her little mouth, which was yet not too little, and the refined and indefinite perfume which exhaled from the ensemble of her silks, her laces, and her gloves, like an odorous version of that otherwise impalpable quality which women call style. She had, with all her flexibility, a certain charming stiffness, like the stiffness of a very tall feather.

"And have you been here a great while?" she asked, turning her head slowly toward Colville, and looking at him with a little difficulty she had in raising her eyelids; when she was younger, the glance that shyly stole from under the covert of their lashes was like a gleam of sunshine, and it was still like a gleam of paler sunshine.

Colville, whose mood was very susceptible to the weather, brightened in the ray. "I only arrived last night," he said, with a smile.

"How glad you must be to get back! Did you ever see Florence more beautiful than it was this morning?"

"Not for years," said Colville, with another smile for her pretty enthusiasm. "Not for seventeen years at the least calculation."

"Is it so many?" cried Mrs. Bowen, with lovely dismay. "Yes, it is," she sighed; and she did not speak for an appreciable interval.

He knew that she was thinking of that old love-affair of his, to which she was privy in some degree, though he never could tell how much; and when she spoke he perceived that she purposely avoided speaking of a certain person, whom a woman of more tact or of less would have insisted upon naming at once. "I never can believe in the lapse of time when I get back to Italy; it always makes me feel as young as when I left it last."

"I could imagine you 'd never left it," said Colville.

Mrs. Bowen reflected a moment. "Is that a compliment?"

"I had an obscure intention of saying something fine; but I don't think I 've quite made it out," he owned.

Mrs. Bowen gave her small, sweet smile. "It was very nice of you to try. But I have n't really been away for some time; I 've taken a house in Florence, and I 've been here two years. Palazzo Pinti, Lung' Arno della Zecca. You must come and see me. Thursdays from four till six."

"Thank you," said Colville.

"I 'm afraid," said Mrs. Bowen, remotely preparing to offer her hand in adieu, "that Effie and I broke in upon some very important cogitations of yours." She shifted the silken burden off her arm a little, and the child stirred from the correct pose she had been keeping, and smiled politely.

"I don't think they deserve a real dictionary word like that," said Colville. "I was simply mooning. If there was anything definite in my mind, I was wishing that I was looking down on the Wabash in Des Vaches, instead of the Arno in Florence."

"Oh! And I supposed you must be indulging all sorts of historical associations with the place. Effie and I have been walking through the Via de' Bardi, where Romola lived, and I was bringing her back over the Ponte Vecchio, so as to impress the origin of Florence on her mind."

"Is that what makes Miss Effie hate it?" asked Colville, looking at the child, whose youthful resemblance to her mother was in all things so perfect that a fantastic question whether she could ever have had any other parent swept through him. Certainly, if Mrs. Bowen were to marry again, there was nothing in this child's looks to suggest the idea of a predecessor to the second husband.

"Effie does n't hate any sort of useful knowledge," said her mother half jestingly. "She 's just come to me from school at Vevay."

"Oh, then, I think she might," persisted Colville. "Don't you hate the origin of Florence a little?" he asked of the child.

"I don't know enough about it," she answered, with a quick look of question at her mother, and checking herself in a possibly indiscreet smile.

"Ah, that accounts for it," said Colville, and he laughed. It amused him to see the child referring even this point of propriety to her mother, and his thoughts idled off to what Mrs. Bowen's own untrammelled girlhood must have been in her Western city. For her daughter there were to be no buggy rides, or concerts, or dances at the invitation of young men; no picnics, free and unchaperoned as the casing air; no sitting on the steps at dusk with callers who never dreamed of asking for her mother; no lingering at the gate with her youthful escort home from the ball — nothing of that wild, sweet liberty which once made American girlhood a long rapture. But would she be any the better for her privations, for referring not only every point of conduct, but every thought and feeling, to her mother? He suppressed a sigh for the inevitable change, but rejoiced that his own youth had fallen in the earlier time, and said, "You will hate it as soon as you 've read a little of it."

"The difficulty *is* to read a little of Florentine history. I can't find anything in less than ten or twelve volumes," said Mrs. Bowen. "Effie and I were going to Viesseux's Library again, in desperation, to see if there was n't something shorter in French."

She now offered Colville her hand, and he found himself very reluctant to let it go. Something in her looks did not forbid him, and when she took her hand away, he said, "Let me go to Viesseux's with you, Mrs. Bowen, and give you the advantage of my unprejudiced ignorance in the choice of a book on Florence."

"Oh, I was longing to ask you!" said Mrs. Bowen frankly. "It is really such a serious matter, especially when the book is for a young person. Unless it 's very dry, it 's so apt to be — objectionable."

"Yes," said Colville, with a smile at her perplexity. He moved off down the slope of the bridge with her, between the jewellers' shops, and felt a singular satisfaction in her company. Women of fashion always interested him; he liked them; it diverted him that they should take themselves seriously. Their resolution, their suffering for their ideal, such as it was, their energy in dressing and adorning themselves, the pains they were at to achieve the trivialities they passed their lives in, were perpetually delightful to him. He often found them people of great simplicity, and sometimes of singularly good sense; their frequent vein of piety was delicious.

Ten minutes earlier he would have said that nothing could have been less welcome to him than this encounter, but now he felt unwilling to leave Mrs. Bowen.

"April Hopes," responsive possibly in its title to "Indian Summer," contains what I am tempted to call Mr. Howells's most vivid portraiture of love. It is noteworthy, without being eccentric, that he should have chosen two of his least substantial characters for the subjects — I had almost said the receptacles — of this auroral life-transforming passion. Dan Mavering, though excellently drawn, is made of gossamer. Alice Pasmer is a sleep-walker whom her ecstasy rather agitates than wakes. Love is a jealous passion; perhaps it is jealous even of individuality.

The classic presentations of young love have commonly been tragic, and "April Hopes" is perhaps the most deeply and irremediably tragic of all the novels of its creator. The hopelessness, the inevitableness, is manifest (as it is not, for example, in the story of Bartley Hubbard); and the inclusion of this fatality in the whole varied, realistic, normal frame of things, its solidarity with hope and love and enterprise and conscience, is brought out with unsurpassable address. The penalties are not explicit; that is the consummating touch. Mr. Howells suffers the lovers to marry, but not before their engagement has laid its pitiless emphasis on those disparities of character which make the reciprocity of passions a menace or a doom. I think of a passage from George Eliot's "Mill on the Floss": "The strong attraction which drew you together proceeded only from one side of your characters, and belonged to that partial, divided action of our nature which makes half the tragedy of the human lot."

The opening chapters, in which the lovers are thrown together at the Harvard Class Day, are very satisfactory, if a trifle deliberate; the story is kept throughout on a low diet of incident noticeable even in so frugal a housekeeper as Mr. Howells. At Campobello, a summer resort, the lovers meet again, and a breathless period of happy expectation is followed by the young man's hasty rejection at the hands of the jealous and incensed girl. Reconcilement in Boston follows, and Mr. Howells forgets both his moral and his melancholy in the voluptuousness of pure surrender to the spell of this celestial madness. This leads off a whole series of delectable chapters, in which the buoyant, rapid, faithful, exquisite narrative shows the full power of the mature hand in its easy mastery of an alluring subject.

I have already remarked that Mr. Howells's longer novels, like actual men and women, have a fashion of aging suddenly in later middle life. This senescence is quite evident in the last quadrant of "April Hopes." The lover's flirtation with another girl, after his break with Alice, is cavalierly despatched, and an opportune lieutenant is summoned from the vasty deep with an abruptness which discredits his reality. The Pasmers reappear with a timeliness that would amuse the satirical, and the renewal of the engagement loses half its interest, dangling helplessly as it does from the end of a foolish chain of misunderstandings and fortuities.

There are delightful moments when Alice Pasmer is only love and youth; but there are times in abundance when she is Alice Pasmer, and at these periods she is very silly, very unreasonable (by no means quite the same thing), and very unlovely in her sacrificial writhings. Like the far more depraved Jeanne in De Curel's "L'Envers d'une Sainte," she shows how much sheer evil — in Alice's case selfishness and ill-temper — may underlie the profession and even the consciousness of self-denying and exalted motives. Mr. Howells has scant mercy for an inflamed conscience.

Dan Mavering is excellently drawn. He is discriminated from the gentler type of Mr. Howells's young men, the Libbies, Coreys, and Dunhams, with whom he would naturally affiliate, by an uncandor or duplicity so tempered as to be always forsaking virtue and never reaching wickedness. In other words, he has just that amount of untrustworthiness which is most natural and least dramatic; and it is notably in the management of these halfnesses and ambiguities, of this trimming or temporizing on the part, not of Dan Mavering only but of life itself, that the artist in Mr. Howells is evoked. Few other novelists could have kept our feeling for Dan Mavering so securely yet so delicately poised. So much forgetfulness as Dan's in the wake of so much fervor is unromantic; it would take some courage to declare that it is untrue.

The mother, Mrs. Pasmer, so engages Mr. Howells that he can hardly keep her from an undue prominence in a novel in which, after all, she is a secondary and not very influential figure. This want of influence is the defect in a nearly faultless portrayal. The efficiency of Mrs. Pasmer is continually extolled and never depicted. The sympathy between her and Dan Mavering is a charming invention, or rather discovery, and both — in contrast to Alice — are made to emphasize the possible coexistence of much goodness with little virtue, or at least with the minimum of scruple and an almost total inertness of the conscience. "I believe this minute," says Mrs. Brinkley, whose exaggerations form a covert, but not a screen, for Mr. Howells's personal opinions, "that that manœuvring, humbugging mother of hers [Alice's] is a better woman, a kinder woman than she is."

I shall avail myself of this contrast between Alice and her mother to introduce a remark on one of the notably modern elements in Mr. Howells's curiously blended ethics. He is loud in his condemnation of ideal and romantic morality. He opposes the exaltation of sacrifice as sacrifice, the worship of suffering, the greed of martyrdom, the craving to expiate where expiation can neither revoke nor repair. He cannot tolerate the conventional heroine who opposes "duty, as she did love, to prudence, obedience, and reason." He coins the contemptuous word "dutiolatry." He is impatient of remorse in the sense, no doubt, of self-laceration. The elder Mavering, in this very novel, clearly speaking for Mr. Howells, says of this passion: "There 's nothing so useless, so depraving, as that." When it comes to romantic self-sacrifice, the merciful philosopher throws mercy and even moderation to the winds. In his criticism, Lady Castlewood's attempt to marry Beatrix to Esmond is "idiotic and detestable self-sacrifice." Sydney Carton's sacrifice in the "Tale of Two Cities" is an "atrocious and abominable act." Let no uninformed reader hasten to infer that Mr. Howells is obtuse to ethical distinctions, or that he values only what may be called morality in large type. He is intensely occupied with moral questions; he is obsessed by the shadings and overtones of morality. The key to the difficulty is simple: Mr. Howells is subtle, but he is sane; and his sanity is constantly showing the door to one set of high-keyed ethical requirements, while his subtlety invites another set to enter in and take possession. It should be easy to discriminate, in theory at least, between the spurious morality which grows up in contempt of the facts and the delicate morality which profits by the discernment of the undertones in actuality. Mr. Howells may overstrain his morality at times, but only where his view of reality is likewise overstrained.

To return to the characterization of "April Hopes." The power in the secondary figures is considerable. Mr. Pasmer's vacuity, indeed, is overdone: like Percy Mackaye's "Scarecrow," he seems kept alive only by his smoking. The Maverings are a strong group: the father appealing, the mother incisive between her prostrations, the girls both distinct, the more quietly touched Minna being quite as vivid in her way as

Eunice, in spite of Eunice's unfair advantage of the rasping tongue. Boardman is perfect, until in an evil hour Mr. Howells is tempted to make a character whose laconism is his breath and being the fluent mouthpiece of his own philosophy. Mrs. Brinkley, crammed with intellect and wit, retains her place in nature, and her husband, negative at first, is permitted at the end to unfold a delightful individuality, which does not in the least overstep his preordained limitations. Miss Anderson hardly counts.

"April Hopes" is a passionate love-story with tragic implications; both its character and its incidents are the reverse of tragic. Two years later, after "Annie Kilburn" and "A Hazard of New Fortunes," comes "The Shadow of a Dream," in which the approach to picturesque and romantic tragedy is more noticeable than in any other work of Mr. Howells. This is perceptible in the Shakespearean title; in part of the setting (a ruinous garden by a lonely coast); in part of the incidents, and much of the atmosphere; in the names of the characters — Faulkner, Hermia, Nevil; in the characters themselves, one of whom, Faulkner, is more like a figure in Scott or Hugo than any other offshoot of its author's brain, while the two others are kept in a neutrality which neither confirms nor dispels this impression. If I said that the book reminded me of Hawthorne's "Blithedale Romance," I might be tempted to unsay it the next moment; and yet, when I recall the bold juxtaposition of romance and modernity in that remarkable book, and remember how curiously the tentative, half reverent and tender, half wilful and mocking, disposition of Coverdale prefigures the attitude of Basil March, I think I should persist in my audacity.

The story falls short of greatness, but the power displayed in this novel venture by a man of forty-three is a rare proof of versatile capacity. Where else than in the chapters descriptive of Faulkner's death is ruin, physical and mental, portrayed so vividly, yet with so sure a skill in the evocation of romantic and picturesque effect from material that teems with pain and horror? The accent of the book is often solemn. I believe that Mr. Howells possessed the tragic sense in a quite unusual degree, though he could not dramatize his tragedy; his drama, which I use in the broad, general sense of the interaction of human beings by speech and conduct, had its source in lighter phases of his being. But the tone of certain passing allusions or observations expresses a Shakespearean depth of awe and wonder in the face of the mysteries of pain and guilt that embitter and enlarge our lives.

In the face of these capacities, what has kept "The Shadow of a Dream" from ranking as a great novel, at least in the conventional sense? The reasons are precise. First, the three main characters are all imperfectly worked out, and two of them, Hermia and Nevil, are inadequately conceived. Second, the action is too slight, and is conveyed to us too uniformly by the circuit of the Marches. Third, whether from the search for relief (where relief, be it respectfully said, is impertinent) or from a realistic conscience almost as unreasonable and querulous as the ethical conscience he so persistently deplores, Mr. Howells has allowed both the Marches to lower and lessen themselves by the indulgence in speech of feelings which their whole conduct belies. Mrs. March's outburst on page 31 (Harper's Edition, 1899), against the man whose house she occupies as a guest, is a wound which her abounding generosities cannot wholly salve; and Basil March's *puckishness* in the talk with the old lady in the sixth chapter of the third part has an effect of ghastliness in the light — I should rather say in the gloom—of the enveloping situation. The streaking of nobility with meanness may be lifelike, but is displeasing in a drama which treats passion on the grand scale in a generous way. Lastly, the drama is too constantly taken to pieces and reconstructed, in a never-ceasing hum of analysis and commentary.

The conduct of the tale, diffuse in time and space, is nevertheless chiefly faulty in the prominence it bestows on the Marches, who are essentially mere spectators. They resemble, however, those high-born spectators of Elizabethan times who sat on the stage and intercepted the common man's view of the performers. It is, of course, quite possible that Mr. Howells felt that the sort of tragic effect which he was qualified to induce would be helped by dropping a veil of distance and indirection between the reader and the persons of the drama.

Here first emerges that interest in crepuscular psychology which time has brought out and fostered in Mr. Howells. I am not sure but that his novel and his lesson pull opposite ways. The author's intellectual interest in the story is unrelated, if not antipathetic, to his sense of its dramatic possibilities. A man is visited by a dream in which he imagines an attachment between his wife and his friend. He dies, and the real love which is born in due time feels itself both inhibited and maligned by the knowledge of the sinister illusion. Now, as artist, Mr. Howells is bound to magnify this obsession; as teacher, he is zealous to rebuke it: the discord slightly mars his work.

"The Shadow of a Dream" is interesting *per se*, and evokes the further interest proper to works which disclose unripened possibilities in natures already ripe.

I have spoken of tragic feeling in Mr. Howells. It is a singular comment on the limitations of that feeling that, in the next novel on our list, "An Imperative Duty," a subject capable of tragic enlargement and solemnization should be treated, in one hundred and fifty moderate-sized pages, with an incidentality that approaches lightness. That subject is the disclosure to a young girl of the slight strain of negro blood that clouds her ancestry. The facts include or imply a great deal of suffering, and the author, in his fashion, sympathizes deeply.

But he feels, and his hero feels, that the two sufferers, the remorsefully secretive aunt, Mrs. Meredith, and the young girl, Rhoda Aldgate, are both rather foolish; and, while the intensity of the anguish is not blinked, it is handled with a deft provisionality. True, Mrs. Meredith dies in her distress, and Rhoda's grief survives the happy marriage by which its first poignancy is allayed. But my former assertion is true: the grief itself is profound, but we are allowed to perceive, without realizing, its profundity.

The story is simplified and possibly lightened by the fact that, while the girl has two lovers, neither finds a problem in her descent; one is uninformed, and the other's generosity is complete. The girl hesitates only for a moment on the question of accepting the man she loves. The successful lover's magnanimity is viewed as so inevitable that its romantic effectiveness is partly lost. Olney, in the midst of the anguish of the aunt and the girl's despair and his own love, preserves the capacity for lightness which so singularly crosses and belies the seriousness of the young hero in Mr. Howells. The author and reader are sometimes at cross-purposes in this regard. The disinterestedness in which the reader discerns the acme of romantic generosity is, for the higher standard of Mr. Howells, only the natural and decent thing. He, therefore, has no hesitation in flecking such a personage with levities and infirmities, in total oblivion of the fact that for the reader, whose eye is fixed on a Bayard or Sidney, these peccadilloes are affronts and blasphemies.

Olney is partly a type, though a type individual to his creator. Mrs. Meredith, another case of the inflated and inflamed conscience, is a weariness to Mr. Howells, and his touch is unwilling and gingerly. Rhoda Aldgate is effectively individualized by the magnifying of two traits, her gayety and her vindictiveness. Her misfortunes only just balance her truculence. She is a little uncanny both in her lightness and in her fierceness, a trait in which her African ancestry may be dimly legible; it is less her filiation to that race than to Mr. Howells himself that we note in her subjection to impulse, in that gustiness in which the conscience, for all its assertiveness, is only another wind in the Æolus cave which represents the personality.

In the small compass of "An Imperative Duty" Mr. Howells's capacity for structure reaffirms itself in a workmanship that is nearly flawless. Room is found for much sketching of negro life and for a liberal portrayal of the sumptuous Bloomingdales on that border of leisure which Mr. Howells never fails to attach to the rapid evolution of a succinct plot. His own affection for the black race no doubt had its influence on the promptitude with which the young physician decides that the tincture of negro blood only strengthens the claim of Rhoda Aldgate on his compassionate and loyal tenderness. The author suggests a little hesitantly that a conscience more robust than Mrs. Meredith's might have spared an innocent young girl the torture of that tardy revelation; and he acquiesces contentedly, if not gladly, in the social dissimulation of Olney and his wife.

A line or two from this novel may be cited in illustration of the pensive, not to say melancholy, fortitude of the outlook upon life characteristic of these love-stories of the author's thoughtful and judicious middle age. "He did not consider either love or life valuable for the happiness they could yield. They were enough in themselves." The riper ethics of Mr. Howells are perceptible in the following comment on Mrs. Meredith: "Right affected her as a body of positive color, sharply distinguished from wrong, and not shading into and out of it by gradations of tint, as we find it doing in reality." The same path of thought leads Kane, in "The World of Chance," to the bolder affirmation: "In our conditions no man can do right without doing harm." So again, in an Easy Chair paper: "In the nineteenth century, especially toward the close of it, one is never quite sure about vice and virtue; they fade wonderfully into and out of each other; they mix and seem to stay mixed, at least around the ledger." We might put the Howells view in our heavier dialect thus: when duty mediates between an inflexible principle and variable circumstance, it must reflect the plasticity of the circumstance no less certainly than the fixity of the law.

VII

Dives and Lazarus

In the present section I shall handle four novels, sometimes far separated in time, but bound together by their common emphasis on social problems of a civic or industrial stamp. They are "Annie Kilburn," its partial sequel, "The Quality of Mercy," "A Traveler from Altruria," and its much-delayed continuation, "Through the Eye of the Needle." A survey of Mr. Howells's economic theory must not overlook the economic side of "A Hazard of New Fortunes" and "The World of Chance"; but these two works are classed more naturally, in the order of review, with the literary and artistic group of novels to be dealt with in the ensuing section.

The theme of "Annie Kilburn" is the relief of poverty. This is a weighty, even an oppressive, theme. But poverty itself is only dimly visible in the book, just as possibly it is only dimly visible in the perspective of much of the benevolence that aims at its relief. Not poverty, but the follies of the charitable, are the theme — an object of satire which amuses mankind at large and convulses the parsimonious. This suggests a light treatment, and the selection of most of the characters from the well-to-do and fashionable classes of a prosperous town connives with the reader in his dismissal of responsibility. But complication does not end here. A ghastly accident overtakes a dreary minister, a certain Mr. Peck, whose cold sagacity, moral gauntness, and sheer indigence of soul breed an unjust impatience with the ideas that make use of so gelid a mouthpiece. He is killed finally by a train, and his catastrophe leaves one with a heightened respect for the discernment of locomotives. All this is merely dismal; the true darkness begins in the moving picture of the struggles of the self-reforming drunkard, the lawyer Putney. The trouble with the book is that the satire can no more digest these drearinesses and horrors than they can assimilate the satire.

"Annie Kilburn" is badly made. It presents some twenty not unimportant persons in illustration of the types of life in a provincial community in New England. Even so, it might have possessed the adequate if restricted unity of George Eliot's "Middlemarch"; but in George Eliot the strands are continuous and solid, while in "Annie Kilburn" they are desultory and piecemeal. Again, the activities are predominantly philanthropic; and here there seems a basis for another kind of unity, the unity of direction or trend exemplified in Mr. Galsworthy's "Fraternity." But to this end the philanthropic activities should monopolize the book; what they really achieve is not monopoly but predominance. The unity is still to seek. There is Annie Kilburn no doubt, but the post of Annie Kilburn is mainly honorary. The book is Miss Kilburn's book in precisely the sense in which the theatricals it minutely describes are Miss Kilburn's theatricals. She is the originative force in neither case; she is the late-comer, the spectator, the afterthought. Mr. Howells, justly dissatisfied with the incoherence of his materials, devised her presence — her continuous and ubiquitous, but, for the most part, inactive and ineffective presence — as the means of spreading a veneer of unity over an essentially inorganic work. Is this concealment? It is also confession. This accounts for the singular vacuity of Annie during the better part of the narrative. She comes to Mr. Howells as destitute as Mr. Peck's Idella came to her; and the author, without hurrying himself, finds means to provide his charge with a few plain conveniences — a husband, for instance, and an individuality. Somewhere in his ample wardrobe he unearths an impetuosity which proves very becoming to the hitherto unadventurous heroine.

Dr. Morrell, who relieves Mr. Howells of further responsibility for Annie, illustrates that exquisite intellectual *temper* which enables this writer to give edge to his portrayal of a figure who is distinctively edgeless. A somebody who simulates a nobody without becoming one is sufficiently difficult to draw, but the doctor, who is all *down*, is quite as substantial as Putney, who is all *quill*.

The situation of Putney, the struggling drunkard, is so affecting and his character is so vigorous that the contrast of character with situation is almost too vivid for the ends of art. The union of incisiveness and frailty, the double and equal appeal to fear and pity (exemplified in another form in Heine), makes him unforgettable among the offspring of Mr. Howells. If the picture is not unsurpassable as well as unforgettable, the reason lies perhaps in a superflux of obvious effectiveness, in the fact that his peril and his raillery place him in a kind of limelight by which his figure is at once intensely vivified and a trifle overstrained. The lame child seems a conventional stroke, but the child himself is precise in the half-elfish way peculiar to Mr. Howells's children.

Lyra Wilmington deserved a broader canvas and a more attentive hand. The sheer *quality* in this artist's work is again superbly evident in his grasp of a distinction so securely imbedded in the commonplace. She is undisguisedly vulgar, but her affluence of nature satisfies like refinement. She maintains a temperate flirtation with a young nephew of her senile husband; and I scarcely know another novelist in any country capable of giving point to the pointlessness of an affair "which perpetually invites comment and never justifies scandal."

The dapper Mr. Brandreth and the leathery Mrs. Munger are clear drawings. The old servants, the Boltons, are ably rather than winningly drawn; there is too much putty in Bolton, too much haircloth in his wife. Mr. Gerrish is a wearisome character: his loquacity submerges even his meanness.

The effect of this book is to unsettle one's belief in the usefulness of present charity. It should be remembered that Mr. Howells believes in the wickedness, the insanity, of the existing economic order, and would scarcely rejoice in the success of alleviations which might cajole men into a postponement of its destruction. In the relations between rich and poor, he feels that fellowship must precede service, and he does not hide his fear that fellowship is impossible. He is wise enough to see that heroic remedies are often visionary; he has only compassionate satire for Annie Kilburn's proposal to work in the mills at Fall River; and he declares in another work, that, in a world ordered like the present, Tolstoi's shoemaking is necessarily dramatic. The poor, in his view, can participate in the benefits of social endeavor only by participation in the endeavor itself. The dependence of helpfulness on love is a cardinal tenet of his creed, as it is the final dictum of Brieux in his dramatic exploitation of the same theme in "Les Bienfaiteurs."

To round out the exposition of his views on these points, let me add that in "Impressions and Experiences" he speaks, with a respect that is possibly half good-breeding, of the "organized efforts at relieving want." He knows how sincere and generous they are, how effective they often are, how ineffective. When he is asked for charity in the street, his fear of pauperizing the asker by compliance is checked by the other fear that his refusal may starve alike his neighbor's body and his own soul.

The brief comment I shall make on these and other economic views of Mr. Howells will aim chiefly to bring out the powers and shortcomings of his mind. An obvious reservation may be made to the doctrine that fellowship must precede service (the wording is mine). The service to which fellowship is the condition precedent is a moral service. Attitudes may govern attitudes; they cannot revoke gravitation or magnetism or nutrition. Bread will make tissue; the bread of the unfeeling will even make the tissue of the ungrateful.

Again, allowance must be made for the extreme — let us not shrink from saying the excessive — emphasis which Mr. Howells lays upon social equality in his view of the interaction of rich and poor. In that combination of misery and disgrace known as poverty, he felt the disgrace to be coördinate with the misery. The poor are twice crushed by wealth, first, as wealth, and second, as station. This exaggeration was a noble error, an error in which his fellow was the delicate-minded Stevenson, and which sprang in both men from a fineness of grain which they imputed with generous rashness both to the fortunate and to the unhappy. The cultivation and sensibility of such men first divide them from the poor, and then proceed to torment them with the wickedness and hopelessness of this division. Blunter people, both well-to-do and ill-to-do, feel the strain of class difference less keenly. I am not sure that an endless probing of differences of caste, even in the nominal interest of humility and remorse, is not a final subterfuge of the aristocratic impulse. I fear sometimes that Mr. Howells luxuriates in certain objections to snobbishness and condescension which derive half their reality from the petting they receive, and which might be half destroyed if they could be wholly forgotten. The pride and shame of class are felt mostly on the class frontiers, that is, in the people just below or just above a social boundary: they are less active in the people of confirmed position and least active of all in the incontestable proletariat.

An instance of overstress may be found in the private theatricals which occupy so large, so very large, a place in a novel which has weightier interests to guard. Mr. Howells has apparently the same aversion to these fashionable theatricals that his master, Tolstoi, felt for a charity ball. But he proves altogether too much. As one may damn by faint praise, one may absolve by rank censure. Mr. Howells makes this unfortunate entertainment responsible for Putney's reversion to drink, for a bitter slight to Sue Northwick, and for a rupture (not final) of the engagement of Percy Brandreth and Bessie Chapley. When, in the end of the book, he takes the proceeds of this villainy and applies it to the foundation of a not unsuccessful Social Union, we feel that he is guilty of recreancy, almost of peculation. He waited, cravenly, until Mr. Peck was dead.

The central figure of "The Quality of Mercy" is J. M. Northwick, "a figment of our commercial civilization," as Mr. Howells calls him, who has risked and lost the property of his associates. The story begins with his return to his country place after the decisive conference in Boston in which his defalcations have been proved. He packs his bag with stolen money, and eludes justice by a flight to Canada, where he hopes to reinvest his booty and retrieve his fortunes. His family, whom he had hoodwinked by the pretext of a routine journey, consists of two grown-up daughters, a maturing, tremulous spinster Adeline, and a younger sister Suzette made up of imperious beauty and proud revolt. Northwick, after starting for Canada, had changed his plan of route, and the train in which he had ordered a Pullman chair by telegraph is shattered in a wreck complete enough to efface even the identity of the dead passengers. Reports of the wreck and of the telegram reach the ears of the Northwick sisters, and their anxieties, at first unmixed with any hint of crime, are minutely and vividly depicted. Their ignorance is pitifully brief. Reporters enter the scene; a young sensationalist, Pinney, of whom the book is destined to say much, publishes a flaring account of the transactions in the "Boston Events," while Brice Maxwell, another figure of moment in the book, contributes a judicious account and criticism of the defalcation to the "Boston Abstract."

Suzette Northwick is the intimate friend of Louise Hilary, daughter of the president of the corporation that Northwick has defrauded. Suzette, in a dramatic scene, demands the truth from the paternal Hilary, and meets his compliance with this demand with reproaches in which his own daughter mercilessly joins. Matt Hilary, a young philanthropist, mistrustful of that capital in which his father has his breath and being, is one with the family in its effort to befriend the Northwick girls. He aids and counsels Suzette Northwick, and the pity that he feels for her courageous helplessness expands and deepens into love. A suit is brought by the creditors against the Northwick property. Suzette rejects all legal aid; but the more daring, because more frightened, Adeline seeks counsel of Lawyer Putney, known throughout the little community for his shrewdness, his addiction to drink, and his antipathy to John Milton Northwick. This last feeling adds nothing but savor to his prompt and resolute espousal of the side of the two sisters, and the interest of the case becomes a stay to him in his lifelong wrestle with intoxication.

At this point Part I closes, and the adventures of Northwick, which have been held in abeyance for some eighteen chapters, are resumed in the first seven chapters of Part II. These paint with animation and penetration the psychology of his journey to Quebec, and recount his passive and drifting search for business openings in unexploited Canada, and the rejection of all these chances by the lethargy that numbs his will. At last he mails a letter to a Boston newspaper, in which he promises restitution, and entreats forbearance toward his daughters, and the story accompanies this letter to Boston.

The letter brings certainty to the Northwick daughters on two anxious points — their father's life and his guilt. They have inherited from their mother an estate which the avidity of creditors cannot touch. They agree to relinquish this property to the creditors, after a vain effort to obtain from the state as the price of this concession the abandonment of the proceedings against Northwick. The state might lean to mercy if Northwick himself would relinquish his own booty. A possible channel for the opening of negotiations with the fugitive reveals itself in the enterprise of the reporter Pinney, who plans to discover and approach Northwick in the course of a trip to Quebec on journalistic business. Northwick is found, is lured to Quebec; but here, eluding his companion, he makes a hurried, secret visit to the United States, where he has time for a yearning, ecstatic hour in the arms of his all-forgiving daughters. He makes good his escape to Quebec, only, in a last impulse of remorse or disheartenment, to put his person and his money into Pinney's hands for conveyance to creditors and sheriffs in his own country. That country he barely reaches; he dies on the train.

Meanwhile, Matt Hilary has offered his hand to Suzette Northwick, who, though she loves him tenderly, rejects him with that decisiveness which in Mr. Howells's women is always the prelude to reconsideration. She reconsiders almost on the spot. The Hilary family are informed of the step, and the elder Hilary feels so strongly his new obligations to Suzette, that he resigns from a presidency which would oblige him to prosecute her father, and makes good from his own pocket the undischarged remainder of Northwick's liabilities. Adeline Northwick dies. Brice Maxwell, the gifted young reporter for the "Abstract," spends a restful summer at Matt Hilary's farm, and a pleasant chapter or two are devoted to the record of the growing response of Louise Hilary to his acrid and incisive charm.

"The Quality of Mercy" is a study of crime. The story traces the diverging effects of a man's crime on his destitute but loyal children, on his business associates, on the fortunes of reporters and leader-writers, on the civic organism. The principle of unity to which all these specifications conform is infringed in one weighty particular, the love-affair of Brice Maxwell and Louise Hilary. It is quite true that their first meeting was the result of a call made by Maxwell as reporter looking up the defalcation, and a thread of similar tenuity relates the crime to the decisive visit of Maxwell to Matt Hilary's farm. It is quite obvious that the genesis of a love-affair might be referred to a defalcation exactly as it might be referred to the San Francisco earthquake, to the discovery of radium, or to the theft of Mona Lisa. A curious and, in its unimportant way, quite legitimate study might be found in the tracing of such a pedigree; but this study would evidently have no standing in a picture of the normal or representative effects of defalcation. The love-affair makes the Hilarys central instead of merely peripheral, and the institution of two centres impairs the solidarity of the book.

The interest is well sustained up to the time of Northwick's arrival in Canada. Then comes a kind of relaxation or disintegration: the pace slackens; the suspense abates; the story is approached from at least four points of view, and we lose both the measure, and the sense, of progress. The business plans vary perplexingly; what is intricacy in the author's mind becomes confusion in the reader's.

Two main impressions seem to have controlled the portrayal of the defaulter Northwick: the impression of something shadowy, Maeterlinckian or Hawthornesque, in his entire being, and the impression, in the Canada part, of mental derangement in its less advanced and acute stages. On these bases, the character is skillfully drawn. The impalpableness may seem anomalous in relation both to the materialities which have been the object of Northwick's life and to the solidity with which criminals are normally imagined. But Mr. Howells has a clear purpose in the anomaly. Society, in his view, is mainly responsible for defalcations by its support of an economic order which makes money the paramount end, and by the handing over of large sums to the keeping of fallible individuals. Mr. Howells emphasizes this social responsibility by making the individual merely receptive, by viewing him as the mere conductor through which the collective evil reaches the surface. We might put the case a little differently by saying that throughout the book Northwick seems in an hypnotic trance, a state in which the suggestions of the social organism would naturally be authoritative. He exhibits some of the best psychology in Mr. Howells, and there is something masterly in the way in which the oncoming derangement is foreshadowed in the long and cunning recital of the veerings of his consciousness on the journey to Canada. He acts little; he speaks, by my rapid count, 117 times; his impassivity becomes painful; and death, at last, finds little to extinguish.

Adeline Northwick, the elder daughter, called the "old maid" with an explicitness which Charles Lamb would not have liked, is drawn with that firm hand which is proof against any limpness in the subject. The portrayal is detailed and painstaking beyond the artistic necessities of the case, and there is no idealization to heighten or sweeten the authentic pathos.

Mr. Howells virtually admits that Suzette Northwick, the beautiful younger daughter, is all of a piece when he allows Mrs. Hilary to describe her as acting only from pride. In this view she seems a little empty, but again her passion makes her seem abounding, and the effect of riches in poverty is rather markworthy. The tingle in Suzette is exceptional, and her anger, like Florida Vervain's, is endearing, because it is the smoke to which love is the related fire. It is quite free from the viciousness which imbues Alice Pasmer and tinctures even Rhoda Aldgate and Grace Breen. The suspense of the two sisters after the railway accident is depicted with a cruel, yet a tender, vividness.

The Hilarys make a good group; the *composition* is admirable. Matt is a little aureoled; one feels that he might vex the critics who rage at Daniel Deronda. But his mildness in inflexibility, his sweetness in contumacy, is very engaging; it is part of his paragonship that he has all the needed alertness, resolution, and practical intelligence, but that he should possess these traits incidentally, as it were, like stockings. The father is clear by glimpses, but wavers possibly in the intervals. With Mrs. Hilary, as with Mrs. Corey, the woman is less ungracious than her part. I reserve Louise for future analysis with "The Story of a Play."

Brice Maxwell, the young reporter in whom literature is fed — and underfed — by journalism, is rather too evidently a gentleman who encourages the impression that he is something else. His picturesqueness is too unrelated to his essence. His oddities, his rudenesses, his defiances, his cynicisms, do not sit quite easily upon him; they might fall off if he were thoroughly shaken.

Putney, whom Mr. Howells cannot forsake in his calamities, appears at the outset rather worse, and, later on, rather better, than in "Annie Kilburn." He has the strong appeal of a double contrast, in virtue of the salt which his cynicism imparts to his humanity and the dramatic vigor which his domination borrows from his servitude. The discharge of all his asperities through his talk allows his magnanimity to flow unimpeded into his conduct.

I am inclined to think that the best character in this book is Pinney. He is a reporter, redolent of his trade, yet incorrigibly peculiar. We are all acquainted with the lovable rake whom Dickens drew in Sydney Carton and Mr. Locke tried to draw in "The Beloved Vagabond." We are all acquainted with the man who is professionally or politically shameless, but whose domesticity is idyllic. These are old and facile combinations: Pinney's is novel. He is indeed a freebooter and deceiver in journalism, while his private life might have stepped out of Paradise — or Dickens. But he is peculiar in the fact that he is equally simple and innocent in his turpitude and in his virtue; his sincerity in insincerity is exquisite. He might have seemed the sort of combination that nature alone could hazard, but there is nothing too delicately poised for transference to the subtle art of Mr. Howells. The picture is marvellous in its blending of equity and indulgence.

Mr. Howells is a little extreme in the austere and deprecating view which he takes of a thing that seems to most of us so lovely and good as the mutual devotion of a young married couple. "They thought it a virtue," he says of the Pinneys, "to exist solely for one another as they did; their mutual devotion seemed to them a form of unselfishness." This is indeed the thin air of the mountain-top. The cerulean quality of these sentiments is whimsically belied and neatly supplemented by the diabolic astuteness of a remark in "Heroines of Fiction," to the effect that "love being the simple, selfish, honest thing it is, the pretense that it is anything else is odious." The sanity of this attitude is at once formidable and reassuring. After the rebuke to the immorally affectionate Pinneys, we are landed in the mud, perhaps, but, thank heaven, we are landed on the ground.

Various characters from "Silas Lapham," "The Minister's Charge," "A Modern Instance," and "Annie Kilburn" are seen passingly in "The Quality of Mercy." Bromfield Corey's senility should hardly have been forced again on the pity of the still admiring reader. If Mr. Howells loves him well enough to fetch him back, he should love him well enough to refrain from doing so.

In this book the events are vivid and the opinions weighty, but I do not think that the opinions profit greatly by the events. There is text and there is tale; but I shrink from saying that there is illustration.

Let me summarize Mr. Howells's probable creed, not flinching from a little needful repetition.

1. Crime is an outcome of the aggregate social order for which the criminal is only partially and secondarily responsible. It is worth noting that in a paragraph of "Impressions and Experiences," where his function as novelist cannot trammel his explicitness or color his sincerity, he repeats his arraignment of "the monotonous endeavor and failure of society to repress the monotonous evolution of the criminal in conditions that render his evolution inevitable."

2. The condemnation of the unrepentant offender is morally useless; his voluntary repentance alone is redemptive.

The plain man's obvious question: "What about the deterrent effect on observers of the condemnation?" is not, I think, dealt with in "The Quality of Mercy." Nor are the means of inducing repentance in corrupt minds made very definite. One remembers that the police to whom society remands the production of salutary moral changes, to wit, the clergy, are thought to share the comparative inefficiency of their starred and belted coadjutors. Mr. Howells's thought, however, is not to be dismissed lightly.

3. Unsoundness of mind is both the parent and the offspring of crime.

4. Defalcations (and presumably crime in general) breed conflicts between legality and mercy, in which the deeper right, even the deeper justice, belongs to mercy.

This is part of the inmost tissue of Mr. Howells's mind and soul, the omnipresent stuff o' the conscience.

5. Good is slowly and obscurely brought out of evil, and the order of the world is not so much justified as excused. (Even God is entitled to mercy.)

There is almost no demonstration of 1 and 2, and the proofs of 3, 4, and 5 are not incontestably cogent.

"The Quality of Mercy" is an earnest and weighty book,

with much grave and high speculation not too closely articulated with the facts, imperfect in workmanship, like all the long novels except "Indian Summer," rich but not surpassingly rich in characterization, dignified, especially in the first part, with powerful and pathetic writing on planes of tragic gravity attained elsewhere only in "The Shadow of a Dream" and "The Son of Royal Langbrith."

"A Traveler from Altruria" is not a story, but a string of random and indolent sketches. Mr. Howells's carelessness has a grace that is surpassed only by the grace of his care.

"Random" and "indolent" are attributes that characterize only the method: the matter is weighty, but the author has made the story a myth, the scene a summer hotel, the design formless, the treatment playful, and the alleged narrator a dapper novelist. He has even given the side he opposes the advantage of including his spokesman.

As mere literature, the work has incontestable felicities. There is the character of Mr. Homos, "contemptibly puerile," yet "lovably childlike," so clearly and delicately intimated in the reserves that precede his explanations. He is a traveller from the ideal commonwealth of Altruria who visits America to study our competitive order. Second in interest is the character of Mr. Twelvemough, a novelist who is the public's spaniel, with his bland and trim egotism, his small good-nature, his small meanness, and the self-disguise which issues in incessant self-betrayal. The drawing shows a minute deftness, skill as it were in duodecimo.

Again I cannot omit from the attractions of the book the first conversation of Mr. Homos with the author, the banker, the manufacturer, the lawyer, the doctor, the minister, and the professor. This sounds almost like an extract from the prologue to the "Canterbury Tales"; and the pictures — or, rather, the persons — suggest or typify a civilization. Such a conversation, intelligent, frank, and witty, with the play of character tempered but not hampered by the discipline of breeding, is a seductive mixture of plain matter-of-fact and whimsical impossibility.

I must add that discussion in the Camp farmhouse, in which a curiously assorted body of persons review our civilization with a sincerity that is gratifyingly real and a frankness that is wholly unbelievable. Philanthropy in Mr. Howells appears to have supplied a vent for fantasy; like Portia he assumes the mummer's part in conjunction with the learned doctor's.

I hesitate to inscribe Mrs. Makely, the fashionable woman, as fifth in my series of enticements. She is unluckily introduced, is too clever for her folly and too virtuous for her naughtiness. There are times when her serene evasion of logic is delicious, and the feeling of eminent sense and character which sustains her in her absurdities is half Molièresque. Mr. Howells takes neither her nor his own picture of her too seriously. He even allows her to overstep her character; to confine her within so small an area perhaps seemed almost like incarceration.

The principle of Mr. Howells's ideal commonwealth had been already formulated six or seven years earlier in a phrase of "The Minister's Charge": "The destiny of the future State, which will at once employ and support all its citizens."

In Altruria every one works three hours a day, by state decree, under state direction, at manual labor. Additional voluntary work is permitted, but the proceeds revert to the state.

The hours of compulsory labor are paid for in tickets which are exchangeable for food and goods at the government storehouses.

There is no competition, no private stores, no differences of economic status; employment and sustenance are assured to all.

The ownership of all property, inclusive, I think, of land, is vested in the community.

Many inventions are discarded, and steam is disused. Machinery in certain forms persists, and electric trolleys are conspicuous.

Family life is preserved, but civic life is emphasized. For instance, private family meals, while not forbidden, are somewhat handicapped.

The æsthetic supervision of costumes and buildings is intrusted to the authorities. Fashion is abolished.

The social equality is absolute; private or exclusive social meetings are prohibited.

The theory might be summed up thus: the power of each is the property of all, and the power of all is the property of each.

The plan outlined by Mr. Howells is neither controversial nor technical. It neither answers nor propounds the objections of the critical expert.

It loads a "State," which, in its picture, is singularly nebulous and impalpable, with positive and onerous responsibilities. Now if we are to judge government, as we judge individuals, by its *record*, — its mundane and secular record, — its capacity for wise and righteous dealing is limited or problematical. Mr. Howells apparently assumes that the abilities will come to meet the functions. Take a minor instance. He wishes government to supervise buildings and monuments, as if taste were an adjunct to statesmanship. Yet in "Their Silver Wedding Journey" Mr. Howells has revelled in diatribes on the public statues in the German capitals.

The civic meals and the mandatory costume imply a retrenchment of individual choice which one notes with surprise in an artist's vision of Utopia. A Latin Quarter would be unimaginable in Altruria. Murger would have lost his romance and Puccini his libretto. In a world so exemplary Mr. Howells would never have written "A Traveler from Altruria."

That the dependence of each man's bread on his own thews and brains, with its incidental uncertainty and responsibility, gives drama to life, is beyond question. Mr. Howells might reply aptly enough with the question whether the drama were not outweighed by the tragedy.

The ends for which men now strive — food, possessions, victory — would cease to be objects of desire in the peace and security of Altruria. Would life become apathy, like the long Sunday afternoon to the well-fed and disengaged householder? The family is proffered as the model. But if families do not quarrel and do not compete, are they not dull? Under conditions which assured comfort and security to labor, the family might still be a recess; it could hardly be a refuge.

But when we look at interest, or even individuality, in relation to the price we pay, — in the slums, the tramps, the paupers, and the criminals,—does not all this stress on excitement seem otiose and fantastic? To weigh dullness in myself against hunger in my neighbor is to forget reason and charity alike. If all were winners, or even players, the suppression of the game might be serious. But we know only too clearly that many are losers and many are pawns.

There are men in our day, artists and scientists, who are secure of food and careless of money; yet their interest in life does not wane. These tastes are special in our discriminating order, but there seems no reason why they should be special in a state that educated and refined the whole community.

The settlement of these questions is beyond my power and my province. It is, however, interesting, to turn from "A Traveler from Altruria" (1893) to its belated sequel, "Through the Eye of the Needle" (1907), and inquire how far the misgivings evoked by the *description* are laid to rest by the *picture*. For the second book depicts what the first only reports. Before answering this inquiry, let me briefly summarize the events of the sequel.

In the first half of the volume, Mr. Homos, in his own person, reports sundry dialogues and meetings which issue at length in a love-affair and an engagement between himself and a young American widow, Eveleth Strange. The man is impalpable, and the woman is disenchanted, but the reality of the love-passion in Mr. Howells is attested by the persistence of its charm where the circumstance is unpropitious, even grotesque. The question of future domicile becomes critical, and Mr. Howells's heroine affirms her right to that post by dismissing her lover peremptorily as a prelude to the discovery that he is indispensable.

The second half of the book finds the couple married and settled in Altruria, whence Eveleth Homos writes descriptive eulogies to Dorothea Makely, now furbished up — repaired, if I may use the expression — into a fit confidante for the Altrurian's wife. Mr. Howells has not very much to add to his institutions beyond supporting details and the vivacity of picture. But he helps us to answer our questions. His picture sustains that very effect in his theories which his vivid draughtsmanship should have counterpoised. The general impression is one of amenity and mildness; the civilization is ladylike. The meals without meat, the newspapers without sensation, the theatre, presumably, without tragedy or melodrama, the society without fashion or exclusion — all this seems rather tepid even when the deft pen of Mr. Howells is placed at the service of the devout admiration of Eveleth Homos. I do not care to justify this discontent with the cool, clean, airy, and tranquil civilization of Altruria; possibly it is only the impatience of the vulgar with refinement, the ennui of Paula Tanqueray in the decencies of self-respecting existence, the toreador's doltish sense that the poet's or painter's life is colorless. That Mr. Howells either shares this feeling or dreads its emergence in the reader is confessed possibly in the resort for interest to extraneous incident; and another confession may be traced, if one pleases, in the location of this incident at the points where Altrurian order is invaded by Occidental crudities. Two American ships land in the region, and some fairly dramatic scenes take place.

The above comments are intended less to discredit Mr. Howells's ideas than to suggest their incompleteness. Under the present competitive system we pay far too high a price for individuality: we pay in anguish, crime, and shame. But under the Altrurian system might we not feel that we paid too high a price for fellowship? Must we find happiness in the bosom of quiescence? must we subject even our Utopias to the sway of that religious instinct that puts heaven *after death?* There seems need of a more comprehensive order, which shall embrace the generosities and humanities that ennoble Mr. Howells's picture in the compass of a larger synthesis.

Mr. Howells's economics may be amateurish; so were Ruskin's, so were Carlyle's. I am willing to excuse his silence in the face of objections, his indifference to the question of means, his assumption, as publicist, of a plasticity in our stubborn human nature which, as novelist, he has been alert to disown — I excuse all this in view of the help he has lent to the race in the clarification of its goals. In one point, recalled by the name of Ruskin, his work is deserving of special honor. We have allowed the progress of mechanics to regulate the structure of society, as if the state itself had been cast in the moulds of our foundries, as if the shuttles in our looms had woven, not our silks and woolens merely, but the fabric of our social life. As we have seen, the Altruria of Mr. Howells disuses steam, and tests inventions by their bearing on the evolution of the social order.

Two or three further specifications remain to be made. Altruria is vegetarian, and its crotchet is a fondness for mushrooms. The difficult point of the coercion of recalcitrants is settled rather than solved by the infliction of physical chastisement on the offenders. The chastisement is electrical; but pain is pain, and electricity is only a refined cudgel. Marriage is legally put off until the strength of the mutual attraction has been tested, — the same expedient, by-the-by, which is enforced by the Princess of France at the close of "Love's Labor Lost," — and divorce is sparingly allowed under painful stipulations which are remitted to conjecture.

The absolute social equality which prevails in Altruria contrasts pointedly with that social inequality which has supplied motive and charm to so many of the fictions of Mr. Howells. His relationship to social distinctions is complex enough to require analysis. The son of a struggling Whig editor in a rough-and-ready Western state, he learned a trade, that of compositor, in early boyhood, and the need of earning his bread which faces the middle-class American on the threshold of maturity has been placated in his case only by the industry of a lifetime. But, while still a young man, he obtained the consulate at Venice — a post and a place conducive to the growth of social aptness; and when, on his return to America, he became sub-editor of the "Atlantic Monthly," the aristocracy of Boston and Cambridge opened its doors unreservedly to the assistant of Fields and the protégé of Lowell.

By these liberalities he richly profited. I think he was for a long time profoundly, femininely sensitive to the glamour and witchery of caste. I do not mean that he respected it. His peculiarity — if it be a peculiarity — lay in his power to value it highly without respecting it. This feeling was partly temperamental; but it blended doubtless with the artist's pleasure in seclusion and elevation, comparable to the painter's delight in recesses and towers, and with the analyst's pleasure in a world in which barriers were at once impalpable and immovable, and cobweb had the tenacity of steel.

The fascination is evinced in the extraordinary part which caste plays in the long series of his novels. Until we reach those very latest works which embody the writer's very earliest experience ("New Leaf Mills" and "The Leatherwood God"), there is hardly a novel that does not *finger* the theme of caste; to say nothing of books like "A Chance Acquaintance" and "The Lady of the Aroostook," which avowedly *handle* it. I have already noted the frequency in his novels of the Pyramus and Thisbe type of love, love communicant through the barrier; and his attitude toward the children of his brain seems genuinely parental, when he lets them marry, as the reader suspects, in defiance of his better judgment. It is curious to note the regularity with which the great world is drawn into stories where its presence seems the rashest of anomalies and the happiest of windfalls. The low-born hero of the story never fails, by hook or crook, through swinging door or open keyhole, to gain some sort of shimmering vision or distant earshot of the magic castle from which his betters are excluded.

A point of still greater pregnancy is the aristocratic bias pervading a novel like "The Rise of Silas Lapham." The hero is a human being and eventually no bad man; but the belated and perfunctory respect that is allotted to his belated though not perfunctory honesty cannot offset the part of dancing bear in which he has figured so long for the delectation of the reader and the distress of the Coreys. I do not think that his crudities are overdrawn; rather I should say that they are overcolored. Facts are, in a sense, objective; but proportions are temperamental, and the aristocratic temper is usually inferable from the emphasis on the vulgar side, rather than the human or natural side, of acts which are susceptible of either treatment. Had Silas Lapham been drawn by the creator of Joe Gargery or of Caleb Balderstone or of Gabriel Conroy or of Jadwin in "The Pit," the result would have been less vulgar even if equally accurate, because taste, if a juror at all, would not have been the foreman of the jury.

I have dwelt freely on these facts because they are not the whole story; they are not even the larger or weightier element in the story. The William Dean Howells whom we see in "A

Traveler from Altruria" and "Through the Eye of the Needle" is a democrat — a convinced, an aggressive, an uncompromising democrat. His ideal is the absolute and final removal of all the man-made differences between men. Resources and obligations are to be equal for all men, and the barrier between culture and ignorance, between refinement and crudity, is to crumble in the extension of the opportunities of self-betterment to all. Democracy must not pause at the recast of institutions; it must penetrate the heart. Exclusive social meetings are tabooed in Altruria. "Human nature," he declares elsewhere, "is better than any aristocratic extract or decoction from it" — to which one might demur that a tendency to extract or decoct itself is one of the most ingrained traits in this worshipful human nature.

The sources of this democracy in Mr. Howells are readily traceable. There is the sense of humor which established an instant brotherhood with artisan and shoeblack, and there is the delight in women which overleaped or overthrew the social barrier. Again, his own sensibility to privilege wrought its natural effect in a compassionate and imaginative soul, and stressed — even overstressed — the heartsinkings and heartburnings of the unprivileged. These forces pioneered the way; then came realism and Tolstoi, and the work was done.

The relation of realism to democracy is unmistakable. The plain man is a fact no less than the courtly man, and, on a basis of reality, their claims to portrayal are equal. Moreover, realism, self-excluded from fantasy and melodrama, must seek its compensations; and its search for these compensations will be greatly impeded by any theory that reduces three fourths or nine tenths of mankind to a plane of relative insignificance. Realism is literature in hodden-gray, and is friendly to the wearers of its own garb.

Last of all came Tolstoi, identifying the first of realists and novelists, as Mr. Howells believed, with the first of democrats, and emphasizing by the relinquishments and austerities of his personal life the cult of brotherhood which he enforced in literature.

To sum up the case, Mr. Howells is a democrat by origin, an aristocrat by æsthetic taste and acquired habit, and a democrat, last of all and most of all, by reasoned conviction and spiritual bent. He felt the joy of the palace as that joy is felt by the man born in the hut, and he recoiled from the baseness of occupying a palace in a world of huts as that man only can recoil who has been a sharer in its pleasant ignominies. I wonder sometimes what place could be found for the author of "The Lady of the Aroostook" in the levels and symmetries of the world constructed by the author of "Through the Eye of the Needle." Perhaps the Aroostookian might console himself by the prediction that subtler inequalities would drive their wedges into the heart of that brotherly Utopia, and produce chasms which fiction might span with its aerial viaduct. But this comfort would be penance for the Altrurian.

I should add a word on the characters in "Through the Eye of the Needle." The note of Mr. Homos is a sweet reasonableness, a suave tentativeness on the surface, a meek inflexibility at the core. That of Eveleth Homos is an aggressive enthusiasm qualified by a jovial naughtiness. After pages of rhapsody, she has a moment of self-doubt, and the curtain falls upon this unquieted misgiving. How much this signifies, the reader does not know, nor Eveleth herself. Possibly not even Mr. Howells.

A short extract may illustrate the more ungirt, more interrogative and deprecating manner of Mr. Howells when he speaks in the person of Mr. Homos in "Through the Eye of the Needle." The manner veils an increase of earnestness.

The noise is bad everywhere in New York, but in some of the finer apartment-houses on the better streets you are as well out of it as you can be anywhere in the City. I have been a guest in these at different times, and in one of them I am such a frequent guest that I may be said to know its life intimately. In fact, my hostess (women transact society so exclusively in America that you seldom think of your host) in the apartment I mean to speak of, invited me to explore it one night when I dined with her, so that I might, as she said, tell my friends when I got back to Altruria how people lived in America; and I cannot feel that I am violating her hospitality in telling you now. She is that Mrs. Makely whom I met last summer in the mountains, and whom you thought so strange a type from the account of her I gave you, but who is not altogether uncommon here. I confess that, with all her faults, I like her, and I like to go to her house. She is, in fact, a very good woman, perfectly selfish by tradition, as the American women must be, and wildly generous by nature, as they nearly always are; and infinitely superior to her husband in cultivation, as is commonly the case with them. As he knows nothing but business, he thinks it is the only thing worth knowing, and he looks down on the tastes and interests of her more intellectual life with amiable contempt, as something almost comic. She respects business, too, and so she does not despise his ignorance as you would suppose; it is at least the ignorance of a business-man, who must have something in him beyond her ken, or else he would not be able to make money as he does.

With your greater sense of humor, I think you would be amused if you could see his smile of placid self-satisfaction as he listens to our discussion of questions and problems which no more enter his daily life than they enter the daily life of an Eskimo; but I do not find it altogether amusing myself, and I could not well forgive it, if I did not know that he was at heart so simple and good, in spite of his commerciality. But he *is* sweet and kind, as the American men so often are, and he thinks his wife is the delightfulest creature in the world, as the American husband nearly always does. They have several times asked me to dine with them *en famille;* and, as a matter of form, he keeps me a little while with him after dinner, when she has left the table, and smokes his cigar, after wondering why we do not smoke in Altruria; but I can see that he is impatient to get to her in their drawing-room, where we find her reading a book in the crimson light of the canopied lamp, and where he presently falls silent, perfectly happy to be near her. The drawing-room is of a good size itself, and it has a room opening out of it called the library, with a case of books in it, and Mrs. Makely's pianoforte. The place is rather too richly and densely rugged, and there is rather more curtaining and shading of the windows than we should like; but Mrs. Makely is too well up-to-date, as she would say, to have much of the bric-à-brac about, which she tells me used to clutter people's houses here. There are some pretty good pictures on the walls, and a few vases and bronzes, and she says she has produced a greater effect of space by quelling the furniture — she means, having few pieces and having them as small as possible. There is a little stand with her afternoon tea-set in one corner, and there is a pretty writing-desk in the library; I remember a sofa and some easy-chairs, but not too many of them. She has a table near one of the windows, with books and papers on it. She tells me that she sees herself that the place is kept just as she wishes it, for she has rather a passion for neatness, and you never can trust servants not to stand the books on their heads or study a vulgar symmetry in the arrangements. She never allows them in there, she says, except when they are at work under her eye; and she never allows anybody there except her guests, and her husband after he has smoked. Of course, her dog must be there; and one evening after her husband fell asleep in the arm-chair near her, the dog fell asleep on the fleece at her feet, and we heard them softly breathing in unison.

VIII

UTOPIA AND BOHEMIA

In this section I shall discuss a group of literary and artistic novels, including "A Hazard of New Fortunes" (1890), "The World of Chance" (1892), "The Coast of Bohemia" (1893), "An Open-Eyed Conspiracy" (1897), and "The Story of a Play" (1898). To these I shall add, with insufficient logical justification, "Their Silver Wedding Journey" (1899), on the pretext that two of its main characters are a magazine editor on furlough and a young man beginning the pursuit of letters.

"A Hazard of New Fortunes" is Mr. Howells's bulkiest novel; its two volumes number, in all, 664 pages. I like the book much better in transit than in retrospect. I have not that aptness for reconciling incongruities which would help me in a backward view to find room for a strike, with heart-crushing fatalities, in a book which sets out in a gay vein to tell the story of a modest journalistic venture; and, while I can always read the story of the Dryfooses with tolerant interest, I cannot face them in the retrospect without a shudder. True, there is

Fulkerson, and there is something tonic and antiseptic in that buoyant and outleaping personality. But there are things beyond the power even of Fulkerson: he cannot enliven death; he cannot exorcise the Dryfooses.

I scarcely know how to give the form of narrative to any summary or suggestion of the matter of this novel. It may be helpful, though it is not precise, to say that its movement is spherical rather than linear; it expands simultaneously in various directions, and its ostensible or tentative centre is the office of a New York magazine, "Every Other Week," which Basil March has been lured from Boston to edit through the blandishments of Fulkerson, the factotum and manager. To this enterprise various "lesser things are mortised and adjoined" by ties of varying tenacity. The editor's quarrels with his wife over the removal to New York may be admitted without question, and the passport thus obtained may be stretched to include their house-hunting pilgrimages in the metropolis. The business manager's love-affair with a Southern girl may be allowed entrance on the same easy terms. After this, only criticism of the Aunt Tabitha vein could close the door on two artists, man and woman, both servants of the magazine, in whose eccentric love-affair the retrospective and the prospective unite, to the virtual exclusion of the actual. The next step is not too hard. There is a young Sir Galahad whose chivalry takes shape in social endeavor; when you have succeeded in imagining him as the son of a predatory millionaire, you will have no difficulty in figuring him incidentally as the treasurer of a magazine. The faintest spectrum of a mutual attraction — as Chaucer says prettily of the wind, "unethe it might be lesse" — may then unite him with a young girl of the fashionable classes, and the story marches on unchallenged.

Doubt arises, however, when this literary magazine is made the occasion for an encounter between the ignorant millionaire and a root-and-branch socialist, almost a mendicant. Their quarrel at a dinner issues in the dismissal of the editor (who is afterward recalled), and in various influences, minatory and propitious, on the outcome of the manager's courtship. Now the use of the magazine as an *entremetteuse* in this affair is a charge on our faith. It is true that the situation is mollified by certain plausibilities. The millionaire is made the "angel" or financial backer of the magazine, though his sudden disclosure in this freakish capacity makes us feel toward the diplomatic Mr. Howells almost as March did toward the temporizing Fulkerson. The socialist, moreover, is a cultivated German, who translates foreign articles for "Every Other Week." We feel that the origin of the conjunction would be more excusable if the conjunction itself were less prolific: accident in the paternal relation may be tolerated, but in the rôle of patriarch it awakens doubts. I know that in social and psychic fields pretty much all that is imaginable is possible, and most of what is possible is real. It is not, however, these outskirts of possibility, or even byways of fact, that should attract the steps of the conscientious realist.

The masterly thing in "A Hazard of New Fortunes" is undoubtedly the picture of Fulkerson, a portrayal that interests the student of Mr. Howells almost as much as it delights his admirers. The author is known, accurately enough, as the subtle painter of subtle people; he becomes for a moment the simple painter of a simple man, — at least of a man far too simple to unravel his own complications, — and the proceeds of this venture are munificent. Mr. Howells is prone either to fuse his characters with himself, or to view them, remotely, through the cold lens of a scientific detachment. In Fulkerson his eye is distant while his heart is near, and every touch is at the same time keen and warm. He is in many ways the opposite of his sitter, and the opposite has the signal artistic advantage of being the *vis-à-vis;* but in one master trait, their humor, the resemblance was close enough to ensure sympathy. Fulkerson has for Mr. Howells the delight of a spectacle without the hardness of an exhibit.

He belongs to the great group of sincere and spontaneous humbugs, of men who are intellectually double and temperamentally candid, the men whose candor is always willing to serve their duplicity on the plain though tacit stipulation that their duplicity will return the favor. The breed is fertile in masterpieces. It gave Falstaff to Elizabethan drama, and it enriched the English novel of our time with two of its most lifelike and admirable creations, the father in George Meredith's "Adventures of Harry Richmond" and the uncle in the "Tono-Bungay" of Mr. Wells. Fulkerson shows, of course, his filiation both to America and Mr. Howells: the individual in him is respectable; the genus only is scamp. The author even takes the pains to test the moral soundness of the man, which, in the end, with the aid of friendly circumstance, achieves a kind of Pyrrhic victory.

The effect of the Dryfooses is desolating to an extent hard to parallel in the works of their creator or in literature at large. The Crawleys, in "Vanity Fair," are baser, but the Crawleys are atoningly comic, and, among the Dryfooses, 'Mela alone offers us the reparation of a laugh. They are so abnormally unlike that we cannot even affiliate and simplify our repulsions; and they excite pity and contempt so equally that each passion robs the other of ascendency. They are drawn with a skill that we half resent, and with a knowledge that chills our optimism.

No other presentation of the Marches is so full, or, in the main, so sympathetic, as that with which we are regaled and tantalized in this novel. March's generosity is amply demonstrated, and Mrs. March reaps "the flower and quintessence of change" through two versatile and checkered volumes.

The Southern colonel's dialectic, like his daughter's dialect, is a little tedious. The solution of English which Miss Woodburn pours out may be compared with the accent of Lindau, who mauls the language as if it were a plutocrat. Lack of space forbids a mention of all the characters, but must not shut out a reference to the painful but interesting portrait of the artist Beaton. The allotment of canvas to this figure is moderate and the dole of vitality is scant, but as a monograph in decadent psychology, an exposition of the way in which morality may forsake the man who has never wittingly or willingly forsaken morality, it is one of the most instructive and edifying demonstrations that Mr. Howells has produced. It is not a great picture; it is an admirable study.

The magazine is handled with intelligent precision, though the method does not rival the compact finish with which book-publishing is treated in "The World of Chance," or the fine symmetry that marks the record of dramatic endeavor in "The Story of a Play." The author pictures journalism in the grip of imperious millions, but how far this has formed and colored his purpose, I cannot guess. Millions are plainly assailed in the smothering effect they produce on the humane ideals of Conrad Dryfoos, and social distinction is less clearly indicted in the narrowed scope it allows to kindred aspirations in Margaret Vance. When the strike of street-car hands occurs, Mr. Howells is, rather characteristically, *for* the men and *against* the strike. The book contains vigorous formulations of the evils of the current economic order. "I may have my work taken away from me at any moment by the caprice, the mood, the indigestion of a man who has not the qualification of knowing whether I do it well or ill." "Someone always has you by the throat, unless you have someone else in your grip." The beliefs to be harvested in "A Traveler from Altruria" are already ripe.

"The World of Chance" is a book of dots and particles; it crumbs experience. Literary and journalistic life is granular, if not strictly fragmentary, and the solider bulks which find a place in the story are approached from points where only turrets or gables or coigns of vantage are perceptible.

Unlike "The Quality of Mercy" and "A Hazard of New Fortunes," this novel adheres with perfect consistency to one man's experience. The thread is single, though the beads are multifarious. A young man of letters arrives in New York with a novel, which, after many uncertainties, is accepted by a good publishing house, and, after more uncertainty, achieves rapid sale and wide repute. The hero has the dapper name of Ray, and his bright, mercurial, egotistic but kindly temper supplies the yeast which leavens and lightens the treatment of literary endeavor in the book.

There is, however, another portion of the novel in which his part is mainly observant. Bohemia has affinities with Utopia, and Ray makes the acquaintance of a family with experience of fraternal communities; its head is a deep and generous thinker, ending his great book and his scattered life in the restrictions of a New York tenement. In this household four deaths occur in rapid succession. The young husband, a religious hypochondriac, exposes his two children to scarlet fever; his suicide expiates their death, and the head of the house dies of trouble and old age.

How has Mr. Howells reconciled this debonair and tripping narrative of literary trial and triumph with the inclusion of horrors from which Emily Brontë or Thomas Hardy might have shrunk? The inadequacy of this reconciliation is the fault of the work. He has approached these solemnities, not lightly indeed, but with a desultory and abstemious hand. His sparing and cursory touch seems to claim, and to concede, a dispensation from emotional responsibility. It is very curious that even in this family the light-minded and jesting young mother is the only figure on which he affectionately dilates.

I doubt if it be quite fitting to emphasize light issues in the presence or the imminence of great ones, however decent and reverent be one's bearing toward the solemnities and austerities themselves. I admit that Mr. Howells's difficulties are peculiar. When Thalia gives a feast, she should hardly invite Melpomene; to slight or to court her guest in such an assemblage seems equally a breach of taste.

The theme of the book is the power of chance, and authorship is selected as its favorite hunting-ground. Chance does not imply, of course, the exclusion of law, but merely the opposition to plan or foresight. The question whether Ray's book or Hughes's shall be accepted is settled by the unforeseeable accident of a sleepless night. The question of the book's success or failure is determined by the chance of one timely eulogy. There are plenty of undesigned meetings, but fortuity of this kind is so much the *law* in Mr. Howells's work that the present novel scarcely lifts the average. Another example of chance is proffered us in the mutual attraction of Ray and Peace. They meet, become interested, undergo various unrelated and distracting experiences, find the attraction diminish, and confess finally that they are not in love. The difficulty here does not lie in the sound general proposition that a love, normally capable of maturing, may be checked in its nascence by fortuities quite unrelated to its own nature or its normal history. The difficulty lies in the choice of the fortuities. Were these distractions really competent to distract? The reader may reply that it "just happened," and that its "just happening" is the lesson of the story. But here a distinction is seasonable. In "The World of Chance" we are clearly bound to find houseroom for the unreasoned cause, but we are not pledged to the reception of the unreasoned consequence. When Mr. Brandreth's sleepless night occasions the acceptance of Ray's novel, the sleepless night descends as it were from nowhere, but the acceptance is riveted to the insomnia by links of inviolable logic. The reasons for the mutual detachment by Ray and Peace are not to be blamed because their origins are fortuitous; they are blamable because they are not good reasons.

The best thing in this book — and the worth of it is unquestionable — is the record of literary experience in New York. The succession of clicks by which the bright, swift, sure, often tiny but always pointed, chronicle is carried forward is a notable demonstration of the interest of truth. The truth has a moment of obscuration in Ray's double good fortune with his 'prentice book. The dice of story-tellers, like those of God, are always loaded, and the protégés of novelists, even of realistic novelists, find the route to prosperity miraculously abridged. One may ask where the story would have been, if Ray's book, like nineteen twentieths of the first ventures, had been finally rejected. This is unanswerable. Only, has Mr. Howells left himself the right to put the question?

The three best characters in "The World of Chance" are Mrs. Denton, Mr. Brandreth, and Kane. Mrs. Denton is hardly likable, and her evolution is perplexing, but the mixture of the acid and the placid in that lazy and teasing nature is conceived and carried out in the very spirit of reality. She is too witty for her intelligence or her class, as Kane, who is all wit, is too witty for his welfare as an individual or as a picture. What is strong in Kane is the peculiar accommodation or treaty between cheerfulness and melancholy, benevolence and cynicism, trivial self-complacence and large detachment, which makes up his indolent, nonchalant, pathetic personality. He suggests Byles Gridley in "The Guardian Angel," but with a difference — an added tincture of mockery and daintiness, reminding one of Walter Map as Tennyson pictured him in "Becket."

The mixture of sense and silliness in Mr. Brandreth is as effective as it is natural; and he is good, just humanly, spottedly good, without exaggeration or pose. Though light himself, he is solidly conceived; Mr. Howells's hand is never steadier than when it depicts flutter.

Peace, the young girl, is a profile. Mr. Howells does not care for austere sweetness; he deprecates Hilda in "The Marble Faun." His Peace is unaffecting; she has neither the firmness of Mary Garland in Mr. James's "Roderick Hudson" nor the tenderness of Mary Richling in Mr. Cable's "Dr. Sevier." She is friendly, devoted, generous, in her own self-guarding way, which seems half a condemnation of these very qualities in the plebeian form which they assume in other people.

Denton, the hypochondriac, is jerky, shrill, and fantastic; he disturbs and teases us when he ought either to frighten us or to rouse compassion. Hughes is a dilapidated Titan — not very appealing to my sensibilities; the name of his book, "The World Revisited," might almost supply a motto to his namesake in the presidential campaign of 1916.

If the reader finds this species of Utopia a little "mussy," he has a partner in his transgression. Mr. Howells is of a divided mind in relation to these people. They nourish his humor; they offend his daintiness; they impress his conscience. His alienation from the world they constitute qualifies his sympathy for the world they prophesy.

A failure in Mr. Howells, the never-failing, almost justifies itself as a curiosity; and "The Coast of Bohemia" may be characterized as a failure. He wrote the novel for a periodical of another kind and caste than those which he frequented; and one suspects alteration or vacillation of purpose; the book is short beyond custom, and suggests a hurried relinquishment of an unpleasing task.

The story deals with a country girl's experience as art-student in New York and the courtship and marriage to which this experience is preliminary. The difficulty lies in the inadequacy of the grasp both on the art and on the love. Had the art-experience been portrayed with the precise knowledge and vivid fullness that mark the record of literary experience in "The World of Chance," no insipidity in the love-tale could have spoiled the book. Had the love-story been treated with the delicate insight and fine graduation of the courtship in "The Lady of the Aroostook," a sketchiness in the art-records might have been reasonably condoned. But when the art is stinted and the courtship is slurred, the reader can only ask, plaintively or testily, "Where is the book?"

Mr. Howells seems actually less interested in art in "The Coast of Bohemia," where he has made it his business, than in "A Foregone Conclusion" or "The Landlord at Lion's Head," where it is merely his recreation. This, however, is entirely explicable. It corresponds to that abatement of cordiality which follows the perception that a person with whom we have often spent an agreeable quarter-hour is foisted upon us for a day in the Pullman. The artistic society to which we are introduced in the tea-drinkings which figure so largely and so oddly in the book strikes us as being at the same time hybrid and fragile.

Cornelia Saunders is, first of all, the heaven-born genius, and, secondly, she is the village-bred, blunt, candid, massive personality. So far she is within truth and a good subject for portrayal, like that other capable woman artist in "A Woman's Reason," Miss Root, whose first name, by a curious accident or a recurrent divination, is likewise Cornelia. But with Cornelia Saunders we have only started. She is, thirdly, an unquestionable beauty; at which we lift our eyebrows. She is, fourthly, a vortex of Bostonian moods and passions; at which we pout our lips. She is, fifthly, a subject for impossible social transformations, and a proper wife for a man of metropolitan breeding and flawless culture; at which we shrug our shoulders. She is so amplified and diversified that nothing, finally, is left of her, except a wholesome reminder of the fact that the ablest and most conscientious artist is not exempt from dangers and temptations.

The loss in Cornelia Saunders should have been made good

in Charmian Maybough, but the compensation is only partial. In her first advances at the unconventional "Synthesis," the reader sniffs vexation for himself and Cornelia, and this impression of uncouthness and rawness yields slowly and reluctantly to his more agreeable revised sense of her as a woman of fashion, with an impulsive temper and a passion for the semblance of Bohemianism. Again, Mr. Howells, who shoves her back and forth like a property or the unfinished canvas which she really is, has contented himself with piquant surface effects, and left unifications to the thoughtful reader. She sometimes touches the verge of charm; the author's own affection for her is evinced in his refusal to let her smoke. But her expansive costume and sprawling posture and their moral counterparts are an injury to the neatness of the story, and the Mrs. Maybough in the reader makes a protest.

Ludlow, the successful artist and wooer, has plainly taken a degree in the Howellsian academy for the education of gentlemen; he is adequate, but savors of the establishment.

The best portraits in this book are those of Mrs. Saunders, who overflows with reality, and the offensive Dickerson, who is vivified by the fervor of his creator's antipathy. The rusticities are more natural than the urbanities, and, in the metropolis itself, the vulgarities are more interesting than the refinements.

It is singular that the author has found room for some of his deepest and most searching reflections on life in this curiously tentative and makeshift novel. Concealments between engaged couples are reproved, and the same hand has a caress for love and a buffet for romance.

I class the short "Open-Eyed Conspiracy," described by its author as "an idyl of Saratoga," with the literary group because its subject is ostensibly the love-affair of a young man of letters, Kendricks, with a Western girl. Actually, the subject is the experiences of the editor of "Every Other Week" and his wife in the supervision of this perplexing idyl. The art profits by the reduction of its scale, to return to a goodly measure of that felicity which figures as the habit of its youth and the variant of its later practice.

The only fault I have to find with this compact and well-wrought story is the readiness of chance to be obsequious to the designs of the Marches and Mr. Howells.

The lovers themselves are so slight and faint that their presence in their own love-story comes to have almost the effect of a liberty or intrusion. Their passion is seen from the point of view of the Marches, which means that it is seen from a fiery succession and bewildering diversity of points of view beside which the experience of the simple-minded lovers must have seemed contemptible in its monotony. Let me get rid of these supernumeraries at once.

Kendricks, like many of Mr. Howells's young men, is made winning at a surprisingly small expense of time and pains on the author's part. He flourishes in his parent's neglect, as Burke said of the American colonies.

Miss Gage seems both dull and sullen, in spite of certain extenuating moments out of which the reader may extract a feeble solace. Even her beauty has the effect of being put on, and put on badly in contrast with her hats and gowns. She becomes illogically intelligent in those straits of conversation in which most of us become illogically stupid.

Simple as the book is in its main fabric, I own to a certain difficulty in tracing the sinuosities of the Marches. (I understand that in history marches or frontiers were always the scenes of uncertainty, contention, and shifts of authority.) The fickleness of the husband is almost equal to that of the wife, but, not being ashamed of fickleness, he is less Jesuitical than a woman bound by her Bostonian tradition to relate a mass of waywardness to a stronghold of principle. The reasons for the fluctuations are few and small; indeed, their pointlessness is their point. One may smile (or frown, if he will) at the spectacle of so much intelligence and conscience employed to so little purpose, to less purpose, indeed, than might be found in a consistent stupidity which other people knew how to find and which knew where to find itself. Their scruples do not hinder their imprudence; they only rob it of the excuse of impulse.

Mr. Howells is very like himself and very unlike most other people in the abrupt solemnization of the note on which this Saratoga idyl concludes:

" 'She is very beautiful, and now he is in love with her beautiful girlhood. But after a while the girlhood will go.'

" 'And the girl will remain,' I said."

This is an insight of terrible clarity, but at the close of a book whose key is struck in the assumption that it is almost calamitous that a foolish young girl should miss the good time she came to Saratoga to seek, the utterance is a breach of charity, almost a breach of contract. A night of Offenbach should hardly close with the "Dies Iræ."

Mr. Archer's epithet of "admirable," applied in his "Play-Making" to "The Story of a Play," would not greatly exaggerate my own estimate of this penetrating and skillful novel.

The stage part is beautifully done. In all dealings with the theatre there is a provisionality which the temper of Mr. Howells exactly qualifies him to seize and reproduce. The details are right, and the atmosphere of fortuity, deviousness, and unconcern, the mixture of calculation, generosity, and perfidy, is conveyed with unfaltering precision. The matter is biting, but the tone is lenient. The profession is blackened fondly — so fondly that the black, in the end, takes on almost the aspect of burnt cork.

The story deals with the composition and disposition of a play by Brice Maxwell, the young journalist of "The Quality of Mercy," now securely married to Louise Hilary, with the reluctant sanction of her high-bred family. The actor with whom Maxwell negotiates is a certain Godolphin, whom I should define as an essay with incomparable vignettes rather than a portrayal pure and simple. At all events, the analysis is consummate. I do not quite see the man, but I see the logic of him, the need of him, the fitness of him, with gratifying clearness. The non-existence of any line between pose and fact in his constitution is admirable. I falter a little in my assent to his alleged perfect comprehension of serious drama.

Maxwell's play is all hovering and wavering, but that has no effect on the firm compactness of the story. Everything is pendulous except the art — an exception which makes everything appear stable. Another trait symptomatic of Mr. Howells is the skill with which the actual value of the play is kept indeterminate, so that every one of the varied points of view may have its moment of plausibility.

The story is short, and, with a single proviso, the compact elegance of its structure might instruct our younger artists in the possibility that a novel may belong to a loose and free type, yet be finely observant of its proper restrictions. The cohesion of the work is adequate, though there is no plot and no process, nothing but an irregular movement with a fortuitous culmination.

The proviso to which I refer is a use of coincidence so reckless that it is worth while to particularize the examples. A lady bathes in the sea at a spot not far from the resting-place of the Maxwells on the sand. It is Mrs. Harley. A few months later, Louise encounters a striking woman in a street in New York. It is Mrs. Harley. A few days afterward Louise observes with interest a lady purchaser in a provision store. It is Mrs. Harley. A few minutes pass, and Louise discovers a new lodger in her apartment house. It is Mrs. Harley. A few days pass, and the manager, Grayson, mentions an available leading lady to Maxwell. It is Mrs. Harley. The same day a woman aids Louise, who has strained her ankle and fallen in a faint. It is Mrs. Harley. A little later, Louise, without Maxwell's knowledge, answers a "want" advertisement in which a prominent star solicits a play. This star is Mrs. Harley. Some time later, Grayson suggests to Godolphin an actress as leading woman in Maxwell's play. It is Mrs. Harley.

All of which proves the difficulty of moderation in the use of questionable aids. "The eschewing is only the remedye."

Brice Maxwell is milder and more agreeable than he showed himself in "The Quality of Mercy." A plain, homespun, honest sense underlies the variations of his artistic temper; he is regular, domestic, philosophical up to the point where philosophy ignites in the general conflagration.

Louise Maxwell, born Hilary, is a creature hardly to be matched outside of Mr. Howells. She approaches charm, as the admirable skill with which she is drawn approaches mastery. Yet I doubt if either charm or mastery be *quite* attained. She most nearly conquers us, perhaps, in "The Quality of Mercy," where her variety, wilfulness, and warmth of heart blend with her languor and nonchalance in a combination that might easily have proved irresistible. Later on, she abounds, she wantons, in contradictions. Attached to society, she marries a social outlaw. Disdaining drama, she glorifies Maxwell's career. She tells lies and practises base concealments when she has time to spare from reproving the disingenuousness of her husband. She is all self-abnegation when she is not all senseless violence. She is implacably fastidious, yet there is something in her which only a brute would call vulgar, but which makes one instinctively think of her in that defect of footgear in which she found herself in her first talk with Maxwell. I doubt if Louise ever found both the shoes. That bit of incompleteness in her dress is the master-stroke that completes her being as an individual. Her favorite slang phrase is "Come off," which seems to relate itself by the most obvious suggestion to the shoes. Louise's character lies largely in the refinements of her class; her individuality, in her shedding of part of those refinements.

There is one element in this book which, even in retrospect, affects one with a pain almost beyond that which literature is authorized to inflict. From time to time, this newly married and deeply loving pair put their talons into each other's souls. They are of a make so fine that they are rent almost equally by the taunts they utter and the taunts they hear. They could rise to George Eliot's saying: "Hard speech between those who have loved is hideous in the memory, like the sight of greatness and beauty sunk into vice and rags." The terror in these outflashes lies in the fact that to the eyes of Mr. Howells they are awful and yet are matters of course. We feel that the high sanctities which these quarrels profane should be vindicated by some searching repentance or some fateful rupture. The fact is that, as these differences are without reason, they are also without result and without remedy. Time may appease, but will, but love, but character, are ineffectual. And the weight of tragic purport is carried by a novel whose theme is lively and cheerful and whose conclusion is — I would have said "happy"; but, since it is Mr. Howells with whom I am dealing, I will erase the word and write "fortunate" instead.

"Their Silver Wedding Journey" convoys the Marches to Europe, and divides its 601 pages pretty evenly between the record of a summer's travel in Germany and the mementoes of a thistle-down courtship. Two thin sources of interest are recklessly expanded, yet the interest is not demonstrably thin. The book's deeper motive is a study of the passage from advanced middle-age to old age in a married couple.

The book exhales content — content in disappointment. We are visited by a thin, bright cheer, reminding us of sunshine on dismantled tree-boughs, or, more rarely and more piercingly, of worn hands stretched out to a dying blaze. The

Marches travel through Europe like deposed royalties through the lands once subject to their sceptred youth; they review past experiences with a sense at once of delicious recovery and immitigable loss. They like to be pleased, readily resign themselves to inadequacies, or burlesque an impatience which is nothing at bottom but a little coyness in the resignation. The curiosity of both is still alert, but it is that subdued curiosity which is conversant with the limits of wonder in the world and of excitement in itself. Each vacillates between antipodal certainties, and they elude and disown each other's intentions in their mutual progress toward a common goal. Mrs. March (like Arlington in Charles the Second's saying) is always tactfully in the way and tactfully out of the way of the germinating love-affair, and overflows with a sympathy which her husband mocks and shares.

The love-affair need not be taken so seriously by the critic. My notes suggest that it is a rivulet cutting its narrow gorge through deposits of anecdote and description — a figure which doubtless exaggerates its tenuity. I do not feel moved to reproduce the incidents which lead to reunion in New York, and a few words may clear us of our obligations to the actors in the comedy. Burnamy, the young man of letters, makes plenty of false steps without altogether losing the tameness which belongs to a pocket edition of all the virtues. Agatha Triscoe is Mr. Howells's form of Scott's Rowena, in virtue of a certain empty stateliness and incapacity for initiative. There is a boy called Rose Adding, in whom an eager and sensitive innocence is effectively though lightly touched.

The best-drawn figure in the novel is the one whose claim to a place in it is the most contestable. An American millionaire of German descent, who employs Burnamy as secretary, is painted to the life, every vulgarity and every brutality unflinchingly realized, yet all steeped in that humanity which tempers them so invariably in life and so sparingly in fiction.

The other persons are seen in the March perspective: Stoller is superb in the objectivity he almost shares with buffaloes and grizzlies. Yet he is not ultimately bestial; he is a man on an animal's plane of feeling.

I think there is an artistic error in giving the Marches so much centrality, and then inserting passages from which they are shut out. We do not mind exclusion in the company of the Marches, if that is the plan, but we do not care to be clandestinely admitted where we are officially debarred.

IX

SUMMITS

I shall take up in this section two novels, several years apart in time, but comparable as the last two fictions that are really distinguished, and doubly notable in the fact that the earlier was written in Mr. Howells's sixtieth year and its companion about seven years later. They are "The Landlord at Lion's Head" and "The Son of Royal Langbrith."

A Boston painter named Westover spends a week in a farmhouse in northern New England, to paint the Lion's Head, a picturesque summit in the adjacent mountains. The family at the house includes, besides a consumptive father and a consumptive elder son who die off at fitting intervals, a stalwart mother, Mrs. Durgin, and a sturdy lad of thirteen, Jeff Durgin, the future Landlord at Lion's Head. A neighboring family, the Whitwells, consists of a spirited little girl, Cynthia, whom Jeff Durgin intermittently torments (Jeff is decent enough between his spasms of impishness), a very small brother, and the father, a rustic wiseacre, who dispenses sagacities to this world, and obtains advices from the next by the aid of an industrious planchette. Westover's visit ends in a shower of stormy apples, a bit of valedictory malice from his friend and quondam follower, Jeff Durgin. The apple-shower is little in itself; it is a mere symptom; indeed the entire book is symptomatic.

Some years later, the returning painter finds a summer hotel replacing the old farmhouse, the profits of which are to sustain young Jeff Durgin in a career which embraces Harvard, the law school, and legal eminence in a seductive future. These are the mother's plans. Jeff himself is indifferent to Harvard and averse to study, and manages in his first year to incur suspension and — rather through bad luck and bad company than actual misconduct — to spend a night in a Boston police station. A vacation trip to Europe brings him within eye-shot of the Vostrands, Europeanized Americans, mother and daughter, whom he rediscovers and grows to like among the summer tenantry of Lion's Head. In Boston he renews the acquaintance; but his hopes of the girl are cut short by the mother's final determination to sacrifice her to an Italian count whose character is as worthless as his property. It may be well to explain that, through Westover's patronage, Jeff Durgin, known in Harvard as a "jay," has obtained a precarious footing on the chilly edge of Boston society. Disappointed of Genevieve Vostrand, Jeff makes love to Cynthia Whitwell, who has ripened into beautiful and self-reliant womanhood. She yields to his courtship, approves his wish to forsake law and betake himself to hotel-keeping, but sends him back, rather against his will, to obtain his degree at uncongenial Harvard.

Once more at college, Jeff works off his latent resentment at the insistent Cynthia by flirting recklessly with Bessie Lynde, a Bostonian aristocrat, fruitlessly pretty and ineffectually clever, tired, incautious, and disposed to find in flirtation with a jay the same sort of stimulus that her brother Alan seeks in the bottle. There is a mid-year party, in which Jeff provides drink for the brother and diversion for Bessie — a combination that rouses Westover to an indignation which Jeff thinks irrational and even the reader finds a trifle overstrained. The girl cannot keep herself from flirting with Jeff Durgin within sight of the lethargic body of her drunken brother, whom Jeff has brought in a carriage to the Lyndes' door in the early morning. A kiss which, on another occasion, the girl meekly suffers and indeed tacitly invites, leads to a flimsy engagement, which is brought to a speedy and timely end by the man's unfeeling but clairvoyant selfishness. He is a blackguard, but after all he is a blackguard in the Howells world, and this means that about half the time he is a gentleman. He owns the truth to Cynthia, who wisely puts an end to the engagement. When he returns to Cambridge, the flirtation with Bessie Lynde is casually resumed, but is stopped by a horsewhipping inflicted upon Jeff Durgin by Alan Lynde, Bessie's indignant brother.

Mrs. Durgin follows her elder son to the grave after a finally ineffectual effort to reconcile Cynthia to Jeff, and the passage of the estate into the hands of the younger son prepares the way for his experiments in hotel-keeping. He starts on a preparatory trip to Europe, but not before, in a chance encounter with Alan Lynde, he has thrown that young man to the ground, and barely mastered the homicidal impulse which drove his hands toward the throat of his enemy. In Florence he meets and courts his old flame, Mrs. Vostrand's daughter, whom the death of the worthless count has released from a disastrous marriage. The young widow hesitates, and a rather odd application to Westover for an indorsement of Durgin's character results in a still odder letter from Westover to Jeff, which satisfies the mild requirements of the Vostrands. Marriage follows, the inner grimness of which for the wife is poignantly suggested in the specious picture of success and geniality at Lion's Head. The book closes with Cynthia Whitwell's consent to accept the offered hand of Westover.

The "Landlord" is the most robust of all the novels. Westover is the manliest of Mr. Howells's travelled Bostonians, Cynthia is the most clean-limbed and strong-fibred of his heroines, and Jeff Durgin himself is kept half respectable by the soundness of his animal vitality. One little trait is worth noting: Mr. Howells does not paint pure country, he paints only the rusticity of fashion. It is almost comic to see how, when his eye falls upon Lion's Head, that lonely wilderness trembles like a guilty thing surprised, and converts itself with obedient swiftness into a fashionable resort. Dr. Holmes says somewhere that, if a young man were cast upon a desert island, a young woman in full evening dress would be found the next evening leaning upon his arm. If Mr. Howells were cast upon a desert island, a hackman would meet him on the edge of the surf, and a waiter would offer him a menu on the first available grass-plot in the primeval forest. In spite of this, the ozone in the atmosphere of the "Landlord" is unmistakable. It is curious that, whether by chance or design, the social life of Boston exhibits in Alan and Bessie Lynde the least reputable figures Mr. Howells has drawn from its ranks.

The story — I use the term without irony — is comparatively rich in effective incident, though when, after emergence from the final exit, you turn back to survey the edifice, the edifice has vanished. There is cohesion, but there is no perspective.

This book is more definitively the study of a single character than any other novel of Mr. Howells that I recall. That character is Jeff Durgin. As the author's view of Durgin requires careful exposition, he deputes a second person, the artist Westover, to formulate his convictions and his hesitations. The remaining figures are occasions or opposites for the protagonist, though several become valuable for their own sake to the author. The fairly abundant and rapid action is almost wholly illustrative; its impetus covers its deviousness.

Jeff Durgin is worthy of his preëminence. There are characterizations that resemble sculpture rather than painting: Jeff Durgin is carved "in the round." The portrayal of Jeff, who stands as firmly on his feet as Rawdon Crawley, should end the notion, if the notion still persists, that Mr. Howells is a mere cabinet-maker or silversmith in the guild of novelists. Even from the page Jeff Durgin inspires fear. He is decisive, but he is also desultory; he passes from mood to mood, but each mood takes on in turn the massiveness of his constitution. By some inscrutable magic, his lounging convinces us of his efficiency. Possibly his calling harmonizes these incongruities, and satirists would no doubt observe with pleasure that the stuff which made highwaymen in the fourteenth century keeps hotels in ameliorated times.

Admirable as picture, Jeff Durgin is perhaps a little incomplete as demonstration. The aim of his maker has been subtle. He wished to draw a scoundrel, but a scoundrel incognito, so to speak, without the particular deeds which attract that unseemly label. The *stigmata* were to be excluded. How different is all this from the handling of predatory types by other authors, from Smollett's handling of Peregrine Pickle, even from Balzac's handling of Philippe Bridau, who, with many differences, is like Jeff Durgin in his combination of cunning and swagger! Now, in the task of keeping Jeff relatively innocent, Mr. Howells's success has been complete. What evil has Jeff done? As a boy he teases Cynthia, and tricks the painter, Westover. In college he has bad companions, and is arrested on a groundless charge of breaking a street-lamp. Engaged to Cynthia Whitwell, the country girl, he flirts with Bessie Lynde, a Boston scatter-brain, with whom he forms a brief, parenthetical engagement. He encourages Bessie's spineless brother, Alan Lynde, to befuddle himself while he dallies with the sister. Horsewhipped by Lynde, he inflicts a pugilist's vengeance. Only two of these counts are serious, and both have extenuations. On the other side is a fairly extended list of good turns, decencies, and candors.

At bottom Jeff Durgin is the good-natured, selfish calculator, with controllable passions, and with the inactive moral sense replaced, and, in its way, efficiently replaced, by a cool estimate of the degree to which good is useful and evil practicable in a society tethered to laws and usages. Jeff's is in a sense the unprejudiced eye; what it sees is actuality extricated from moral preconceptions. It seems to me a great proof of insight that Mr. Howells, without relinquishing his own preconceptions, can imagine with perfect clearness the world as it appears to a mind denuded of those aids, or, as the mind itself would say, released from those trammels. In one way Jeff Durgin would be intelligible to a stable-boy; but what in the stable-boy is instinct is wisdom in Mr. Howells.

I have diverged a little from my purpose of pointing out an inadequacy in the character of Jeff Durgin conceived as a demonstration. Mr. Howells has kept him technically innocent, or, at least, decent; and he has impressed us, nevertheless, with his turpitude. Is not this the acme of art, to convince, not the mind, but the nostril, so to speak, by the effluvium distilled from the personality? It might well be so, if Mr. Howells had left the reader's nostril to make its own undisturbed observations and decisions. But, in obedience to a dubious habit, he has so pursued and harried me with his own view of Jeff that I cannot be sure whether my divination of evil is really an intuition or is simply the echo of his dissertations. Of what use is the magnanimous refusal to brand the defendant with explicit deeds, if Mr. Howells is to tag his person from top to bottom with compromising labels, signed Howells or Westover, as the case may be? This cannot warp the *drawing;* it only clouds the *proof*. Jeff remains a triumph of skill and insight, and Mr. Howells's fairness to a character that has magnetized him by its repulsiveness would be a theme of wonder, if the feat were single in his work.

Cynthia Whitwell is a noble figure in all that we are permitted to see of her self-poised, upright womanhood. Mr. Howells dares neither give her, nor deny her, refinement; he dims that section of the canvas. He is more reckless in the bestowal of intellectual sagacities which suggest that the Lion's Head overhangs Beacon Street. This prepares her for the marriage with Westover, accomplished, like some other marriages, while the duenna, Realism, is asleep.

Whitwell's laxly genial mind and spirit excite in me a discomfort exactly like what I should expect to feel in the presence of the slouching reality. Jombateeste is a particle, but a particle of pure joy. Mrs. Durgin, admirable in the grim taciturnity of her first appearances, declines in interest as she fails in rigor.

Westover, a Bostonized Westerner, is almost the best of Mr. Howells's gentlemen, because his delicacies are not advertisements of caste. The Vostrands are shadowy, and I am puzzled to say whether an effect of oscillation in Mrs. Vostrand means wavering in the novelist's art, or means rather its perfect steadiness in the face of the waverings of the subject.

Alan Lynde, the patrician inebriate, is for once a figure hardly credible. I can scarcely find room for his gentlemanliness in the clefts of his bestiality. Bessie Lynde, skillfully disposed at the side of the passive and dissipated brother, is in the main successful. All the preparations for her folly, her slight over-ripeness, her isolation, her orphanhood, her parity with Alan, are diviningly conceived. Her most original trait is not the facile, experimental, zest-loving and hazard-wooing disposition, but the indolent, deprecatory, not unpathetic spectatorship with which she watches the gambols of that prankish kitten, Bessie Lynde.

"The Landlord at Lion's Head," written, as I have said, in Mr. Howells's sixtieth year, is remarkable among his other novels for power and for difference. Its type, as character-study, is unique, and its fibre has a novel health and soundness. Power and difference — a little less remarkable — are characteristic of the novel we next consider, "The Son of Royal Langbrith."

I propose to analyze "The Son of Royal Langbrith" with detail enough to allow the uninitiated reader a glimpse of the close-woven, yet on the surface rather inconsequent and desultory, web which obtains in the later and longer novels of our author. There are thirty-seven chapters; I summarize each chapter in a sentence, leaving the segments to cohere or fall apart, as the story pleases.

Dr. Anther, mature and able physician in Saxmills, a town famous for its make of paper, courts Mrs. Langbrith, widow (as we learn later) of a rich debauchee and peculator whom Saxmills reveres as a public benefactor. Mrs. Langbrith declares she must speak to her son, who worships his father to the point of finding impiety in the project of a second marriage. This son, James Langbrith, home from Harvard for the Easter holidays, plans an elaborate dinner for his friend Falk, a laconic and sardonic artist. The dinner plans are made in conversation. The son, a little pompous and fatuous on a basis of high-hearted magnanimity, admits to Falk his interest in Hope Hawberk, daughter of an unfortunate inventor whom the elder Langbrith had plundered and whom opium has robbed alike of manhood and of memory. The young men pass a jovial evening with three town girls, including Hope and a certain Susie Johns to whom Falk is noncommittally attracted. The dinner takes place, and James Langbrith is prodigal of attentions to the beautiful, wayward, and incorrigibly humorous Hope Hawberk. Dr. Anther, at the party, fraternizes with Falk in tacit mockery of young Langbrith, and is cold to Langbrith's suggestion that a medallion likeness of his father be inserted in the public library, his father's gift to Saxmills. Langbrith woos the unconsenting Hope, and meets her brain-sick father, just returned from a stay at a retreat.

In a conversation with James, his mother says nothing of Dr. Anther's proposition; her reason, which comes out later, is her son's keen resentment of Dr. Anther's cool reception of his plan. The young men leave Saxmills; James's love for Hope pastures on conversations with Falk and on his private meditations. Mrs. Langbrith explains James's attitude to Dr. Anther, who is nettled by her suggestion that he should humor James in this particular. Anther receives notice from his landlady, and tries to elicit a little of the dead Langbrith's past from Hawberk's crazy mixture of aureate dreams and wild hysteria. The dead man's character is explained by Anther to a lawyer, Judge Garley, who postpones his opinion and advises prudence; Anther wants to promote his own marriage by a revelation of the facts to James. He begs forgiveness of Mrs. Langbrith, and is cheered by the sight of the three young girls on a laughing visit to the post-office. At Hope's entreaty the doctor seeks to cure the distracted Hawberk by a treatment in which laudanum alternates with less destructive potions. James Langbrith, consulting Hope by letter about the memorial tablet, is mocked by the girl, and mocked again for the superfluous telegram in which he acknowledges the justice of her satire. In an access of pique he renounces the entire plan, to the distress and remorse of Hope, who seeks, through Mrs. Langbrith and the doctor, to persuade him to return to his idea. The Episcopalian rector, Dr. Enderby, and his wife imagine past disagreements between Dr. Anther and the elder Langbrith. James Langbrith, having forsaken his plan and quarrelled with Hope, returns to both; a Jewish sculptor achieves art by betraying nature in the sculptured likeness of the dead father.

There is a brother of the dead man, John Langbrith, manager of the business and aware of the facts, with whom Dr. Anther pleads in vain for candor on the subject with his nephew; Judge Garley advises Anther to desist from interference. The judge and the rector have been asked to speak at the dedication of the tablet, and the Enderbys consult Dr. Anther. Dr. Enderby, having heard the physician's story, decides, after cruel indecision, not to recede from the promise he had made to speak; Mrs. Langbrith entreats Anther to be present at the ceremony. The tablet is unveiled; Judge Garley is adroitly hypocritical and Dr. Enderby adroitly noncommittal; James treats Hawberk with distinguished courtesy. Hope, grateful for this kindness, accepts James, who tells her that he means to study playwriting in Paris; he plans to offer Dr. Anther his father's office. Mrs. Langbrith accepts Dr. Anther; they are discovered by the son, who reviles the doctor and leaves the house. Persuaded by Hope, he returns home, acquiesces in the marriage, and is told by his mother that she shall revoke her word to Dr. Anther. She proceeds to break the engagement, and discusses with Dr. Anther the peril to the dead Langbrith's reputation from the completion of the process which is bringing Hawberk back to sanity.

John Langbrith, tortured by dyspepsia, asks the doctor for medicine, and Hawberk exults in the restoration of his faculties; he will give no publicity to his reviving memories of the dead Langbrith. Hawberk becomes an assistant to John Langbrith, and Mrs. Langbrith falters in a tremulous resolve to tell Hope Hawberk the truth about James's father. Anther, now resigned to bachelorhood, refuses Mrs. Langbrith's offer to marry him; Hawberk, after a relapse and a return to self-control, falls a victim to the effects of an accidental plunge into ice-cold water. John Langbrith's dyspepsia necessitates a rest from business; Mrs. Langbrith summons her son by wire from Paris; she cables from Dr. Anther's house, where the doctor is prostrated by typhoid fever. John Langbrith, stumbling upon his returning nephew in the smoking compartment of a parlor-car, is goaded by rage and pain into a revelation to the son of the full infamy of the father's character. Dr. Anther dies; Hope, informed by James Langbrith of the painful facts, instantly rejects the release he has manfully offered, and suggests that they consult Dr. Enderby on the necessity of publishing the secret to the world. The Enderbys advise the young people not to divulge the truth. James marries Hope, and makes paper for a livelihood instead of plays; the secret is confined to the informed and cautious few.

I have risked tedium in this long recital in order to bring out more precisely than any shorter or more interesting summary could do the matter and movement of the Howells novel in its larger form and later period. Does the outline indicate a meagre or a crowded story? Readers would answer this question variously, but it may not be venturesome to suggest that the readers who are not surprised by the scarcity of incident will be surprised by its abundance. There are two measures which give opposite results. More of this when the dictum that "nothing happens in Howells" comes up for estimate.

The tragic sense is a mixture of passion and awe. Mr. Howells possesses the awe; it is not clear that he attains the passion. In "The Son of Royal Langbrith," as in "The Shadow of a Dream," this awe is paramount.

The main woof is hardly tragical. There is nothing tragic in the fact that a scoundrel long since dead is honored as a benefactor by the New England community in which he stole his fortune, and is raised to sainthood in his son's deluded memory. The question is whether this secret shall be divulged by its few possessors. The proposed marriage of a middle-aged doctor to the widow of the miscreant — a marriage hingeing on the revelation of the secret — imparts scarcely any tragic moment to the case. The revelation to the son has a deeper solemnity, of which effective use has been made. But the tragedy is incarnate in the person of an opium-ridden victim of the dead sinner, a shambling, grimacing, yet deeply pathetic figure, in the shadow of whose calamity his daughter and her young cheerfulness and young love must find such house-room as they can. Here Mr. Howells has struck his deepest chord. The terror of living, the gayety that both alleviates and aggravates that terror, are caught with a mixture of insight and tenderness which I should find it hard to match in literature. To see at once how the tragedy enfolds the cheerfulness while the great, varied, unreceding intricacy of existence enfolds the tragedy — this is the unshared faculty of Mr. Howells. Moreover, this evil in the past, this evil in the grave, the puissance of its nothingness, is realized with a sort of power which Ibsen's "Ghosts," so rich in other powers, has hardly equalled.

The conduct of the story surpasses expectation about as much as it falls short of demand. There is almost a plot; there are, beyond all doubt, situations. John Langbrith's blurting out of the whole sordid history to his unprepared and protesting nephew would be effective on the stage. Hawberk's gradual recovery of the sanity which restores to clearness the faded memory of the evil secret is a point which a sensationist might have envied. Indeed, Mr. De Morgan, whose taste for sensation is as outstanding as his love of the tenderly whimsical, has twice availed himself of similar restorations, in "Somehow Good" and in "Alice-For-Short." Drama more or less pervades large sections of the work; it arrests that subsidence of power which marks the latter half of the extended novels. Some deductions must be made. The story is rather centreless; its apparent centre, Dr. Anther, is hardly its focus; and the events proceed in that casual, unguided way which Mr. Howells would reprove his readers for not liking. There is a great deal about the memorial tablet which the son dedicates to the father's memory; it serves the plot scantily by its indirect furtherance of the young man's courtship, but its chief purpose seems to be to involve a set of good men in a dreary series of pitiful equivocations.

Mr. Howells's ethical verdict is part of his attitude toward veracity, and that attitude is complex enough to deserve a moment's careful scrutiny. The good characters in all the novels tell social lies with a freedom and alacrity which are apparently not in the least prejudicial to their virtue. Mr. Howells, as we have seen, praises Mark Twain for not being "stupidly truthful," and condones the "merely mechanical falsehood." His grip on actualities, and his preference, wise or unwise, of the comfort of a human being to the propitiation of an impersonal law supported him in this view. The untruth was a phase of the realism. But the same propensities which made him flexible in particulars made him rigid in essentials; in cases where there is a mutual right to frankness, he upholds and enforces an immitigable candor. Sincerity is rewarded, or its opposite chastened, in "The Kentons," "The Coast of Bohemia," "April Hopes," and "The Minister's Charge." But even here allowances are proper. If obligations are unyielding, human nature is ductile. The male sex at its best is disposed to temporize, or is so estimated by the other sex, which erects its indignation at this frailty into a bastion behind which it deploys its own tergiversations in happy security. Though the evil in uncandor is inevitable, the guilt is less than the evil. The last coil in the involutions which give an appearance of deviousness and waywardness to Mr. Howells's notion of the duty of straightforwardness is found in the question which is put and somewhat tentatively answered, in "The Son of Royal Langbrith."

We must bear in mind that, at the point in time in which the novel is placed, the revelation of the iniquity would redress no concrete, no palpable injustice. Three men, the shrewd lawyer, the humane physician, the deep-hearted rector, concur in a policy that conceals and temporizes. Mr. Howells gives to the suppression of the depravity of Royal Langbrith the same reluctant sanction which he apparently gave to the concealment of the Ethiopian strain in Rhoda Aldgate. In the absence of any *individual* claim to the knowledge of a painful or guilty secret, the *public* claim to such a disclosure is cautiously and musingly disallowed. Mr. Howells is a man to whom truth is dear, much dearer than veracity, but who would make a strong distinction between the truth enjoined by sentiment and the truth enforced by duty.

Hope Hawberk is the exquisite reply to a difficult question. How shall a novelist dare to be just at the same time to a girl's tenderness for her father's unspeakable calamity and to her youth and that youth's uncanceled claim to hope and joy? This is not all. The novelist has given the problem an edge by adding an inspiration as subtle as it is daring: he has made the girl the impersonation of bubbling laughter. Can she be kept human, kept woman, in the face of these convergent contradictions? Those who answer this question in the negative have not fathomed the potency of Mr. Howells.

The father, Hawberk, is well done, but is a little too slatternly, not for truth, but for the depths and murks of which he is the slipshod incarnation. Mr. Howells will not costume and panoply his tragedy; it must borrow its wardrobe from the facts.

James Langbrith, the son and lover, is a fine example of Mr. Howells's power of keeping a character on the edge of a fatuity which it narrowly but securely avoids. Mrs. Langbrith, the widow and mother, is too limp; you can hardly make a human being out of a sofa-pillow. Falk, the caricaturist, is a pungent drawing to which his own art has lent a touch. John Langbrith, similarly pungent, is also a trifle overdone. The cayenne in both is overcharged. Dr. Anther is lovable, but a little too patently the epitome of all the insights and the virtues.

"The Son of Royal Langbrith," written at or near the age of sixty-seven, exhibits a dramatic force hardly perceptible in earlier work and expresses much of its author's profoundest insight into the pathos and mystery of life.

X

RECESS AND INTERLUDE

In this section I shall treat of "Ragged Lady," "The Kentons," "Letters Home," "Miss Bellard's Inspiration," and "Fennel and Rue," five novels, or novelettes, of advanced date and reduced significance.

"Ragged Lady" (a phrase which, I am assured by the dictionary, is a name for the fennel flower, and serves here doubtless as a symbol for rustic charm and innocence) is the story of a beautiful untaught country-girl, who wins the regard of a rich couple, and is wooed by a large and varied assortment of suitors, two of whom, both Americans, enter intimately into her life. Of these two, the first-comer, a young clergyman, holds her heart and her half-promise for a time, is rejected in favor of a young inventor from Ohio, and reclaims her finally from the widowhood in which her first marriage prematurely closed.

"Ragged Lady" is the one novel of Mr. Howells to the purport of which I am unable to find a satisfactory clue. I cannot see that it means anything but Clementina, and Clementina is not a solution; she is a problem. Incidental meanings may be ascertained or conjectured. In the Lander couple the book undoubtedly means to show the mingled pathos and ugliness of people born poor whom riches have sentenced to inaction and futility. A contrast may likewise be intended between the hectic scrupulosity of the young clergyman and the moral soundness and wholeness of the young inventor who supplants him in Clementina's mobile affections.

These things are clearly subsidiary; the central interest is Clementina. But what and who is Clementina? Why is this little western flower, against whom or around whom Cupid looses so many love-shafts, transported to Florence and Venice, when her main business is to decide between the opposing claims of two Americans? Is the object to show the relation of the largest number and diversity of characters to a simple-minded, pure-souled American girl? Is it the triumph of American artlessness over European wile? Is it Cinderella at the Prince's ball? Is it an impersonation of pure candor? Is it Daisy Miller without the recklessness?

Clementina's leading traits are a sweetness of temper which masquerades as warmth of heart, a fine sense of justice, a scrupulous conscience coherent with incurable placidity and quiescent religion, passivity crossed with a few clear insights and resolves, and an absolute self-poise in relation to externalities. The name Clementina suggests a long white tunic fastened at the throat, and we imagine sometimes that Clementina herself, at a pinch, could be folded up and laid away in the drawer of a fragrant linen closet. She is best in her wild-flower girlhood; she palls a little on acquaintance. A more active Clementina might have found a kinswoman in the Cicely Jupe of "Hard Times"; on the platform she might have betrayed a sisterhood or cousinship to Verena Tarrant in Mr. James's "Bostonians."[1]

The effect of patchiness or sketchiness in this book is quite unexampled in Mr. Howells. There is no visible dependence, ascension, unfolding. I do not know that there is any involuntary looseness in the web. There is so much voluntary looseness that it is difficult to say. Artistic intention in our day coincides so nearly with artistic unintention (in the keener writers) that it is hard to discriminate the crude from the subtle.

On the characters little need be said. Minor figures stroll

[1] Since the above was printed I have found the following explanation from Mr. Howells himself: "In the 'Ragged Lady' I began with the idea of a girl who had a genius for society, a delightful social creature." — *World's Work*, 18, 11547: "Mr. Howells at Work at Seventy-two," by V. W. Brooks.

on or off the stage with the most disconcerting inconsequence, to be replaced now and then by major figures equally at a loss for useful occupation. Mrs. Lander is very well done, and the clergyman Orson is excellent. Mr. Lander, Mr. Milroy, Clementina's parents, Gregory in his headwaitership, are pleasingly touched; the rest is silence, or, at best, undertone.

"Ragged Lady" is a story of American rusticity and European worldliness. "The Kentons," described by Mr. James as "that perfectly classic illustration of your spirit and your form," is a story of American provinciality and European travel. The reviving interest in Europe calls up, if it does not quite call back, the days of "A Foregone Conclusion" and "A Fearful Responsibility." "The Kentons," though a mild, slightly plotted novel, with an effect, at a distance, of improvisation, has a persistent interest — a fact demonstrated in my own case by the fairly severe test of reading it twice, once for pleasure and once for study, within a period of a few months.

More than any other book of Mr. Howells (its only competitor is "Silas Lapham"), this is the story of a family, and he has placed them, by a pleasing association, in Ohio, the state of his own birth and nonage. The stress and drama of the tale are confined to the first hundred pages, with the briefest revival of tension in a pivotal situation near the end. An extremely troubled love-affair is succeeded by an extremely placid one. There is not story enough to suffer from the maladies which attack Mr. Howells's long stories in the course of their approaches to a close. After the first hundred pages, there are so many episodes, so many occasions for tameness, that it is quite unreasonable in a story so handicapped to be interesting; but even in this point it defies logic.

The profound thing in the book is the likeness between Bittredge and Breckon, which so subtly yet simply rationalizes the transfer of Ellen's affections from the hound to the clergyman.

A refined girl has her head turned by a facetious blackguard; she is cured by a new passion for a facetious Unitarian minister. The introduction of a third character, another blackguard, to whose mirth she is faintly responsive, is possibly an *embarras de richesses;* but the reader could not sanction its withdrawal.

The first love-affair is exhibited as the family's problem rather than the girl's. The treatment of the parents offered a problem of some difficulty. They are underbred, by the Howells standard, and they are well-bred, and the problem is to be just to both aspects. The solution is in the main adequate. They are a little humdrum, a little heavy — which means, as I shall take leave to whisper in my reader's ear, that their talk is not so *very much* brighter than that of alert and clever persons in real life. Their helplessness before their children and their problem, and a certain erectness in their helplessness, are well pictured. They are equipped with individualities which never rasp the conventions in which they securely fit, and neither of them perhaps is quite so individual as their mutual relation.

In the sea voyage and the sequel, Ellen is truly, if lightly, drawn, but the early portrayal is warped by Mr. Howells's quite sincere belief in the possibilities of insanity and cruelty latent in the tenderest and purest women.

Lottie seems astray in the Kenton family, astray almost in the Howells clan. Neither seems to have a place reserved for the young woman in jack-boots.

Boyne, the younger son, is the artistic feat of the novel. He has affinities with Rose Adding in "Their Silver Wedding Journey," and his solemnization of the world and himself is handled with a sympathy which loses no jot of the humor. I doubt if anyone else could quite do this — not Tolstoi, not Turgénieff, not Meredith, not James. We ask ourselves if we are not all Boynes, imperfectly mature, with reversions to simpleheartedness.

Bittredge, the hound who pursues Ellen, is an almost impeccable portrait. Mr. Howells looks on him with a detestation which destroys his philosophic tolerance, but rather aids than hinders the objective precision of his touch. The note of the workmanship is rather tragic than comic. The same power in handling blackguards reappears in lighter form in the brief but unforgettable delineation of Trannel.

Breckon is put together inexpensively out of two salient traits — his overflowing humor, and his doubt of the seemliness of this overflow in a Unitarian clergyman. He is the pattern gentleman who does shabby things; he plays a silly trick on a young girl whose sorrow would have made her sacred to anyone but a model gentleman.

The book touches at Scheveningen in Holland, in order to take aboard some agreeable reminiscences of Mr. Howells.

In "Letters Home" Mr. Howells showed instant mastery of an untried instrument — the epistolary form. The six writers are an elderly Bostonian *flaneur* sojourning in New York, a young journalist self-exported from the West, a lower middle-class and super-middle-aged house-tenant and his wife from the same region, a young girl of Puritan tradition established in a rich parvenu's family, and the expansive daughter of the parvenu. The bulk of the letters are written by the three observers, the Bostonian, the Puritan girl, and the journalist, who is actor as well as looker-on. Here, as elsewhere, the spectators are half the spectacle.

The story avows its paternity in its slightness. The journalist and the millionaire's daughter love each other. The man is drawn into some reluctant but compromising attentions to the sixteen-year-old daughter of his struggling landlord. He hesitates between passion and duty, or duty's semblance, decides for the latter, and is rescued from the penalties of his own magnanimity by the magnanimity of the landlord's family. An attempt to buy off the girl's father is thwarted by the mother's courageous independence, and the story ends in happiness — I should say marriage — for the lovers, and incurable disappointment for the girl of sixteen.

The letter method, in Mr. Howells's skillful hands, is abundantly able to carry these light responsibilities. It quickens the pace and unshackles the pen: it lends informality and plausibility to the serried brilliance which in narrative would have seemed less easy and in conversation less credible. The characters are clearly discriminated, and the youthful impulse in the letters of Frances Dennam could not have been bettered if Mr. Howells had written them at Miss Dennam's age. The commentary is stinted. The Bostonian who delights in comment and has, furthermore, a peeping, tiptoeing curiosity which would be vulgar outside of Boston, is too ill-informed to satisfy either appetite.

I find in the book one grave artistic fault. We are asked to treat the young journalist's venial error in relation to the sixteen-year-old girl with about three times the seriousness which such episodes demand in the average novel. I should not complain of this attitude if "Letters Home" as a whole were three times as grave as the average novel. But "Letters Home" in its entirety is care-free and sportive; it rejects pressing invitations to be serious. The millionaire is the soul of a trust, and the sins which starve and freeze the poor are the sins that are least excusable with Mr. Howells. But this millionaire, drawn with admirable spirit, is tolerable, even attractive. He is not Jonathan Wild, but Robin Hood, the incarnation of generous roguery. This is perfectly excusable in comedy; what is less easy to excuse is that the comedy which has just condoned this enormity should put on the mien of John Knox or Jonathan Edwards toward the half-voluntary error of Wallace Ardith.

Mr. Howells wishes to idealize the millionaire's daughter. With masterly tact he keeps her very much out of the way. In the *descriptions* of her admirers, her proportions become continental (her name is America), and her authority sovereign. But in their *narrations* she seems extravagant, hot-tempered, unscrupulous, and coarse. Mr. Howells argues in her behalf that "real feeling is *always* vulgar" — a defence that itself requires protection if it does not demand apology.

Frances Dennam is admirable at first in the impassivity of her social surface and the reckless abandonment of her epistolary outpourings. Later on, in her vast tolerance of America Ralson and her merciless censure of Wallace Ardith, we feel that she is becoming Mr. Howells's blackboard. For a blackboard she remains amazingly vital.

Wallace Ardith knows too much and sparkles too much, but something tender and ingenuous humanizes his accomplishments.

"Miss Bellard's Inspiration" is a novelette — scant in bulk and light in tone. Its subject indeed might have justified a weighty novel: it is the discouragement to marriage produced by the trust of modern youth in the observed facts of life rather than in the illusions of its own moods. It is part of the problem handled by Henri Bordeaux in that responsible book, "La Peur de Vivre." In the Howells work an object-lesson in matrimonial discord is the occasion for the rupture of a congenial engagement between two passionate and happy lovers. The reason is logically insufficient, and its dramatic insufficiency is glaring. The argument which finally reunites them is intentionally puerile, and the puerility is only half excused by the intention.

The girl, Miss Bellard, is Mr. Howells's first sketch of the "new woman." It is a mild treatment of a light case of that subtly graduated malady. Miss Bellard's "newness" consists mainly in self-support by teaching in a Western university, and in a hard-headed prevision of the ills of matrimony. She has all the "oldness" which inconsistency and flightiness can confer. Indeed, Mr. Howells's differentia of the "old" woman might almost be said to be a lyric rationality, an inflammation of logic in the wrong place. This definition exactly fits Miss Bellard.

The English lover, Edmund Crayburne, is charming, though a little ghostly. I hope that, in the Elysian fields to which his sweetness and goodness will inevitably conduct him, he will find a soft couch on the asphodel somewhere between Lord Rainford and Mr. Westgate.

The other characters hardly demand treatment. The matrimonial scarecrow — if I may so express the office of Mrs. Mevison — is so unimaginable that I think she must be true. Here again, the theme is too grave for the handling. "Miss Bellard's Inspiration" is a novel that is almost equidistant from failure and success.

In "Fennel and Rue," another novelette, an outrageous deception is practised on a young author. He writes a stinging letter. He meets the chief culprit, a fragile and remorseful young girl, at a country house where her peculiar office is to concoct amusements for the guests. Recognition and confession follow; and the author sees the young girl carried away from the unspoken plea of his deprecatory, his almost expiatory, love by the energy of a simpler and firmer man.

I think it is the mixture of discomfort and unreality that makes this book so exceptionally wearing. Pain substantiates life; life is its excuse, its compensation. This book heaps up the pain while it scants the vitality. The poor girl shudders away from us and from Mr. Howells. She is over-punished for her offence, and her castigator is over-punished for his severity. The best traits in the novelette are the spirited opening and the comradeship between the young novelist and his mother.

XI

Finalities

"The Leatherwood God" (1916), whether gauged as history or as fiction, is hardly to be classed among powerful narratives. The record of the bedevilment of a raw Ohio settlement in the eighteen-twenties by a religious mountebank is not carried out with consecutiveness, proportion, or adequacy. The failure is not mysterious. The reeking Dylks, porcine rather than vulpine, is the very scum of imposture, as his sorry victims are the lees of dupery. Mr. Howells avoids the effluvia by eluding the subject, and seeks a restorative in the society of the unbelievers with whom as artist his concern is less immediate. The evasion is forgivable, if we are to thank for it the admirable portrait of Matthew Braile, the humanely humorous skeptic, whose character might be reached by bisecting a right line drawn from Squire Gaylord in "A Modern Instance" to Owen Powell in "New Leaf Mills." He dominates the tale from the tilted chair-legs of his covered porch-way by the acrid charm of his reality. With him the author is at home, but to certain other people and things his relation is lateral rather than frontal; he has even an effect of glancing at them over his shoulder. The proportions are not wholly sound. Nancy Billings's bitter and tragic problem seems undervalued in its relegation to the post of an adjunct, and Jane Gillespie's part seems of that ambiguous type which is too slight for prominence and too large for subordination. The resurgence of Dylks after a downfall which should have been final may please the realist, but can only disconcert the artist and the logician.

The *aversion* of Mr. Howells from his central theme (using "aversion" in both its literal and its derived sense) is a check on the thoroughness of the psychology. In a single chapter, the sixteenth, the mere analysis of imposture is masterly; but analysis is distinct from portrayal, and the half-heartedness of the portraiture of delusion becomes evident in a comparison of "The Leatherwood God" with Browning's "Return of the Druses," or the nearer and clearer analogue presented by "La Colline Inspirée" of Maurice Barrès. It is in the psychology of disbelief or half-belief that the tried hand reasserts its cunning.

After Matthew Braile and Matthew Braile's wife, whose laconic speech has the mysterious property of leavening her capacious silences, I incline to give another married couple, Abel and Sally Reverdy, the first rung in the scale of characterization. They are wedded so absolutely that their individualities seem little more than offshoots of their mutuality; and a critic is interested to observe how the character which in nature has the formlessness of dough can put on firmness of contour and crispness of crust in its passage through the bakery of art. The slatternliness, a little too faithfully specified, of the civilization as a whole is a hindrance to the reader's attempt to find invigoration and cheer in its robustness. The style in these latter days is shrinking — I might almost say shrunken; but the skill that vivifies local custom is paralleled in the spare touch which fairly burnishes the landscape.

Two things on which Mr. Howells delighted to enlarge were Shaker communities and summer board. In "The Vacation of the Kelwyns," a novelette published just after his death, he had the happiness of combining these delights. The Shakers, indeed, merely fringe or tuft the story: they lease a summer abode to a professor in historical sociology called Kelwyn, and at their suggestion a rustic couple, the Kites, are hired to cook and work for the professor's family. The Kites are wretchedly, shamelessly inefficient; the legalities and moralities are all with the Kelwyns; and the point of the story is the constant eagerness, the unfailing reluctance, and the final refusal, of the Kelwyns to enforce their rights by dismissing these offenders. Mr. Howells does not prescribe, does not expressly ratify, this conduct; he indicates a fact, the recoil of moral delicacy from a personal share in the inhumanities by which a brutal social order puts pressure on its shirks and sluggards. It is easy to reply that more Kelwyns in the world would mean more Kites, and that more Kites would mean more trouble for the Kelwyns, and even for the Kites themselves, since incompetence is its own enemy and victim. Mr. Howells would not deny this; but I think he would say that where the same act was brutal and necessary, if nine hundred and ninety-nine men affirmed its necessity by their conduct, it was more than time for the thousandth man to proclaim its brutality by his abstention. He might also say that a social order which identified the necessary with the brutal was a disorder which cried aloud for remedy.

Novels that do what the Yankees call chores often show the heaviness and unwieldiness of the persons by whom chores are done. "The Vacation of the Kelwyns" is a clear exception. Mr. Howells loves the *technique* of life, its rigging or tackle, the ways and means of living; at least he loves the crossings where physics intersects psychology. He is rather shamelessly joyous in the squalor to which he introduces the innocent and hapless Kelwyns. But even the Kelwyns take misfortune easily. The spirit of the tale is found in a speech of Kelwyn (who as professor and sociologist has every right to be heavy if he so chooses) to his visitor, the Shaker elder, Nathaniel: "Take a stretch of turf." The book, for all its grave implications, seems to have been written in one of those lulls of responsibility in which Mr. Howells faces destiny with a smile. It is a book of facts, an industrious, expeditious, unhesitating book, yet its rapid sureness in the appropriation of its material is so quiet and easy as almost to take on the air of unconcern. The irresponsible Kites, to whom their accomplices the Kelwyns are so irresponsibly indulgent, are a social fact which may be viewed loftily from a pulpit or rostrum or loungingly and whimsically from a stretch of turf. The oddest people come straying in from all sides, to nibble at the comfort which nests perversely in the heart of discomfort. Shakers we might expect, but there are gipsies, and a bear-leader with his bear, and Italian organ-grinders, and an Irish linen-peddler, and a burly negro tramp, and a beguiling Frenchman. All enter or pass very much as the Kites stay, by right of a certain salubrity in the moral atmosphere to which nothing you might care to shut out is quite so unlovable as expulsions and exclusions.

Where so much is let in, a love-story could not well be kept out, and the story is here, perhaps rather as favored guest than as inmate. Here one might expect convention, the "sweetening to taste," which is part of the undeviating recipe. But the mark of this love-affair between Mr. Emerance, as he is usually called, and Parthenope Brook is a half-achieved, perhaps a half-thought-out, originality. Parthenope, born in Naples, is Mrs. Kelwyn's cousin, rich in what she calls experience, a rather lordly young woman with evanescent severities. Her lover, born on a farm, self-cultivated, with much rotation of crops in the process, a little perplexed by the very multitude of his capacities and inclinations, remains curiously restful in his manifold efficiencies and sunnily placid in his very doubts. We might here expect the not unfamiliar conflict between the well-born girl and the low-born but high-bred man, whose personality reminds one alternately of his birth and of his breeding. This may very possibly be the essence of the conflict, but it is not the form. Parthenope finds the man immature, uncertainly masculine, unfixed in his ideals, submissive to impulse. Her doubts are finally removed, or, at least, overcome. The idyl is pleasant enough, but Parthenope is only half realized, and Emerance, though better imagined, is one of those sons of Mr. Howells in whom the parent seems a little too obviously to live again. But inheritance goes with sonship, and in this instance the bequest is — charm.

XII

SPARKS FROM THE CHISEL-EDGE

The short stories to be considered in the present section begin with "Tonelli's Marriage" (1868), and "At the Sign of the Savage" (1877), Atlantic stories, republished in conjunction with "A Fearful Responsibility." There follows a long silence. "Christmas Every Day and Other Stories," drolleries for children, was printed in 1895. In 1901 appeared "A Pair of Patient Lovers," containing five short stories; in 1903, "Questionable Shapes," with three stories skirting the supernatural; in 1907, "Between the Dark and the Daylight," mostly frequenting the subways of consciousness; in 1916, "The Daughter of the Storage," a miscellany, of which stories form a part. I shall condense my treatment of this secondary work.

The two most interesting stories — to the critic at least — are the two earliest. "At the Sign of the Savage," a simple record of an amusing trick, is perfect in its conduct, and settles once for all the question of Mr. Howells's intrinsic faculty for the short story. "Tonelli's Marriage" is equally perfect on lines of far greater delicacy and far less power. Story is discarded; a few absolutely credible and logically disconnected facts are recorded in relation to the hesitating marriage of a middle-aged Italian; and the advance in truth coincides with the retreat in vigor. I am not sure but that this tiny narrative is the most perfect expression of Mr. Howells's ideal as fictile artist.

It is remarkable that neither of these tales had a competing successor. Mr. Howells never reverted to perfection in the conduct of the traditional short story; he never quite reverted to the simple boldness of the new type developed in "Tonelli's Marriage."

The "Pair of Patient Lovers" volume, published more than

twenty years later, is of a milder interest. These tales are long, in deference possibly to the example of Mr. James and Mrs. Wharton; their subjects are quiet; the treatment is distant — I might almost say, preoccupied; the tone is leisurely even when the speed is high. The author cherishes his preliminaries, and his major scenes are not lengthened — not even heightened — in relation to the preparatives. The story seems to disappear rather than to conclude.

The best of these tales is "A Circle in the Water," in which the encounter of a released convict with his uninformed daughter affords a solemn, half-tragic note of which Mr. Howells is quick to avail himself. The Marches run the story, but the father and daughter, who rank only as the principal characters, are permitted to appear for measured periods at discreet intervals; there is nothing mean about the Marches. The story, though truncate at the close, is touching, and embodies the deep and subtle idea that our sorrows and disgraces are not only liabilities and taxes; they are properties and rights.

Next in merit perhaps is "A Difficult Case." I do not admire the unfolding of this story, but its basic conception, that of the solitary old man in his forlorn domicile, battling with his fears of immortality, is pathetic and vigorous.

"The Pursuit of the Piano" is happily whimsical in its accounts of the recurrent instrument; but the love-story into which this comedy merges is so faint as to be almost inaudible. "A Pair of Patient Lovers," in which the Marches are again nursing an invalid courtship, is a rather languid treatment of a fairly incisive motive — the recovery of a young woman who has obtained her mother's consent to marry in view of the supposed nearness of her death. "The Spell of a Voice" is dim — not obscure but simply dim.

"Questionable Shapes," which contains only three stories, is of greater average interest. The supernaturalism in all three is illusory.

"His Apparition" sketches keenly the psychology of a man who supposes he has seen a ghost, and is effective in its satire of the bargaining American. A freakish but amiable heroine scatters pungencies through the novelette, which offset in a measure the tameness of the hero and the slow pulse of the tale.

What "The Angel of the Lord" vouchsafes us is a fine mood, a mood that diffuses a wine-colored autumnal flush over a story almost too slight to engage the analytic attention of a group of after-dinner talkers in a Boston club. The coterie is strident, but its leading spokesman, the psychologist Wanhope, is of a lovable and admirable repose. There is a great air of philosophy in the recital, but somehow the fencing — not to say boxing — in the club and the poetry of the Ormonds are the only things that rivet the memory.

"Though One Rose from the Dead," a slight but notable venture, contains perhaps the best description (or descriptive narrative) of the romantic type to be discovered in the works of Mr. Howells. I see no reason why the hand that drew the two "call" scenes in this story should not have mastered, if it had so willed, the secret of that romantic mysticism which gives effect to Beckford's "Vathek," to Brown's "Wieland," to Poe's "Ligeia," and Mrs. Wharton's "Moving Finger." The story, tenuous at best, is further attenuated in the leisurely narration. The problem is, briefly, the extension of telepathy to the next world, or rather to the two worlds, and a married couple, exceptional in the force of their mutual passion and in their seclusion from the normal world, are chosen as the subjects of the exposition. Having reached the proper end by realistic standards, Mr. Howells adds the postscript demanded by romantic expectation; the difference is illuminative, and the concession piquant.

"Between the Dark and the Daylight" consists mainly of stories drawn from the penumbra of consciousness. In "A

Sleep and a Forgetting," which reaches sixty-one pages, the story of a lapse of memory under tragic auspices is faintly, almost dreamily, recorded, as if the tale, whose motive is embodied in its lovely title, were itself hardly more than reverie. "The Eidolons of Brooks Alford," another story in which Wanhope takes the chair, which his person, moral and physical, seems to cushion, is interesting, if a little shapeless. A sincere pleasure in the ending is qualified by a sense that, however often marriage with a widow may have proved a dose, it is a little unfeeling to suggest it as a prescription. "A Memory That Worked Overtime" and "A Case of Metaphantasmia" (which means apparently dream-transference instead of thought-transference) are short, rough-and-ready stories of psychic experience, in which the wonder felt by the characters in the story is imperfectly shared by the questioning reader. The three remaining stories emerge into daylight. "Editha," a tale whose careless brevity belies its weight and saps its power, impales the young woman who drives her reluctant lover to premature death in a questionable war. "Braybridge's Offer" is a morsel of psychology rolled in comment. "The Chick of the Easter Egg" is "local color" in a double sense.

"The Daughter of the Storage," in addition to plays and poems mentioned in another section, contains twelve specimens of story or sketch, with the sketch undeniably predominant. It is unusual that minor work of an advanced period should all but incite the critic to a reconsideration of weighed and cherished estimates, but this book offers rare testimony to the persistence, in the output of Mr. Howells, of that change which is the index of vitality. The two stories which take no part in the provocation to retry the Howells case are the two longest in the book, "The Daughter of the Storage" and "The Critical Bookstore." The motive of the first, a girl's marriage in a storage warehouse, has a journalistic dash which we rather pardon than admire in Mr. Howells; but the cheapness of the groundwork is offset by an edging and frilling of a delicacy which literature only could supply. "The Critical Bookstore," in which literature and woman are the objects of a parallel and interflowing courtship, is the most agreeable of the twelve fictions, and exhales precisely that tranquil charm which one likes to associate with the mellowed age of a fortunate man of letters. The curious thing is that it is exactly in the rebuff of any such expectation that the other experiments in the volume achieve their tart originality. They mix two qualities which in combination rather frighten one — desolation and vivacity.

They show this mixture, however, in very unequal degrees. Possibly I am alone in divining the property of desolation in the rough-hewn but vigorous satire of "The Return to Favor," in the excellent sketch of a mischievous boy, "The Amigo," and the whimsical reflectiveness of the less successful Central Park colloquy, "The Escapade of a Grandfather." The element of liveliness, on the other hand, retreats to a discreet abeyance in "A Presentiment," a club story which reads like a loose and drifting leaf from "Between the Dark and the Daylight," and which loses effect through the slowness — not to say stagnation — of its current. "Table Talk" and "A Feast of Reason," lively pictures of social entertainments, have not the slightest excuse for ruefulness, but they leave the reader with a sensation as if "the mouse behind the mouldering wainscot shrieked."

There are four other sketches in which the grimness is more evident. "Somebody's Mother," a formless bit, in which earnestness seeks relief and finds aggravation in persiflage, leaves the reader faint and gasping. In "An Experience" the gropings of a shapeless reverie, and the sultriness of a day in which the air is half gum, blend sordidly yet portentously with the half-grasped, half-visioned fact of sudden death. "The Mother Bird," a brief sketch of a questionable woman on a ship, is an experiment which Mr. Howells would have declined in 1860, in 1880, perhaps even in 1900; it is, none the less, a legitimate motive, and it is handled with an art whose perfection is merciless. "The Boarders" has much less merit, but even greater significance. The simple union of desolation and liveliness is sufficiently painful; but when the desolation becomes sordid and the liveliness cynical, the result is not to be forgotten or endured. Had I read this sketch in ignorance of its authorship, I believe I should have ascribed it to the reckless ferment of undisciplined and untamed youth rather than to "the depths of a mellow heart" out of which the publishers assure us that this amazing volume has been distilled.

In one of Lord Byron's early revels at Newstead Abbey, it is reported that wine was passed to the guests in a skull. After reading the prose of "The Daughter of the Storage," with its mixture of gayety and horror, I can imagine myself a partaker in that feast.

Sketches like the above involve the question of Mr. Howells's attitude toward life. Is his mood cheerful or gloomy? The answer is a little hesitating.

The novels of this realist are at least superficially cheerful. They attract us by the amenity and tranquillity of the tone, by the gleam and ripple of humor, by the presence of youth, the rapture of love and the brightening certainty of wedlock, and, lastly, by a liberal allowance of those social gatherings, excursions, receptions, dances, teas, which enliven the distant and solitary reader, however little they amuse the participants. Cheering estimates are not very scant in his books. He praises "the large, cheerful average of health and success and happy life" in America, has a kind word for optimism in "Imaginary Interviews," and tells us, in the preface to "Literature and Life," that he has "seldom seen a sky without some bit of rainbow in it."

His life has been almost exempt from misfortune, and he himself tells us that its "smiling and prosperous times" have been plentiful. He has had the safeguard and the solace of work, and the years which have spared his faculty have confirmed his fame. Realism in his time has been ascending, he would say culminating, though its sway is far from universally acknowledged; and, if the social reorganization for which he yearns is still only a hope, it is a hope which the rising conscience and clearing perception of America render every day less visionary. A life so favored seems almost under bonds to be happy, because it represents conditions rather more promising than those which we seek to universalize in the hope that they may benefit the race.

Let us now turn to the other side. There is a tendency in the novels, visible rather than prominent in the earlier group, gathering strength and distinctness from the time of "A Modern Instance," which penetrates the reader with an inward and abiding discomfort, very different from the sugared pathos and voluptuous despair with which romance has so often beguiled the palate of sentimentalism. What their fatalism portrays is not so much the disaster of life as its disease, and not so much its violent and mortal disease as a dull, smouldering, irremovable, and patient malady. It is less the magnitude of the distress than its certainty, its contumacy, its obduracy to the old romantic charms and sedatives, that pursues the reader with formless disquiet.

The occasional utterances take on, by degrees and with intermissions, a perceptibly sadder coloring. Until we reach the poems the feeling never leaps out; it *creeps* out rather, or *peeps* out, in a momentary self-disclosure which does not arrest the smooth, sunny onflow of the self-possessed and courteous page. The terror of these utterances lies in their seeming inadvertence. "I would not live my life again," he says passingly in "My Literary Passions." "Life," he remarks in a preface, "seems sad in Trezza because life is mainly sad everywhere." Self-unbosomment becomes explicit in that sincere and terrible volume of poetry, "Stops of Various Quills," though I must not here anticipate what I have to say of the heartbreak which imparts to that cluster of lyrics its dread significance and sombre beauty.

We must not, however, be too ready to infer that disenchantment and despair is the be-all and the end-all of Mr. Howells's later attitude toward life. This Howells is the same man who, in "London Films," as late as 1905, approached the metropolis in the rich, housewifely content with which one might unfold the fragrant contents of an historic cedar-chest; the same man who, in "Familiar Spanish Travels," as late as 1913, seemed himself almost to shake the castanets in a blithe upward spring of youthful gayety. How shall the critic harmonize these diversities?

I should say that Mr. Howells was a man with a quite exceptional capacity, not for joy precisely, but for enjoyment. Life, in its daily passage, offers him a thousand appeals, enlivenments, diversions, pungencies; the tiny recreations are innumerable. This alone was enough to breed reactions in a sensitive mind, and the reactive impulse found a perpetual subject and occasion in the sight or the thought of his burdened fellow-men. His was a spirit infinitely pitiful; the poverty of others weighed upon him as it weighs upon few of us — as it weighs rarely, I fancy, upon the humanitarians who devote their lives to contention with its evils. No doubt, he felt in a sense branded by his well-being, and viewed his happiness (or his fortune) as a kind of perfidy to his race. There are two points, however, in which our judgment should be wary. We are all prone to think that a man is more fully himself in his generalities, his views of life and the world at large, than in his particular experiences or perceptions, and we imagine a greater significance in his despondent moods, which commonly review and assay his pleasures, than in the happy hours which are normally uncritical. Both views may be misleading. The breadth of the field which the generalization covers is unfairly taken as a measure of its power in experience; but the briefest reflection shows that a generalization is a thought like another, that a thought is momentary, and hence that its claim to represent the man must depend on the degree of its recurrence and insistence. Precisely the same thing is true of the critical mood; it may be less characteristic than the mood it judges. The test of a man's real disposition is the form which his mood takes in the equipoise of circumstance, in the absence of strong biases or deflectors from the outer or the inner world. I am unwilling to believe that the cheerfulness which animates the great bulk and the sound norm of Mr. Howells's work is wholly fortitude, and, even granting that his despairs are his most vivid moments, I distrust the inference that they are likewise the most typical, since extremities of all kinds are rarely typical and are usually vivid. They differed from such passing disasters as occur to many men in love or business, in the fact that they were permanent liabilities; but a permanent liability need not even approach the character of a continuous experience, and a house may be sunny in a climate that has thunder-showers.

These speculations establish nothing; they merely admit the possibility that life may have been less inclement to Mr. Howells than one might infer from his darker intervals or his ampler generalizations.

XIII

THE TRUTH-TELLER

I have now concluded my review of particular novels and tales, and shall restrict my generalizing summary to a single topic. On characterization I have been expansive to a degree which makes it needless to expand further by the addition of a summary. Style, a major topic, may be better handled in an estimate of the whole man. A single topic, that of realism, calls for elucidation at this point.

In his later days especially, I think that Mr. Howells's realism became prejudicial to his art. He allowed the cult of truth to excuse artistic lapses which it could not justify. For instance, I do not think that the meagre bulk and scattered results of the phenomenon called coincidence in real life will uphold Mr. Howells in the ample scale and unity of direction which he assigns to that influence in "The Story of a Play." I feel that he errs again in "The Quality of Mercy," in the introduction of the love-affair between Louise and Maxwell — an indirect and random consequence of the Northwick defalcation — into a group of sequences which are clearly intended to be direct and typical. I do not feel that the raggedness of "Ragged Lady" is justified by the discovery in real life of shreds and tatters in a profusion and confusion even more strongly marked; I cannot but think that art stands for the progress we have made in the sifting and sorting of the scrap-bag. I know that inconsequence in *theme* passes by insensible degrees into inconsequence in *treatment*, but is it not the part of men like Mr. Howells to remind their duller brethren that the empires which that shimmering boundary divides are as unlike as order and chaos? Realism in narrative cannot forsake art. When a man writes a book, he merely puts certain ideas together, and this is done in the faith that they gain in meaning by their neighborhood; that meaning becomes his sieve, his test, his law; the fruit of his obedience is art; he can forswear art only by disowning intelligence.

Mr. Howells remains a true artist in the face of these partial reservations, as he remains, likewise, an eminent realist in spite of the deflection from truth I am about to name. The facts will not bear him out in the grade of intelligence, and, more especially in the brand of conversation, supplied even to average characters. If one compares well-bred and intelligent speech in Mr. Howells's Americans with the same grade of speech in the Russians of Turgénieff and Tolstoi, he discovers that the Americans have been blessed in their endowment or fortunate in their painter. His countrymen may watch these pictures with a patriotic glow, not unqualified perhaps by a personal shiver. The brightness of these performers seems to say to the reader, like Emerson's gay equipage, "Who are you, sir?" Mr. Howells's fools are a grave embarrassment to his reader. It is difficult to maintain a decent and seemly contempt for imbeciles who move in an order of ideas and expressions which arouses one's envy in real life.

The modification is in part unconscious. Every man instinctively makes himself the measure of his race; and a bright man's power to attract and arouse capacity in others will raise still further his estimate of the normal alertness of the human mind. It is hard to believe, however, that this conversation is mimetic of any experience, even the special experience of Mr. Howells. I cannot persuade myself, that, quality and evenness both weighed, our author ever heard from Dr. Holmes conversation equal to Mr. Colville's or from Mark Twain himself outpourings so richly and variously whimsical as Mr. Fulkerson's. It must be admitted, doubtless, in extenuation of this fault, that Mr. Howells's characters talk very like people in real life even when they talk very much better; that is to say, the verisimilar tone and movement restore half of that effect of nature which the literary value of the conversation has obscured.

I would not press this point unduly. To apply the whetstone or the strop to human nature is a forgivable weakness, and it is piquant and pleasing to catch Mr. Howells, whose interest in tips is irrepressible, in the act of bestowing a *douceur* on the race. There is an incidental mistake which to my mind is graver than the general error. Mr. Howells is prone to raise the intellectual level of certain of his characters without warrant or prologue. Mrs. Erwin, the silly aunt in "The Lady of the Aroostook," is commissioned to say certain things that are very far from silly. Lemuel Barker, who is stolidity incarnate in his first appearances, becomes quick and happy in retort. Again and again we are moved to address these characters of Mr. Howells in the words used by the blind Gloster to his son Edgar:

> Methinks thy voice is alter'd, and thou speak'st
> In better phrase and matter than thou didst.

It is evident that such a practice contravenes art and realism alike.

I wish now to mention certain points in which the author's realism is novel — points in which his work resembles nature and differs from that of his competitors. Of course, the most novel resemblances are not necessarily the deepest or the weightiest; they are, nevertheless, the clearest signs of independence and sincerity. The points I shall note are sometimes little, sometimes large, and the particles are almost as interesting as the blocks.

Mr. Howells has an eye for those vividly irrelevant perceptions, which impress us, by a curious anomaly, in proportion to the depth of our engrossment with other things. Mr. Sewell has a painful confession to make to his wife.

"She stood with the pillow-sham in her hand which she was just about to fasten on the pillow, and Sewell involuntarily took note of the fashion in which it was ironed." This has now become a habit, almost a trick, of the expert story-teller.

He is wise again in those peremptory associations which bring grotesque trifles to the mind in its crucial moments. Rhoda Aldgate's life has been convulsed by a shattering revelation.

"She turned from the chill of its [the day's] pale light, and looked at Olney. Through the irresistible association of ideas, she looked for his baldness with the lack-lustre eyes she lifted to his face."

He understands how the inertia of habit will impel men to acts that belie the situation and their own mood. Bartley and Marcia Hubbard are parting after furious words.

"She could not make the buttons and the button-holes of the child's sack meet with her quivering fingers; he actually stooped down and buttoned the little garment for her, as if they had been going to take the child out for a walk between them."

He can fix an act like this (Ray is carrying a paper in which his novel is favorably reviewed):

"He threw the paper into some bushes; then, after he had got a long way off, he went back and recovered it, and read the review once more."

Acts of this kind are almost unknown in fiction; their pertinence in nature will be instantly recognized.

Several details in the matter of conversation reveal a curious fidelity. Comedy reports unsparingly the miscarriages in the speech of its butts, but serious art has rarely taken account of the fact that these failures and ineptitudes pervade the conversation of the serious. In Mr. Howells, people who are not ridiculous grope for replies, grope for witticisms, which they do not find. The obvious fact that conversation is a shifting game, in which the bad player sometimes wins and the good player often loses, is clearly reproduced. In other artists the talkers always win or always lose; they are infallible or hopeless. In these books people say bright things and fail to cap or match them — a misfortune to which every reader of this book will modestly confess that the brightest talkers are liable. Again, the inequality of fortune which often divides two witticisms of equal desert is noted in these conscientious pages. Still further, a man is convinced by utterance of the untruth of a proposition which he uttered sincerely. "I found myself talking sophistries," says March.

The reciprocal misconceptions of two speakers are hackneyed in comedy, but, as an element in the verisimilitude of serious aspects of life, they are almost unknown to art; Mr. Howells has not overlooked their claim. The special case of the two persons who part on a common understanding, and meet again in a mutual bewilderment caused by the acquirement of new data on one side, is reflected in the amaze of Sewell and his wife at the close of Chapter 32 of "The Minister's Charge."

Closely allied to this delusion is the misreading of the facts illustrated in the effort of the Laphams to read into Irene's letter an intimation of her willingness to be pleased with an attentive cousin. The amusing and fruitful misunderstanding is a device which age has withered and custom staled in the repertory of comedy, but the passing, the serious, and, more especially, the *sterile* misconception is a commonplace of life that remains a novelty in art.

There is a form of the unexpected in which freshness, if not absolute novelty, may be claimed for the work of Mr. Howells. Here again our novelty is antique; art has taught us from its earliest rise to expect the unexpected. But the surprises of art have mostly been invoiced and registered; they are stereotyped, like the marvels of the juggler, in their very novelty. The surprise I have in mind may or may not electrify; its peculiarity is that it baffles. It is as if we put a question to life and received from that authority, not the momentous Yes or No for which we had prepared ourselves, but an answer in an unknown foreign tongue. The reply is inapt; expectation is *thwarted* almost in the literal, material sense of the term. Mr. Ferris, in "A Foregone Conclusion," is in quest of his fate at the door of the Vervains, and learns that his fate has not yet returned from Europe. "He laughed to himself at this keen irony of fortune; he was prepared for the confirmation of his doubts; he was ready for relief from them, Heaven knew; but this blank that the turn of the wheel had brought, this Nothing!" A more piercing illustration is found in the passage where Ferris brings his stored and nourished fury to the door of the priest, to be met by the ghastly irrelevance of his death. The uncandor of life has deeply impressed Mr. Howells, who declares that nothing happens as you expect.

There is another element in reality to which possibly no one but Mr. Howells has rendered full justice: I mean the element of uncertainty. Art has always acted on the presumption of its own omniscience. Indeed, one of the superiorities of fiction lay in the circumstance that the novel, though unreal, was sure of its unreality, whereas the fact, though real, was uncertain. One might say of Mr. Howells that he has deprived art of its latch-key. But this would overstate the truth. Rather let us say that he has robbed art of that skeleton key which fitted equally into all locks, and he has allowed it omniscience only in the case of leading characters. He will not tell us explicitly that Margaret Vance loved Conrad Dryfoos; he will not tell us whether Jeff Durgin spared Alan Lynde from an impulse of pity or in recognition of the approach of Jombateeste; he will only suggest that Mrs. Vostrand may have overruled her daughter in the successive acceptance of two questionable suitors. Life poses many questions which it never answers, and realism comes finally to adopt the reticence of life.

Beside the halfness in our knowledge of the facts must be placed the halfness of the facts themselves. Human nature appears to have the most perverse ingenuity in stationing itself in the exact cleft or interstice between right and wrong; or, to vary the figure, it frequents the river that divides the two governments whence it can land at its convenience on the ports of either shore. A curious anomaly ensues. The posture which is most congenial to our dispositions is least tractable to our intelligence, and, in law and opinion, our logical instinct — in other words, the convenience of our thinking — gains the upper hand, and imposes the brutality of its hard-and-fast categories on the shifting and slipping dubiety of fact. Art, or the æsthetic sense, originally sides with logic against life; it paints a definite goodness and badness, a pronounced wisdom and folly; it is only when the fullness of time has made its eye sharp and its hand supple that it ventures to forsake the solid illusion for the wavering reality, that it sees its advantage in the mixture and the doubt. In my treatment of the characterization of Mr. Howells, I have often praised the skill with which his portrayal has defined — has fastened, in a sense — a character on the frontier between two categories. To fix a tremor — that is the problem he has solved.

Earlier literature has its affinities or proximities to the type. The susceptible young man whose pliabilities are liabilities is as old as Tom Jones and Captain Booth, to trace his ancestry no further. Scott's Rodericks and Byron's Conrads illustrated the character which forms, so to speak, a picturesque gorge between contrasted heights of good and evil. But the hovering character — hovering, I mean, between two definitions or categories — is infrequent in the annals of belles-lettres; and if figures like Molière's Alceste or, possibly, Prévost's Manon Lescaut obscure Mr. Howells's title to the fame of a discoverer, they cannot rob him of the honors of a pioneer.

Another point in which Mr. Howells's realism is novel is its critical attitude toward the passion of love. He has felt that passion profoundly, and, in his refusal of any countenance to loveless marriage in its most beguiling forms, he has taken a stand which worldlings would describe as sentimental or romantic. But this man, whose pictures of that passion in "A Foregone Conclusion," let us say, or in "April Hopes," are hardly surpassed in glow and color by any novelist of our time, is as stern toward love as he is devout, and never relaxes his purpose to sift and test that many-tinctured passion.

No other contemporary, except possibly Meredith, has made his exposure of the shams and pyrotechnics of that singular emotion a pendant to so profound and sympathetic a sense of its sacredness and reality. He says in "Criticism and Fiction" that the "gaudy" heroine,

> long taught by example, if not precept, that Love, or the passion or fancy she mistook for it, was the chief interest of a life, which is really concerned with a great many other things; that it was lasting in the way she knew it; that it was worthy of every sacrifice, and was altogether a finer thing than prudence, obedience, reason; that love alone was glorious and beautiful, and these were mean and ugly in comparison with it.

The following is from "The Coast of Bohemia." "They flattered one another with the tireless and credulous egotism of love; they tried to tell what they had thought of each other from the first moment they met, and tried to make out that they neither had ever since had a thought that was not the other's; they believed this." Mr. Howells sees that all great passions are mendacious, since a great passion might almost be defined as the claim of a part of life to be the whole; and he sees, no doubt, that the greater the reality, the greater is the imposture. To me sentimentalism and cynicism are cheapened almost equally in the clear light of Mr. Howells's unequalled mingling of veneration and perspicacity.

In a single point insight yields to sentiment. Courtship between persons of unequal breeding is a favorite problem in the novels, and, while Mr. Howells can put the objections to such a union with astonishing and disconcerting force (see "Out of the Question," IV, 1), he ends, in every case but one, by permitting the disparities to wed and sending them off with that ambiguous benediction which married couples receive from the conscientious realist.

The treatment of marriage is the same combination of exposure and defense. Marriage is to Mr. Howells a holy and a terrible thing; in one passage in "Silas Lapham" he makes the anguishes and brutalities which it can live through and live down the measure of its divinity. His presentation of the sobering facts in marriage is not to be classed as a realistic innovation; the novelty in Mr. Howells is the emergence after the descent, and this falls only by a certain allowance within the compass of our present topic.

The insight which tested love is applied to the analysis of grief. Ceremonial grief is as hollow as romantic love. Dr. Olney, in "An Imperative Duty," is surprised by the fitful gayety which checkers the gloom of Rhoda Aldgate in the crucial days that follow her aunt's death.

> He was himself too inexperienced, as yet, to know that we grieve for the dead only by fits, by impulses; that the soul from time to time flings off with all its force, the crushing burden, which then sinks slowly back and bows it in sorrow to the earth again; that if ever grief is constant, it is madness, it is death.

The reader will remember that the present section aims to confine itself to the differentiae in Mr. Howells's realism, the points in which he outsteps his forerunners. He will remember that the novel insight is not necessarily the profound one, that the last truth to be grasped in a new field, like the last lands to be appropriated in a new country, may owe its postponement to its inferiority. In fact, the matters I have touched upon differ greatly in value. Some are mere details. Some deal with the irrelevancies and incoherencies which represent the inorganic element in life, and which art, itself an organism, has long eschewed for much the same reason that a cow rejects pebbles. To my mind, these points are of more interest than value. They are elements of reality which art perhaps has rather blinked than missed, which it is well to remember sometimes and permissible often to forget. The points which relate to hovering characters and to the dissipation of romantic fantasies are of quite another order of significance; they touch the kernel of reality.

When we add to the above traits a perfect observation, a marvellous psychology, and a friendliness with truth that makes her accents dear and cordial like a mother tongue, the high place of Mr. Howells among contemporary realists is clear.

A word further must be said. Mr. Howells is one of the very few novelists — more than that, he is one of the few realistic novelists — who are capable of the strictly realistic point of view. That point of view is very simple, so simple that it is achieved with some difficulty by a complex generation, and that even to define it with trenchancy requires a little art. The material of the strict realist is the *human fact;* he is related to that fact as the botanist is related to the botanic fact. It is enough for the botanist that the fact is a fact and is botany; it is enough for the strict realist that the fact is a fact and is human. The point lies in the word *enough.* Other men, plenty of them, delight in the human fact, if you will let them add something else to it — interest, logic, charm, passion, greatness, profit. The strict realist may love these things too; but he is a strict realist because he can get on without them. He looks abroad over the world. He sees a billion or more of human beings; each of these beings has, let us say, sixteen hours every day when consciousness rolls up its inner curtain and stages its interior drama; in every conscious second, something *occurs* on that stage. Now a man may care to know *what* occurs in any conscious moment to anybody. That man is the strict realist. The two remarkable things about this intellectual curiosity are that its *scope* is so vast and that its *unit* is so diminutive. The vastness of the scope does not mean that the novels must be long; if your whole is too large to be handled in its totality, you must break off a part of it, and it is just as reasonable to break off a small part as a large one. Nor does the smallness of the unit mean that combination of the units into edifices is forbidden; the point is simply that the edifice, like a child's house of blocks, can be unbuilt, and that, when this happens, the blocks of which it is composed remain genuinely interesting to the architect.

The inquirer may here put in a modest question: "Why does n't everyone feel this *human-fact* curiosity?" or, turning objector, may ask more aggressively: "Does n't everyone feel it?" The answer to this is, of course, that the interests and desires which equip us for the contest of life confuse, confine, and, to a great extent, expel or efface these universal values. These interests and desires include some of the most respectable parts of our being — the logical impulse with its artistic correlative; the love of the unusual; the love of beauty; the ethical, religious, or didactic impulse; the sense of humor; the eagerness for life. These are, or, more strictly, they create, *derivative* values, and each of these new values winnows the human facts for its own purpose. They enlarge and reduce; they go further; they eliminate, and, as we all know, they invent. Now it is difficult for a man to suppress, to alter, or to belie the unreinforced, the unembellished human fact without losing much or all of his respect for its integrity. Zola, Flaubert, and Balzac were realists. What does Zola care for the facts that contravene his thesis? What does Flaubert care for the facts that circumscribe his art? What does Balzac care for the facts that chasten his exuberance? The men who maintain a high respect for the bare human fact in the face of these competing purposes and passions are few. Tolstoi, in his undidactic moods, is one; Arnold Bennett is one; Mr. Howells is distinctly of their number.

This by no means implies that Mr. Howells is without partialities, specialities, or favored topics. On the contrary, his store of these conveniences or inconveniences is noticeably large. He favored the subtle and the delicate, and loved the class in which these graces are distinctive; he had a partiality for art and letters as a topic; he had an interest in women that marked him off even from other males and other artists; he was ethical to the core; in his later years he developed a profound concern for the influence of the social organism on human welfare. But this is by no means all; the case may be put with even greater force. The earliest group of novels, the playfully subtle love-stories, by which his celebrity as writer was confirmed and his reputation as novelist was created, owed their charm and their fame to the exploitation of a novel interest of the most narrowly select and special kind. That interest was exceptional refinement and subtlety developed in a favored social class by the suavity of circumstance. Discerning judges have assigned to this group the first place among his novels; and even judges like the present writer, who are unwilling to say that it contains his best work, admit without cavil that it reveals his best workmanship.

This fact has to be reconciled with the thesis that Mr. Howells's interest in the human fact was universal. Strictly speaking, no reconciliation is necessary; a sympathy that cares *somewhat* for *all* men is entirely compatible, is indeed not infrequently combined, with a sympathy that cares *more* for *some* men. But if the question be put in this way: where was the universalist in Mr. Howells when he wrote "The Lady of the Aroostook" and "A Foregone Conclusion"? the critic is bound to reply. His answer will be a suggestion, not a dictum, and he will leave the estimate of its worth to the reader. Mr. Howells was an observer born to poverty amid plain people in a rude country. The observer in this setting could not be dainty; he became omnivorous. The eye was catholic, and the heart and mind, if not impartial, were at all events comprehensive. A man thus reared is brought in his riper youth into contact with persons of subtle insight and exquisite breeding, and the circumstance defines an epoch in his life. He came into his own, not like a foreigner into some bright, new land, but like an exile to his native country, or, let us say, like a French colonist born in Siam or Algeria to Paris. For the time being his literature is controlled by the new enthusiasm; the universalist is submerged; and the tide has to recede before the love for the simple human fact can reappear and take its place beside the ardor for the specialty. I put the case too crisply and too crudely. Mr. Howells, even in his devotion to the elect, never quite forgot his fealty to human nature. "The Lady of the Aroostook" is a short novel; it contains at least six persons alien to the class that supplies the novelist with his point of view; and five at least of these persons are sympathetically treated. The odd thing is that, even in later fictions, where interest is conspicuously widened, Mr. Howells never seems to feel quite at home with the very persons with whom his birth and breeding had fitted him to feel peculiarly at home. He draws them very well; indeed, they furnish him with his best portraits; but he is never quite wonted to them; he has the effect of continually repressing slight starts in their society, of politely hiding his disposition to treat them as a branch of anthropology. It is only in some of his latest novels, "New Leaf Mills" and "The Leatherwood God," that the reversion to early attitudes and habits becomes complete enough to abolish this bodiless but efficacious barrier.

This aloofness from the uncultivated man, which often consorts with admiration or sympathy, is merely incidental to my present object. That object is to suggest that, when the specialist receded (he never disappeared or ceased to emphasize his presence), the universalist, the Howells to whom nothing human was unrelated, resumed his place. The world was searched by a heart to which every overture of the senses was a boon, by an eye that found its contentments everywhere, by a curiosity that found its solaces in the very objects that distressed the heart. He has been called a man of details, and, while the dictum is unsound if it be held to include an indifference to wholes or sequences, it is correct enough in the sense that other men's fractions became his integers. The test of greatness in a man is the unit of consciousness, the solitary perception: the man is great and vital as that is great and vital; in like manner and measure is he small and weak. Mr. Howells made a mansion of the fact; indeed, he went further — he made of it, in a sense, an abode. Observation is normally a traveller, but this man could give to sojourn the effect of settlement; he was like Sothern and Marlowe, who rent a house in every town they visit, and contrive to dwell in the very spots through which they flit.

The crudest view of realism imagines that the realist must love dullness since the bulk of reality is dull. A view slightly less crude imagines that the realist must be fond of littleness since the bulk of reality is little. But little or dull in this context must be measured by the effects on the author's mind, or, more precisely, by the amounts of himself that the author can put behind an object which passes for little or dull among his listless or trivial associates. The amount of Howells that contrived to get itself behind a plain particular was singularly large, and the destined reader is quick to adapt himself to the new dimensions of this pleasing world. Observation in one aspect is creative. A word, a gesture, has a groundwork in the mind. If in relation to the word or gesture — the external sign — observation is a mere recorder, in relation to the mental groundwork it is a diviner, an interpreter, a clairvoyant. The keenest of observers cannot hear or see his neighbor's mind, and when, at the entrance of that mind, his senses desert him, it is clear that either the quest must cease, or its conduct must be remitted to imagination. In the fullness of this realization of the psychic basis for the external sign, in this pursuit of the fugitive far into the dim interior, Mr. Howells is akin to Dickens, whom he hardly liked at all, and to Meredith, whom he liked with ample reservations. In all three writers the process involved a transfer to their characters of segments or portions of themselves; and doubtless one reason why they found the minds of other men so habitable was that they had eked out the shabby accommodations with loans from their own furniture. Mr. Howells undoubtedly overrated the brains of the common folk whom he met in life and pictured so acutely, and it was doubtless partly to this overestimate that he owed his happiness in their society.

The processes of observation differ widely. There is an observation that resembles a scoop or shovel, that observes, so to speak, by the paragraph or page. This is Hugo's observation, at least in his diffuser moods. There is an observation that reminds one of a fork in the hand of a well-bred Englishman in the leisurely composure of its withdrawal and return; this is the observation of Trollope. There is another observation which reminds one of the use of a fork or its fraternal implement by a Western American at a *table d'hôte;* that is the observation of Balzac. There is an observation that suggests a nut-pick, the delicate extrication of fragments of pure pith; that is the observation of Mérimée. There is an observation that resembles a straw in lemonade; that is the observation of Mr. Howells. Temperamentally, it is not unlike the observation of Mr. Hardy. The straw does not so much connect two surfaces as connect two interiors. The word *infiltration* might describe the process; or, if the reader is tired of metaphor and wants a plain version of the facts, let us say that while observation and experience mean two things to many writers, in Mr. Howells observation *is* experience. It was once commonly said that nothing happens in Howells.[1] It might be retorted that in Howells

[1] This idea is happily touched in *Indian Summer* (Chapter 20). Mrs. Amsden, the old lady, is speaking to Colville and Imogene Graham.

"I feel that we are a very interesting group — almost dramatic."

"Oh, call us a passage from a modern novel," suggested Colville, "if you 're in the romantic mood. One of Mr. James's."

"Don't you think we ought to be rather more of the great world for that? I hardly feel up to Mr. James. I should have said Howells. Only nothing happens in that case!"

"Oh, very well; that 's the most comfortable way. If it 's only Howells there 's no reason why I should n't go with Miss Graham to show her the view of Florence from the cypress grove up yonder."

"No; he 's very particular when he 's on Italian ground," said Mrs. Amsden, rising. "You must come another time with Miss Graham and bring Mrs. Bowen."

everything happens. If nothing in his works is an event, — and to admit this is to admit a gross exaggeration, — everything, a smile, a glance, a turn, a word, a silence even, tends to become an *incident*. What is an incident? Let us define it as a break or shift in the external course of things which demands a shift in the mental attitude of the observer. An incident is that which produces or invites a mental readjustment. Let the curious reader note the mobility, the flexures, in the situation depicted in the following dialogue from the thirteenth chapter of "A Chance Acquaintance." Kitty Ellison has asked for time to consider an offer of marriage from Mr. Arbuton, a Bostonian of formidable distinction.

Besides, it was somehow very interesting to Kitty to be there alone with him, and she thought that if all were well, and he and she were really engaged, the sense of recent betrothal could be nowhere else half so sweet as in that wild and lovely place. She began to imagine a bliss so divine, that it would have been strange if she had not begun to desire it, and it was with a half-reluctant, half-acquiescent thrill that she suffered him to touch upon what was first in both their minds.

"I thought you had agreed not to talk of that again for the present," she feebly protested.

"No; I was not forbidden to tell you I loved you; I only consented to wait for my answer; but now I shall break my promise. I cannot wait. I think the conditions you make dishonor me," said Mr. Arbuton, with an impetuosity that fascinated her.

"Oh, how can you say such a thing as that?" she asked, liking him for his resentment of conditions that he found humiliating, while her heart leaped remorseful to her lips for having imposed them. "You know very well why I wanted to delay; and you know that — that — if — I had done anything to wound you, I never could forgive myself."

"But you doubted me all the same," he rejoined.

"Did I? I thought it was myself that I doubted." She was stricken with sudden misgiving as to what had seemed so well; her words tended rapidly she could not tell whither.

"But why do you doubt yourself?"

"I — I don't know."

"No," he said bitterly, "for it really is I whom you doubt. I can't understand what you have seen in me that makes you believe anything could change me towards you," he added with a kind of humbleness that touched her. "I could have borne to think that I was not worthy of you."

"Not worthy of me! I never dreamed of such a thing."

"But to have you suspect me of such meanness —"

"Oh, Mr. Arbuton!"

"— as you hinted yesterday, is a disgrace that I ought not to bear. I have thought of it all night; and I must have my answer now, whatever it is."

She did not speak; for every word that she had uttered had only served to close escape behind her. She did not know what to do; she looked up at him for help. He said with an accent of meekness pathetic from him, "Why must you still doubt me?"

"I don't," she scarcely more than breathed.

"Then you are mine, now, without waiting, and forever," he cried; and caught her to him in a swift embrace.

She only said, "Oh!" in a tone of gentle reproach, yet clung to him a helpless moment as for rescue from herself. She looked at him in blank pallor, striving to realize the tender violence in which his pulses wildly exulted; then a burning flush dyed her face, and tears came into her eyes. "I hope you 'll never be sorry," she said; and then, "Do let us go," for she had no distinct desire save for movement, for escape from that place.

Her heart had been surprised, she hardly knew how; but at his kiss a novel tenderness had leaped to life in it. She suffered him to put her hand upon his arm, and then she began to feel a strange pride in his being tall and handsome, and hers. But she kept thinking as they walked, "I hope he 'll never be sorry," and she said it again, half in jest. He pressed her hand against his heart, and met her look with one of protest and reassurance, that presently melted into something sweeter yet.

If the reader avers that this is very quiet drama, perhaps the best reply would be that it is very dramatic quiet. It may not suit all minds, but its *sufficingness* — how different that word from mere sufficiency! — for the qualified and preadjusted reader is complete.

People have allowed themselves to regret the passage of Mr. Howells from the delicately secluded love-tale of his first period to the freer and wider topics of his maturity and age. Mr.

Howells was a strong man who grew, and it may be frankly conceded that his growth carried him away from that special phase of life which was *supremely* favorable to the flower and quintessence of his mere art. The record of this larger self is worth much, very much; for the masculine type of reader it far more than outweighs the abatement in artistic felicity which was its penalty or tax. Let it never be forgotten that the artistic difference in question is a difference, not between perfection and deficiency, but between perfection and efficiency. To do the smaller thing consummately is doubtless better than to do the larger thing ill; but this is far from implying that it is better than to do the larger thing well. Mr. Howells was not a lute-player, as some people fancy, in the world of art; still less was he a mere flower-girl; he was a grown man whom life profoundly and diversely interested. It is better to be catholic than nice; it is better to diversify and enlarge the human than to perpetuate the exquisite. To write six novels like "The Lady of the Aroostook" was admirable; to have written thirty would have been effeminate. Had the novelist pursued this course, perhaps the very readers for whom the sacrifice was made would have come to lament their triumph, as Enid mourned in Geraint the failure of that manly prowess which had sprung from his surrender to her beauty. After all, the Howells who wrote the six novels was not the original, not the inborn, Howells, though he spoke the new tongue with all the fluency, and almost more than all the delicacy, of a native. Two of these novels had their scene in Venice, and from that fact we may evolve an allegory. If one is young and a poet, Venice may well call one away from boisterous America; but, if one is a man and a doer, America will call one back from Venice. Its memories will remain priceless; its reality would have ceased to remain so.

CHAPTER V

Plays and Poems

Mr. Howells's plays, measured in words, are not extensive; the letter-press could probably be packed into a volume not much larger than "The Quality of Mercy." They comprise, however, between twenty and twenty-five titles, and their range may be gathered from their possible classification under headings so various as comedy, farce, sketch, comic opera, and serious blank-verse playlet. They begin at least as early as 1877, the date of "Out of the Question" and "A Counterfeit Presentment," and they close not earlier than 1911, the date of "Parting Friends." I purpose to follow affinity rather than time in the disposition of the plays for criticism, but I am fortunate in the support of both principles when I begin with the two comedies of 1877.

I

Comedies

Early readings of "Out of the Question" and "A Counterfeit Presentment" were pleasurable and vivid; but re-readings after many years for critical ends issued in disappointment, moderate in the latter case, keener and more surprising in the former. I find that my affection has survived the removal of its props, and the look and touch of the little volumes still invite me to forget that they did not altogether verify the most fallacious of hopes — the hopes of memory.

These two idyls of the summer resort are called comedies, but they substitute bare numerals for acts and scenes, they intersperse dialogue with description and narrative in a fashion anticipative of Mr. Shaw, their dialogue is flowing and ample, and the draperies appropriate to the novel replace the tights, if the word be forgivable, by which the normal stage-drama both emphasizes its contours and quickens its speed. The characters are mostly Brahminical in the Dr. Holmes sense, and, in both plays, a love-affair of undoubted interest pursues a troubled course to a fortunate outcome.

In "Out of the Question," Mr. Howells, for whom processes are more inspiriting than issues, has been content with a mild suspense. He has allowed himself certain classic expedients. The invention which sends the young Westerner to save the Boston young woman from aggressive tramps and, later, intrusts the care of his wounded arm to her grateful interest, is of the sort that managers would find hopeful; and the subtlety which identifies the sister's wooer with the brother's rescuer might have evoked the plaudits of Mr. Clyde Fitch. In Mr. Howells, however, these things are not the play; they are merely the trestles on which the observation and divination are supported. There is another scene in which the offer of a business partnership from the young girl is mistaken by the Westerner for an offer of another kind which is too painful to be either comic or pathetic. In still another place, the girl's mother on the topic of ill-assorted marriage is impressive to the verge of tragic solemnity, but the scene reads like a passage of "Ghosts" dropped by inadvertence into a comedy of St. John Hankin. The real comic felicity is finally reached in the conference in which Mr. Charles Bellingham, the heroine's brother, attempts to play the diplomatist with the astute Blake, in a scene as innocent of contribution to the real outcome as even Mr. Howells could desire; but by this time it is too late to be care-free, and we enjoy the drollery furtively, like a joke in school hours.

I am sorry to have outlived my response to the vernal

enchantment of Leslie Bellingham. To my soberer sense she is too voluble, and she manifests a self-complacence, a prearranged and resolute niceness, as she understands niceness, which suggests that convention faces convention, when she throws down the gauntlet to society.

Blake, the Westerner, quite out-Bostons Boston. He reminds one of that chauffeur in Mr. Shaw who coolly corrected his master on the point of the authorship of a French quotation. True, Blake is much more agreeable than a shameless aggregation of unbelievable virtues has any right to be; but it is quite clear that his endowments beg the question. It is ridiculous to ask whether Beauty ought to marry the Beast, when it is quite clear to the meanest intelligence that the Beast is a young prince in disguise. Nevertheless, this question of social disparity is no light matter to Mr. Howells. The difficulty seems to be that the question which is serious for the author is sportive for the comedy. The resulting difference of key is unlucky.

The minor characters may be briefly despatched. Mrs. Murray's speech is like "a brazen canstick turn'd"; Mrs. Bellingham is a salve where salves are undoubtedly wanted — little less than indispensable; Charles Bellingham, always good in Mr. Howells, through whose works he saunters with the air of a man having nothing better to do, is quite up to his mark in his first appearance.

In pure interest of situation, "A Counterfeit Presentment" is one of its author's most fortunate conceptions. A young girl, recently jilted in Paris, encounters in the parlor of the Ponkwasset Hotel a young man who is the living picture of her former betrothed. The circumstance is striking, human, and pathetic; and it borrows no more from accident than it repays and overpays in vitality and suspense. There are three grades of seriousness in the play: the coincidence is inherently light; the situation of Constance is essentially tragic; but the treatment occupies a middle zone, lightening and darkening as occasion serves. As often happens in Mr. Howells, the depth of the suffering exceeds that of the story.

The opening scenes are excellently done, but a difficulty supervenes when the reciprocal interest of the young lady and the "counterfeit presentment," in other words, the second man, begins to assert itself. The problem, at this point, is to retard the impatient — the hastening — outcome, and the brakes are oversubtle for a play. Scruples of this kind present themselves. "It is enormously indelicate to think of loving a woman who would never have looked twice at me if I had n't resembled an infernal scoundrel who tried to break her heart." "Why," the reader, hazarding his own reputation for delicacy, is constrained to ask, "why enormously indelicate?" And if the reader in the sobriety of the closet is constrained to such question, he cannot but feel concern for the bedevilment of his luckless brother in the parquet or the balcony. Delicacies of this sort may furnish an airy nourishment to the refined novel with its ladylike appetite, but they hardly appease the stomach of robust drama with its ploughman's hankering for beef and pudding. Lest my meaning be misconceived, let me hasten to add that the serious in drama should be equally distrustful of the vociferous and the inaudible. The circumstances that the story of the Wyatts by accident reaches Ponkwasset shortly before the Wyatts themselves, and that the man whose name the miscreant forged is the cousin of Bartlett's friend, are bits of "innocent naughtiness" which the critic need not hasten to condemn. I suspect a theatrical reluctance in the comedy as a whole, interspersed with points of vantage for a capable actress among which the girl's instinctive recoils from Bartlett would be especially inviting.

The conversation in both comedies would be better if it were not so good; realists and managers would probably agree that perfection is its infirmity. Of both plays it may be said that they are not dramas pure and simple, but attempts of the novel to annex the drama. I part from both with a tenderness which admits and condones their faults.

In the briefer comedy of much later date, "A Previous Engagement," there is a sort of compendium of Mr. Howells. If a cultivated Icelander or Samoan, absolutely ignorant of the novelist, wished to learn what he could of the man in a half-hour, I am not certain that I should not refer him to "A Previous Engagement." I do not call it very good, though its opening is perfect; but it is pretty good and it is highly characteristic. A young girl, asked in marriage, insists first on making confessions, later, on extracting them; she ends the inquest by a motiveless rejection, to be followed in its turn by a motiveless acceptance. On all this an admirable comment, which condenses Mr. Howells's woman into a sentence, is offered by the sagacious Mrs. Winton: "Women not only have to hoodwink men; they have to hoodwink themselves too. A girl — such a girl as Philippa — enjoys putting herself through her paces before a man; she likes to exploit her emotions, and see how he takes it; though she may not know it."

This is searching, but not ruthless, not even unkind. In the young girl of Mr. Howells, the waywardness which in simple natures appears as mere coyness or coquetry arrives with equal certainty at the same goal by a wider circuit, in which the reason and conscience — more exactly, the phantasms of reason and conscience — are involved. The sincere and robust ethics of Mr. Howells himself must never be confused with the aggressive and masterful ethics of these young women, which are mostly to be classed as meteorology. The Philippa of this courtship is particularly unreasonable and ill-tempered, and does all in her power to embitter an attractive little comedy. It is noticeable that the *victorious* motive in the swirl-dance is apt to remain as indistinct in the reader's mind as it might eventually become in that of the distracted heroine. With so much shading there is naturally some shadow. The other three members of the quartette that forms the cast are entirely pleasing, and the attractive Mr. Camp sustains the vicissitudes of courtship with a resignation almost marital.

"An Indian Giver," a fourth comedy, contains some very happy and pointed psychology. Mrs. Inglehart's determination to give away her lover is surpassed in naturalness and felicity only by the celerity of her recantation. The trouble lies in the dissipation of her attraction in the maze of her duplicities, and in the twofold pain with which we see in her marriage with James Fairford the punishment of a man we value and the reward of a woman we have come to despise. The latter half of the play is weakened and cheapened by a manœuvring the ingenuity of which is less impressive than its guile. Apart from the heroine, the characterization is vigorous.

II

FARCES

The farces of Mr. Howells are conspicuous for the persistence with which four characters, the Willis Campbells and the Edward Robertses, are brought on the stage with their satellites in a variety of diverting situations. All four of these persons are in fashionable life, and possess that virtue and refinement which Boston spares even to its aristocracy. They are drawn with a care and success unusual in farce; Mr. Campbell and Mrs. Roberts are the most amusing, while Mr. Roberts and Mrs. Campbell are the most lifelike. The two first-named are the author's trick ponies, so to speak, and they have an effect sometimes of prancing too high in obvious response to the stage-manager's whip-crack. The page is sometimes almost too crisp with the percussions of Mr. Campbell, and sometimes almost too fluttering with the palpitations of Mrs. Roberts. Roberts himself, who is rarely overdrawn, is excellent in the worldliness that sheathes his essential innocence, and the hesitant mildness which, like a soft and noiseless matting, overlays his whole disposition, even his troubles and excitements. Mrs. Campbell, who appears in two farces as Mrs. Somers, is happy enough in the restraint with which she dignifies her recurrent outbursts, and in her singular air of being coerced into dictation.

The masterpieces among the farces in which these characters figure are "A Letter of Introduction" (1891) and "The Unexpected Guests" (1892), and, for the reader at least, they rank very high in their kind. We are not surprised to discover that in these eminent successes the motive should be social in the narrow or fashionable sense of the word. The field had not been overworked. Farce, and even comedy among English writers, has commonly found its characters in persons whose titles and jewels could not veil the boorishness of their deportment; the gentleman's cane has borne a suspicious resemblance to the swain's cudgel. It might be difficult to decide which of the three baronets, Sir John Brute in "The Provoked Wife," Sir Anthony Absolute in "The Rivals," or Sir George Crofts in "Mrs. Warren's Profession," is most successful in aping the manners of a carter. Even the obvious and effective contrast between inner heartlessness and surface breeding is so rare on the English stage that almost the only examples that offer themselves readily are "The Importance of Being Earnest" and its clan. But who before Mr. Howells, in our race at least, thought of embodying in farce the fun that grows out of the contrast between the feelings and the professions of people who are really well-bred, upright, generous, and humane? Outside of charlatanry and swindling, it is hard to imagine where that ready, off-hand, and pertinacious lying which historically is a mainstay of farce can find so close a parallel in reality as in the sacrifice of truth to politeness which figures so largely even in honorable and scrupulous lives. The work of comedy or farce is simplified in such cases by the fact that the drawing-room is already half a theatre.

The cunning of the workmanship in "The Unexpected Guests" is a partial screen for the fearless simplicity of the materials. Two guests at a dinner-party are not expected by the hostess; she undertakes to hide her surprise; and a series of malignly artful circumstances strips off the mask from her hypocrisy. Can a spirited farce keep within the confines of the probable? "The Unexpected Guests" has very nearly attained that credibility the achievement of which in farce is so all but incredible. In "A Letter of Introduction," the contrivance is a trifle more pronounced. An absent-minded man is made to believe that he has affronted an Englishman by mistakenly putting the wrong inclosure in a letter of recommendation which the Englishman is to carry. The Englishman's return confirms the supposition, and the group of superserviceable relatives are tireless in their efforts to distract the guest from the perilous topic. A turn of admirable unexpectedness is given to the case by the substitution for the alleged error, not of innocence, but of a quite *unforeseen* mistake — the absence of any inclosure in the envelope. The play of humor and character in the not wholly probable decoy scene is very charming, and the delectable Englishman would be quite wasted on farce, if a farce that had been pampered with Campbells and cockered with Robertses could find any viands too costly for its palate.

Of the two farces, both of which endear themselves to the reader, I should slightly prefer "The Unexpected Guests," on the ground that it is a little more tense, if I were not haunted by a misgiving that I prefer "A Letter of Introduction," for the reason that it is less tense. In both plays a fine mockery, which is partly truth, represents the social, formal intercourse as the essential thing, and the domesticities as provisional.

It is in this specialized farce — farce made human and fashionable at the same time — that Mr. Howells's mastership is unqualified. This will appear, I think, in a brief review of the other farces in which the Robertses and the Campbells enliven a group of situations which may be handled in the order of merit rather than of time.

In "A Likely Story" Mr. Howells has given his invention its head, and the result shows that his scorn of theatrical complexities is not the defensive or vindictive scorn of incompetence. How "clever" he might have been with a little more silliness! Like Sardou and Pinero, Mr. Howells is alive to the value of the letter as the mechanical inducement to moral complications. A lover puts a love-missive into an envelope, which he automatically directs to another lady whose invitation to a lawn party he intends to refuse. The arrival of the letter is the signal for breakfast-table vivacities between husband and wife. Afterward, the wife, in a glow of inspiration, sends the supposed letter to its probable object, in an envelope supposed to bear that object's name. Discovery that the lady-love has been wrongly identified is the source of an aftermath of complications. But blunder repairs the havoc wrought by cleverness; the letter has been despatched on its second mission in the old envelope. It is returned with the seal intact, and explanation restores happiness.

The second mistake is handled with what is possibly a shamefaced rapidity. Mr. Howells, in this net-weaving, betrays a disrespect for his trade, which no doubt embraces his customers. I think this might be a bar to his success in the practical theatre: what the average audience wants is seriousness in the pursuit of levity. Very different from this brusque despatch is the luxurious leisure with which diction is unrolled and character laid bare in the fluid whimsicality of the initial dialogue. To put it tersely, "A Likely Story" consists of a single scene of sedulously wrought and thoroughly successful comedy of character, followed by a comedy of intrigue which imitates the swiftness and spareness of a scenario. Its appeal is relatively popular.

The conception of "The Elevator" has force; the object is to show a fashionable party under the stress of a physical anxiety which strains without subverting the yoke of ceremony. A party of dinner-guests is detained for a few quaking minutes by the mysterious stoppage of the elevator in which they mount. Farce hardly knows itself in the mirror of so vivid an anxiety.

Next, in my own order of preference, comes "Five O'Clock Tea," in which Mrs. Somers, afterward Mrs. Campbell, serves tea daintily to dainty guests, to the noiseless accompaniment of the falling snow. The setting is delicate, and the fall of wit in the little parlor is as incessant and quiet as that of the snow on the roofs and windows. The brilliancy overshoots the mark, if the mark be nature, but the tone maintains its kinship with reality. A proposal of marriage has to get itself made, heard, and answered amid the social interruptions furnished by five-o'clock tea. This involves periodic tête-à-têtes between the lovers, and the tea-room has to be emptied and refilled about as often as the teapot — a process in which the nimbleness of the guests is more laudable than the dexterity of the author. The conclusion is hardly so good as the earlier scenes: Mrs. Somers's refusal (merely temporary) of Mr. Campbell because Mrs. Curwen's magnanimity has left them alone together is a subtilization which farce can hardly digest.

I should rank next "The Garroters." In this play the propelling incident is mechanical, as the title suggests, and is both very ingenious and very improbable. It is highly characteristic that the emphasis should fall on the social perplexity to which the physical embroilment leads. A man who thinks himself robbed snatches what he believes to be his own watch from a supposed garroter who is really an acquaintance. The comedy is accentuated by making the watch-snatcher the host, and the acquaintance the guest, at the ensuing dinner-party. There are happy scenes of an incidental and explanatory nature, in which character is skillfully brought out. The conclusion is relatively weak; the fencing between Campbell and Dr. Lawton is unwisely clever, and the *scène-à-faire*, the mutual confession between host and guest, is hurried out of sight with a disdainful celerity which Francisque Sarcey would have hesitated to forgive.

"The Sleeping-Car," relatively early among the farces, ranks next in my table of merit. The subject is an incentive to horseplay; on the other hand, in the scope it gives to fashion in undress, both moral and physical, it admits the portrayal of manners. Mr. Howells has adopted a middle or, possibly, a double course. The incidents are madcap, though one divines a certain reluctance in the capers; the manners are more seriously drawn; and the characterization, while it frisks more or less with the incidents, remains quaintly true in the midst of unbelievable absurdities. Mrs. Roberts combines the vital and the incredible in a fashion reminiscent of Dickens; to which Mr. Howells might reply, with partial justice, that equity was achieved when *his* farce reminded us of Dickens's earnestness. We are not spared, or not denied, those indecorums which a literature, itself decorous, may reproduce; and the farce as a whole suggests the mixture of kinds and the merging of levels.

"The Mouse-Trap" is lively — lively to excess. Mr. Howells may be forgiven for standing Mrs. Somers in a chair where a mouse is in question, but he forgets his manners when he puts Mrs. Roberts upright on a piano-stool. Undoubtedly, Mrs. Roberts has an aimless mobility, a yielding obstinacy, a gyration about her own axis, which are amusingly suggestive of a piano-stool, but the fitness does not cancel the unfitness. The conclusion is happy.

"Evening Dress" marks the extreme to which the Howells farce will go in the attenuation of the subject. A man is kept from an evening party by the inability to find his dress suit. The stage properties are manifold, and the stage business importunate; the movement is giddy, even a little slapdash. But the loudness is not half so penetrating as the undertone, and the least boisterous parts, which include the opening dialogue between the Robertses — both effective in this play — and the charming skirmish with Bella, are foremost in attraction.

"The Smoking-Car" calls for little comment. Responsibility for an unclaimed baby evokes some crude alarms in the Roberts-Campbell quartette. In the broad burlesque parts, the high-bred Mr. Howells has the air of a man pursuing a handicraft in evening dress.

"A Masterpiece of Diplomacy" is inaptly, even ineptly, clever. An available source of comedy is lost in the chase of the far-fetched and the fine-spun. "The Albany Depot" is a rather ineffective handling of a somewhat boisterous subject.

This concludes the Campbell-Roberts farces. The others are few, and not highly significant. In "The Register," the characters are of one grade of farce, the incidents of another, and the terminal confession, which perfects the ingenious plot, demolishes the characters. Much of the detail is highly spirited. In "Parting Friends" the issue is sentimental and minute, and the characters all impress us as having been up too late the night before the action.

"The Parlor Car" explains in needless detail how a girl whom we strongly dislike renews her broken engagement with a man whom we barely tolerate. "Room Forty-Five," the broadest of all the farces, magnifies the sufferings of a married couple in their hotel quarters from a gentleman in the room below, who sleeps, as Mr. Howells has elsewhere put it, with passionate intensity. "Self-Sacrifice: A Farce-Tragedy," a study of courtship that mixes the subtle with the antic, shows a vivacity that is tireless, and yet — one suspects — a little tired. "The Night Before Christmas," nominally a morality, but actually a farce, is an outpour of gifts and objurgations in which the exuberance of Christmas feeling is turned with some exaggeration but much effect against Christmas itself, or rather against the worldly travesty of a religious festival. "The Impossible," in which the Fountains are retapped, combines farce and parable in such a fashion that the farce warps the incidents while the parable distorts the motives. In this drawing-room sketch, the lightest and gravest selves of Mr. Howells confront one another, and each turns haggard and spectral in the shock of their reciprocal encounter. It is a piece which grips the memory through the conscience.

In farce Mr. Howells was master and originator of a charming vein — the farce of high-bred, virtuous people embodying the psychology of the drawing-room. He left psychology, left the drawing-room and its purlieus, at his own risk. Farce that involves mess or noise seems doubly messy or noisy in an author who has trained our senses to enjoy the cleanliness and seemliness of his exquisite literary housekeeping. I should not mind the clutter of "Evening Dress" in Dickens; I should not mind the trotting of the baby round the railway station in Mr. Kipling: but in Mr. Howells these things affect me as penances. His farces show more invention in the vulgar sense than the whole field of his narrative fiction; and in this vein I should call him fertile and happy, but undiscriminating. He does not sift his improbabilities, for the same reason possibly that he would not sort a waste-basket. Much of his farce hardly exceeds the moderation of comedy, but parts of it here and there (in the "Sleeping-Car," for example) overstep the bounds of farce. He is quite sufficiently ingenious, but he lacks that heartiness, let us say that naïveté, in ingenuity, which the public loves to ascribe to its entertainers.

He has been happy in finding out-of-the-way settings for his farces, in which the novelties in the setting of the great world-drama of contemporary life are interestingly mirrored. There is the sleeping-car, the smoking-car, the parlor-car, the railway station, and the elevator. In three or four of these plays — whether with intention or not, I cannot say — he has seemed to exhibit the fashionable atmosphere in conditions that imperil its continuance. "The Sleeping-Car," "The Elevator," and "The Garroters" may be instanced. The characterization, taken as a whole, is possibly the very best that ever gave lustre and value to the persiflage of farce; I should put it above that of "Le Médecin Malgré Lui," of "The Critic," and even of "The Comedy of Errors." The farces have a success with amateurs which is quite unshadowed, I believe, by the fear of competition from the boards.

I must here find room for a passing allusion to "Bride Roses," a so-called "Scene," enacted in a florist's shop, where three people order roses for a young girl whose death is known to only one of them. The execution does not correspond in merit with the touching and original idea. The sub-title of "A True Hero" is "A Melodrama." This is confession, a confession possibly intended as prophylactic — one of those lightning-rods which attract the electricity of criticism only to carry it harmlessly to earth. I think the sin would be more forgivable if it were more thorough. Mr. Howells's application to this burly and blatant form of his habitual indirection of motive and abstruseness of moral reminds one a little of those airy gyves with which the stout Norsemen bound the wolf Fenris. The wolf, in this instance, is a trifle rebellious.

III

COMIC OPERA

Mr. Howells has cherished an unalterable fondness for the work of W. S. Gilbert, and the wish to voice an element in his nature which his ordinary work had silenced or at least quieted urged him to a single experiment in comic opera. "A Sea Change" contains two acts and an epilogue. Act I provides ingenious and droll complications in discreet subordination to lyric and dialogue. Act II is a dream fantasy embroidered on romantic burlesque, the ornament being scarcely more fantastic than the ground.

Lyricism is endemic on the ship in which the action is laid, and the lyrics disclose an unguessed faculty in Mr. Howells. They have a Nereid-like flexibility, they are moist and supple, they wind and coil, and the rhymes are prolific, nimble, and surprising. If I may trust the witness of a not too circumstantial memory of Gilbert, Mr. Howells is pliant where the Englishman is sturdy. The dialogue is insinuating, and the characters are slippery. In being silly, the personages of comic opera exercise an hereditary right; but I regret the extension of the franchise which permits them to be mean as well as silly.

In the treatment as a whole I suspect that what Mr. Howells wants is not faculty, but faith. He is in the position of the unbelieving man of science, to whom religion and superstition were identical, who should masquerade as prophet for the exploitation of the faithful; he would be embarrassed to fix the point where credulity in the credulous stops. "A Sea Change" is rather curious than valuable.

I conclude my estimate of the plays at this point, reserving two or three poems in dialogue for later treatment under the head of verse. Let me subjoin the interesting fact that Mr. Howells collaborated with Mark Twain in a never published and never presented dramatization of Colonel Sellers in "The

Gilded Age." Nor should it be forgotten that the same alert and skillful pen is responsible for "Yorick's Love," the English adaptation of "Un Drama Nuevo," by the Spaniard, Don Manuel Tamayo y Baus, which proved remunerative to Lawrence Barrett and not wholly profitless to Mr. Howells.

IV

THE VOICE AT PRIME

The early aspirations of Mr. Howells were poetical. His deviation into prose elicited in later life a gentle reproach from E. C. Stedman, which in turn evoked a retort from the "Editor's Study," to which all readers who love salt and hate acid in literature are referred for an example of amenity in reprisal. In early youth he collaborated with John J. Piatt in a volume entitled "Poems of Two Friends," which, in his own self-bantering phrase, "became instantly and lastingly unknown to fame." He is lavish of eulogy for his collaborator, but it remains doubtful if Mr. Piatt is responsible for the price of ten dollars affixed long after to a stray copy of the unreprinted work in a bookseller's catalogue. Its later rarity seconds its early obscurity in defending it from criticism.

The first poems of Mr. Howells accessible to the present writer are the J. R. Osgood (afterwards Houghton Mifflin Company) volume of 1873. As the collected or even the selected verse of a man of thirty-six who had served the Muses almost from his cradle, the two hundred and twenty-three pages scarcely show a prolific inspiration, and the verses, in which the narrative factor is emphasized and somewhat diversified, disclose youth, experiment, and insecurity. The poems are finished, and they are crude; they show crudity in the caprice and inequality of their finish. The rhythm is sometimes of an erect and high carriage — *et vera incessu patuit dea;* and it is sometimes rough-shod or slipshod.

The favorite metre is probably the English hexameter in the form popularized by Longfellow. Mr. Howells has expressly told us that he believes this hexameter to be "one of the measures best adapted to the English speech," and recourse to it in his very latest years has proved the fidelity of his attachment. To my mind it is a measure at once indolent and perfidious; it caresses and rebuffs the ear alternately; it abounds in lines which subject the reader who pronounces them aloud or internally to the painful dilemma of allowing the syntax to warp the prosody or the prosody to rend the syntax. It is a measure hazardous even for the vigilant, as Longfellow's frequent cacophonies in "The Courtship of Miles Standish" plainly proved; and it is deadly for the easy-going. Now the metrical virtue of Mr. Howells takes the form of zeal rather than punctilio; he had rather improve a good line than reform a bad one; and he is not proof against the invitations to shiftlessness so lavishly offered by this compromising metre.

He will pass the following line:

> I could make out the much-bepainted Biblical subjects,

a phrase which a fastidious prose-writer would reject; or the following:

> Life, if he would, might have had some second question to give him.

Of course, there are agreeable lines in plenty, and metrically beautiful lines are discoverable; for instance:

> Hung, like a tear in the sky, the beautiful star of the evening.

The metrical form next in favor with Mr. Howells is probably the four-line stanza, with rhymes in the second and fourth lines and a rhythm which is fitfully iambic and anapæstic — the form known to Germans in Heine's lyrics and to Americans in Longfellow's "Bridge." Here is a second case of the unlucky adoption by a half-vigilant metrist of a prosodic form which only the perfection of vigilance can keep from turning into a pitfall. Observe the fourth line in the following stanza, the main idea of which is suggestive and appealing:

Without is tender yearning,
And tender love is within;
They can hear each other's heartbeats,
But a wooden door is between.

"Between us and music, certainly," the reader assents.

Again, there are those voluntary deviations from the normal melody which are supposedly agreeable to the expert in the precise measure, if not for the precise reason, that they are unpleasing to the layman. In the fourth line of each stanza of the subtly attractive poem, "Before the Gate," there is a crumple or balk which suggests the bowing or bending of the reluctant stanza under the unwelcome and disconcerting addition of an extra foot.

The better or more continuous melodies, which are not infrequent, occur oftenest in the least characteristic poems, such as the dreamy "Vagary," and the trolling and pendulous "The Bobolinks Are Singing." But sometimes felicity concurs with distinctiveness. The italics in the following are mine:

Of the river where we used to swim
Under the ghostly sycamores,
Haunting the waters smooth and dim.

In these early poems there are lovely phrases and felicitous turns in a measure which hardly prophesies, but which certainly does not belie, their profusion in the mature prose. In that state of half-maturity in which the capacities are larger than the man, the ingredients are sometimes finer than the poems. The touches in a poem glow, while the poem itself only glimmers. The phrase is maturer than the feeling, and complex impulses divide the uncertain will. These poems are too tolerant, too inclusive, too pliable; they hearken willingly to diverse promptings. It is when a poem becomes protestant and remonstrant in the face of its creator, when the thing formed says unto him who formed it, "Why hast thou made me thus?" and is obdurate in its high self-will, that we feel that a living creature has been born. An excess of motive, which means finally a defect of motive, is an appreciable drawback even to poems so shrewdly conceived and wrought as "The Mulberries" and "The First Cricket."

There are types that are destined to have no sequels. "Avery" is a record of adventure. "The Pilot's Story" is acute melodrama alleviated by landscape. In "Clement," illicit love has the door rather gently closed in its face; in the later works it scarcely gets within sight of the knocker.

There are two tendencies, however, in which the later man, the individual, emerges from the routine of literary adolescence. Ohio proves little and Venice proves nothing in relation to poetic individuality; but to link Venice and Ohio, as Mr. Howells has sought to do in "Louis Lebeau's Conversion," is a rebuff to convention which demanded courage. Similarly, America is pitted against Venice, conspicuously in "No Love Lost" and "The Mulberries," less emphatically in "Pordenone." Another point that foretells the waning of pupillage is the introduction, in serious or semi-serious narratives like "No Love Lost" and "Pordenone," of an infusion of unmistakable satire. The result is not uniformly happy; it is not happy in "No Love Lost," an epistolary narrative from several fictitious hands, which begins on the tragic plane of "Lady Geraldine's Courtship" and ends on the smiling levels of "The Fudge Family in Paris." Still, the doing of it, well or badly, is a harbinger of liberation.

Further, Mr. Howells is most effective at this period in poems in which the wildwood borders the park, and you pluck the rhododendron or syringa with one hand while the other reaches out for a cluster of choke-cherries. This union is most intimate in "The Mulberries," in which the lounger on the

Rialto in Venice buys American landscape and boyish reminiscence and mature regret in the basket of berries for which he vastly overpays the Venetian fruit-seller. But the length of that poem is unfriendly to quotation, and "The First Cricket" must be chosen in its place.

Ah me! is it then true that the year has waxed into waning,
  And that so soon must remain nothing but lapse and decay, —
Earliest cricket that out of the midsummer midnight complaining,
  All the faint summer in me takest with subtle dismay?

Though thou bringest no dream of frost to the flowers that slumber,
  Though no tree for its leaves, doomed of thy voice, maketh moan,
Yet with th' unconscious earth's boded evil my soul thou dost cumber,
  And in the year's lost youth maketh me still lose my own.

Answerest thou, when nights of December are blackest and bleakest,
  And when the fervid grate feigns me a May in my room,
And by my hearthstone gay, as now sad in my garden, thou creakest, —
  Thou wilt again give me all, — dew and fragrance and bloom?

Nay, little poet! full many a cricket I have that is willing,
  If I but take him down out of his place on my shelf,
Me blither lays to sing than the blithest known to thy shrilling,
  Full of the rapture of life, May, morn, hope, and — himself.

Leaving me only the sadder; for never one of my singers
  Lures back the bee to his feast, calls back the bird to his tree;
Hast thou no art can make me believe, while the summer yet lingers,
  Better than bloom that has been red leaf and sere that must be?

This is the earlier Howells at his best, and the reality of its charm is incontestable. The leaven of civility, of sophistication, is supplied by the allusion to the library, and the poem, as often happens with reflexed or implicate natures, is more sincere than others of the same stock that are more artless. But if we test the author's basic inspiration by this favorable and winning specimen, I think we must conclude that a man has done very skillfully something that is not his proper business. As yet, he is only the playfellow of the Muses.

V

THE VOICE AT EVE

A careful judgment of this order on the poetry of a man of thirty-six is not often retracted by the judge or disproved by the outcome, and such reversal becomes doubly improbable when for twenty years or more the man has deserted poetry and applied himself to fiction, criticism, and travel. It is a strange and wonderful thing, a revelation of the admirable lurking potencies in Mr. Howells and in human nature, to find originality, passion, power, genuineness, asserting themselves on the further side of middle life in the work of a man whose best at thirty-six is represented by the excellent but unauthoritative "First Cricket." He had built in youth and early manhood a pretty boat which he could not launch; it was placed too far up on the beaches. In "Stops of Various Quills," published in 1895, he was able to launch that boat, and the reason is manifest: *the tide had risen.* A water-shed divides experience from poetry in the young, and experience must rise to the appointed level before it can crest the barrier and flood the poetic basin on the adverse side. This usually happens between twenty and thirty if it happens at all; in Mr. Howells the adjournment was remarkable. In poetry at thirty-six he was adolescent. Even the novels which he wrote between thirty-five and forty, while mature in beauty and art, may be viewed as preparatory in relation to his message, his philosophy, his character. In poetry, fruition was even later; its May was autumnal; indeed it was in a sense the falling of the leaves that allured the delaying spring into tardy blossom. Illusion has often made poets of the young; Mr. Howells is one of the rare instances in which disillusion has made a poet of the ripened man.

I will quote first "Society," the best-known poem in the volume.

I

I looked and saw a splendid pageantry
 Of beautiful women and of lordly men,
 Taking their pleasure in a flowery plain,
Where poppies and the red anemone
And many another leaf of cramoisy
 Flickered about their feet, and gave their stain
 To heels if iron or satin, and the grain
Of silken garments floating far and free,
As in the dance they wove themselves, or strayed
 By twos together, or lightly smiled and bowed,
Or curtseyed to each other, or else played
At games of mirth or pastime, unafraid
 In their delight; and all so high and proud
 They seemed scarce of the earth whereon they trod.

II

I looked again and saw that flowery space
 Stirring, as if alive, beneath the tread
 That rested now upon an old man's head
And now upon a baby's gasping face,
Or mother's bosom or the rounded grace
 Of a girl's throat; and what had seemed the red
 Of flowers was blood, in gouts and gushes shed
From hearts that broke under that frolic pace.
And now and then from out the dreadful floor
 An arm or brow was lifted from the rest,
As if to strike in madness, or implore
 For mercy; and anon some suffering breast
Heaved from the mass and sank; and as before
 The revellers above them thronged and prest.

To this the poem on "Hope" may be added.

We sailed and sailed upon the desert sea
Where for whole days we alone seemed to be.
At last we saw a dim, vague line arise
Between the empty billows and the skies,
That grew and grew until it wore the shape
Of cove and inlet, promontory and cape;

Then hills and valleys, rivers, fields, and woods,
Steeples and roofs, and village neighborhoods.
And then I thought, "Sometime I shall embark
Upon a sea more desert and more dark
Than ever this was, and between the skies
And empty billows I shall see arise
Another world out of that waste and lapse,
Like yonder land. Perhaps — perhaps — perhaps!"

In poems like these we face the authentic power, depth, and weight of emotion converting itself into depth and weight of utterance by the rapid act of an aroused and potent imagination.

These poems are intimate without being in the least confidential. In poetry, men can say what it would be impossible to utter elsewhere, since poetry is revelation without exposure. Poetry, as J. S. Mill pregnantly remarked, is overheard; it can remove the barrier because it puts up the screen; and the solitude in which the poet dwells withholds nothing because it proffers nothing. Mr. Howells has been brave and frank, and in the presence of his generous openness the recipient has almost the shame of a thief.

The sadness of these poems is unconveyable by mere description. The mood — which must be distinguished, not dissevered, from the man — is almost without counterpart in literature; it is not the melancholy of Shelley or Keats, not the gloom of the second James Thomson, not the bitterness of Thomas Hardy, not the trepidation of Maeterlinck. There is in it something blanched and wan, something withered and haggard, something penitential and ascetic, disheveled and hollow-eyed, sentient of vigils and macerations, the more impressive as the implied kernel of an experience whose sheath or envelope is the antithesis and denial of these things. This pain is not traceable to failure or shortcoming in love or health or art or fame or riches; and its terror for the reader lies in the aspect it wears of a disinterested, an impartial, estimate of life. If that aspect be trustworthy, the world seems indicted in the anguish of the bystander more piercingly than in the throes of the victim. In the poetry itself the anguish is without alleviation; Mr. Howells is conspicuously the man of letters, and yet in no poems is suffering presented in a more absolute independence of those arts by which literature turns bitters into confections for the spoiled children whom it feigns to treat as patients. The reader may look in vain for the customary sedatives and lenitives, the Byronic comfort in the act and pose of suffering, or the consoling exaggeration which relieves the tension by the intimation it conveys of partial insincerity.

The opinions are less bitter than the emotions. Immortality is left doubtful in "Hope," negation is disapproved in "What Shall It Profit?" theistic guidance is clearly implied in "Parable" and expressly affirmed in "Statistics"— "Your facts are facts, yet somewhere there is God." But the impact of fatality is heavy on the book; there is the autocracy of temperament, the inveteracy of faults, the insolubility of enigmas, the deceitfulness of to-morrow. The sufferer figures himself under the image of a mariner in a dreary sea, a shipwrecked voyager on a rock, a vagrant in a noisome alley.

The art of these poems is strong. When a naturally solicitous artist resolves to be unscrupulous, he may succeed in paring down his solicitude to the exact measure demanded by the needs of his poem. Mr. Howells has not forgotten art, but his effort to forget it has reduced it to that fitting and happy subordination which is more truly artistic than its unchecked supremacy. There is a delicate secret of forgetting and remembering one's instrument in the same breath, a casual watchfulness, an incidental solicitude, which is the happy secret of those to whom art is much and nature more. There are details, doubtless, in which the effect is far from wholly pleasing. I do not mind his speeding or *fledging* his lines with a redundant syllable, as in "How wildly I hurry for the change I crave" — a fashion cherished by our later metrists; but my ear is restless under the strain of a pentameter of this type, "Above me, a boy, in a house far away," and becomes querulous in the digestion of cacophonies like "Wholly or solely one's sheer self again" and "The thing that has been is that which shall be."

His use of the straightforward, immediate word in topics redolent of business or squalor seems on the whole justified by his purpose and his earnestness. Passion has its own franchise, its own impunities, and it may fearlessly use vocables at which the poet of the drawing-room or of the terrace or even of the meadow rightly shudders. There are times when the displacement of the æsthetic sensibility by the moral instinct is ratified by the æsthetic sensibility itself. I quote the following in illustration:

> Within a poor man's squalid house I stood:
> The one bare chamber where his work-worn wife
> Above the stove and wash tub passed her life,
> And the sty where they slept with all their brood.

It will be noted that, while the third line is merely squalid, the fourth line is squalor lifted into dignity. There is one poem in which poetry seems to undergo both death and resurrection; after daring plainnesses and commonplaces, the simple words, "I went up town," are so used and so placed as to bring the whole weight of the inexplicable universe down upon the reader's helpless and afflicted soul.

The casting-away of fineries from the style corresponds to the stripping-off of illusions from the thought; but Mr. Howells cannot entirely exclude luxury, even from his literary fasts. "Question" is loftily and artistically worded, and "Society" is modelled with sculpturesque precision. The difference in effect between the carved and the hewn poems is less than one might have surmised; at all events each merges amicably enough in the effect of tragic reality which dominates and overshadows both.

These poems are rifts in a soul — that is, they are openings made by fractures. They come out of deeps which American poetry has rarely plumbed.

In "Stops of Various Quills," Mr. Howells had given proof that his enterprise was inexhaustible. He is framed like Tennyson's "Ulysses."

> The long day wanes: the slow moon climbs: the deep
> Moans round with many voices. Come, my friends,
> 'T is not too late to seek a newer world.

"The Father and Mother" is a blank-verse dialogue between parents in the house just desolated by the funeral of their child. The lines are over-syllabled and harsh, but sped and suppled by their very dissonance. The diction is ascetic; the aim is to make language alive by making it bare, and the most moving, sometimes the most beautiful, plainness is the outcome of its fulfilment. Add a curious activity of the speculative imagination, setting up new attractions, repulsions, conjectures, aspirations, the restless shuttle of the inquiring mind weaving a checkered woof in which the blackness of sheer denial is silvered on the edge by a glimmering faith. The great ultimate property is the vital emotion; the poem invades and dominates the heart. The powerful combination of traits, the unflinching baldness and harshness, the astonishing intellectual vivacity, the sinking and merging of both of these in a depth of tragic reality which is rarer and stronger than either, attest the originality and profundity of Mr. Howells.

Two other verse-dialogues, "The Mother" and "After the Wedding," complete a piercing trilogy by dramatizing the thoughts of the parents in the hours that follow the birth and the bridal of their child. The three poems are akin but unequal, and the earliest in date is first in merit. All three profess to furnish translations of life; what they actually give is paraphrase, or even parable. The diction and emotion are indigenous to the real world; the thoughts are importations. It was hardly to Mr. Howells that we looked for an illustration of the truth that reality is separable from realism.

In "The Daughter of the Storage," there are five longish poems: three are narrative; one is monologue; one is a dialogue in heroic couplets over a long-distance telephone — a combination in which the bewilderment of latter-day poetry seems curiously and comically symbolized. They are all based more or less on the hypothesis that literature is the great enemy of literature, and they are straightforward, matter-of-fact, and, on occasion, dissonant and commonplace. I do not wholly sympathize with the latter aspect of these vigorous and interesting poems. I feel that the prosaicism is rather too voluntary and theoretic and yet, paradoxically, that it relies too much on luck. To my mind, a poet should be as nice, as cunning, as meticulous, in the application of his baldness and harshness as in the distribution of his ornament and grace. He should be fastidiously homely, he should be punctiliously rough. Now I have a sense that Mr. Howells has not calculated the proportions and applications of his draught very sedulously, but has dispensed an infusion of plainness and roughness as a dose of physic that could not fail to be sanative for a poetry that had been cockered into dyspepsia by the delicacies from its own kitchen. The treatment is in a measure hygienic, disciplinary, expiatory; it is not purely and disinterestedly artistic.

Whatever be the force of this objection, the poems interest us by the precise and vigorous effects secured by a veteran artist through the aid of methods new to his own practice and not hackneyed in the art of the world. These poems *do* things, clean-cut things, diverse things. I am not sure but that the most effective, humanly and artistically, is the monologue whose crudity of subject is advertised in the fearless title, "Breakfast Is My Best Meal." Let us hear the author of

"Venetian Life" and the dean of American letters in his dramatization of an Illinoisan's appetite.

And mother she set there and watched me eat, and eat, and eat,
Like as if she could n't give her old eyes enough of the treat;
And she split the shortened biscuit, and spread the butter between,
And let it lay there and melt and soak and soak itself in;
And she piled up my plate with potato and ham and eggs.

This is the ultimatum. The wheel is complete. The "literature" that has had its hour with Spanish castles and Italian palaces finds itself at last, despoiled of its quotation marks, beside the savory abundance of the provincial breakfast-table. Among the other pieces, I rank next "Black Cross Farm" and "The Face at the Window," in which mystery and pathos of divergent types are brought home to the reader's imagination, in spite of an appreciable prolixity in the first case and a buzz of officious comment in the second. "Captain Dunlevy's Last Trip" makes its point sharply, if rather bluntly ("sharp," in literature, is rather the companion than the opposite of "blunt"); and "City and Country in the Fall" is clever enough, though it suffers from that note of bumptiousness in the assumption — or even in the dramatization — of which, Mr. Howells is not wholly happy or at ease. It is interesting that, in the first poem of this book, "Captain Dunlevy's Last Trip," the author should have returned to the measure (the dactylic hexameter) and to the frame (a river-pilot's narrative) of the first poem in the volume of 1873, "A Pilot's Story."

CHAPTER VI

Criticism

The materials for an estimate of Mr. Howells's criticism are found in the following works: the Atlantic reviews, 1867–1882; "Modern Italian Poets," 1887; "Editor's Study" in "Harper's Monthly," 1885–1892; "Criticism and Fiction," extract and distillation of "Editor's Study"; "Heroines of Fiction," 1901; miscellaneous papers in "Literature and Life," in the "North American Review" and in "Harper's Weekly." The "Easy Chair" is sporadically critical, and three of the autobiographies already handled, "My Literary Passions," "Literary Friends and Acquaintance," and "My Mark Twain," contain data available for this chapter.

I

Reading and Scholarship

The quickest way to give the reader some notion of the scope and tenor of Mr. Howells's reading is to list the authors whose names (or titles) appear in the table of contents of "My Literary Passions." It will be understood, of course, that the list is only a partial epitome of an imperfect record. Where the names of authors appear twice in the table, they appear twice in the list, but are counted only once in the footings; where *titles* appear in the table, *names* are substituted in the list; where the strength and warmth of the passion was exceptional, the name of its object is italicized. The list runs as follows: Goldsmith, *Cervantes*, Irving, Longfellow, Scott, Pope, Mrs. Stowe, Ossian, *Shakespeare*, Ik Marvel, *Dickens*, Wordsworth, Lowell, Chaucer, *Macaulay*, *Thackeray*, Mendoza (author of

"Lazarillo de Tormes"), Curtis, Longfellow, Schlegel, *Tennyson*, *Heine*, De Quincey, Goethe, Longfellow, George Eliot, Hawthorne, Goethe, *Heine*, Reade, Dante, Goldoni, Manzoni, D'Azeglio, Guarini, Tasso, George Eliot, Kingsley, author of "Paul Ferroll," Erckmann-Chatrian, Björnson, *Turgénieff*, Auerbach, Valdés, Galdós, Verga, Zola, Trollope, Hardy, *Tolstoi*.

There are several interesting points about this list. It contains forty-five distinct names; of these eighteen are English, seven American, seven Italian, four Spanish, four German, two French, two Russian, one Norwegian. The culture is cosmopolitan almost from the cradle: the second name is Cervantes. The Romance ingredient is powerful: Italy equals America in contributions. Against this ground of European and Romance proclivities, the indifference to the French is astonishing, but fairly represents the author's attitude toward a people whom his travels encircle but hardly touch, and whose literature held him only by the modern novels. The negation might be explained by his hatred of the indecency which French literature cultivates, were it not that two of the leading exceptions to his unresponsiveness to French letters, Flaubert and Zola, are two of the leading exceptions to his hatred of indecency. He turns his back on Molière to embrace Goldoni. Russian potency is hardly represented in its fullness by two names, but it will be noticed that both names are capital. His Teutonic favorites are those un-German Germans, Goethe and Heine.

Of these forty-five authors, thirty-three belong to the nineteenth century, five to the eighteenth, five to the sixteenth, and two to the fourteenth. The modernity of Mr. Howells is not overstressed in these proportions. He loves the literature of his own day; he believes that the praise of the antique is largely flattery (or self-flattery), and that the ancient is the aristocrat to whom the critic acts the part of snob; and he is willing to let his humor and disdain play about what some critic — Lowell, I imagine — has called the mausoleum of the British Poets.

This distrust may have reached the stature of a failing; but it is only fair to suggest that a reader who suckled his childhood on Cervantes, pastured his boyhood on Shakespeare, and fed his manhood with Dante may have been modern to excess, but was not blindly and ignorantly modern. I doubt if his classical acquirements went much beyond a sufficient intimacy with Virgil to enable him to gauge with intelligence William Morris's translation of the "Aeneid." That he would have profited by immersion in the classic wells is incontestable, but it would be rash to affirm that he did not profit largely — perhaps equally — by the immersions which he sought in their place. A man whose study of the Italians had familiarized him with the inheritors of the antique legacy and the propagators of the classic impulse, a man who could oppose Alfieri to Shakespeare and pit the tense concentration of Dante against Goethe's wandering diffuseness, was in better shape than most of us to forego the discipline and the stimulus of the orthodox curricula. Let me add that form in simplicity is perhaps the distinguishing mark of classic workmanship in letters, and that Mr. Howells is eminent for the love of form in his personal art and the love of simplicity in the art of others. The task of prescribing another education for the man who has put his resources to better use than almost any recent American in his own field I shall relinquish ungrudgingly to bolder spirits.

To return to our list. Of the forty-five authors in question, twenty-six are novelists, twelve are poets, and the remaining seven are mostly essayists or critics. These figures are just — and more than just — to Mr. Howells's undoubted preference for belles-lettres, and dissimulate a sincere liking for history, a pleasure in biography which in autobiography rises to delight, and a respectful interest in scholarship and life-problems.

It is interesting to note that Mr. Howells had his romantic

orgy like other boys, but he had it in the good company of Cervantes and Irving at the age of ten or thereabouts, a period of life when diseases can be had with impunity for the time and immunity for the future. By thirteen or fourteen he is ready for Pope, and he reverts thereafter to his romantic predilections very sparingly in a flickering fondness for Ossian and a more lasting enthralment by the dubious charms of the author of "Lazarillo de Tormes." In his early twenties, while waiting for his passport to Venice, he consumed all the Waverley Novels in a month, on which the only adequate comment seems to be that of Joe Gargery on Pip's sudden disposition of the hunk of bread-and-butter: "such a — such a honcommon Bolt as that." This feast might excuse the suspicion that some of the consumer's later animadversions on Scott partook of the character of eructations.

The humor of Pope hardly appeals to modern boyhood, and a passion for Pope at the outset of one's teens is normally a passion for form. This early subjugation by form is of great interest, and one can understand how the crispness of the antithetic Pope attuned his ear to the related crispness of the antithetic Macaulay, though we may well believe that in the brand of gingersnap provided by that excellent caterer the ginger was quite as enjoyable as the snap. The obvious, the outstanding, forms of any merit are naturally the first to obtain appreciation.

Some of these youthful passions may have characterized the time and place more strictly than the boy who was their subject. In Mr. Howells, as I have previously remarked or implied, one of the significant things is the way in which the faculty of immediate reception is balanced by the faculty of eventual recoil. He did not resist the epidemic; capable of feeling by himself, he rejoiced in his partnership in the feelings of others. I am by no means sure that induction or infection was not a main source of his enthusiasm for Shakespeare. His relation to that master-spirit was peculiar. Shakespearean phrase in the form of a powder permeated his diction; but extended quotations — quotations assuming the verse-form — are rare or non-existent, and the references to plots and characters are singularly few. His page rarely vibrates to the names of Shakespeare's women. With Dickens a like supposition is still more plausible. He was *overrun* by Dickens, carried off, like his compatriots and contemporaries, in the Asiatic scope of that unprecedented conquest. I am not sure that he ever quite forgave Dickens for a capture which may have been involuntary without being reluctant. He was so much the child or the brother of his time that he underwent a "paroxysm" of Alexander Smith, a man now famous only for his fame, whom the youthful Howells read with an "ecstasy unspeakable." The "precious and sacred experience" with Tennyson, while equally inevitable, was doubtless more personal and intimate, since it appealed to an inborn appetite for the sumptuous and picturesque in language, and sprinkled his pages for all time to come with the gleaming dust of that memorable and coruscating diction.

Something analogous to the relation we divined in the companion passions for Pope and Macaulay may be even more plausibly inferred in the two great subsequent passions for Heine and for Turgénieff. The truth is that Mr. Howells, in his youth, was divided between his predilection as artist for the far-sought and the high-wrought, and his inclination as human being toward the simple. The necessity of compromise made him an easy thrall to artists who reached simplicity in external result by complexity in interior process. This union was effected in verse by Heine, in prose by Turgénieff. The rapid growth of Mr. Howells's mind is evinced in the fact that, presumably in the very early twenties (I cannot quite date the passion for Heine), and already in the embrace of Tennyson, his response should have been so instant to the alien merits of an adverse style. He attained this manner himself in admirable passages of his mature prose, but was never secure or consecutive in its use; the mutation which his later style underwent was partly renovation, partly breakdown.

Even the admiration for Turgénieff was destined to a successor, and a partial supplanter, in a still livelier admiration for the formless form of Tolstoi. He delighted in Turgénieff because the wires by which that artist operates his mechanism are invisible; he revered Tolstoi for removing the wires.

In this story of development an order is perceptible, a little vague and shifting as is the wont of actual evolutions, but definite enough to interest the thoughtful. There is the passion for romance, early in its manifestation and largely, though not conclusively, outlived and dismissed in boyhood; there is the passion for incisive form, illustrated in Pope and Macaulay; there is the submergence by the passions of the time, exemplified possibly in Shakespeare and Dickens; there is the passion for the exquisite in language to which Tennyson offered stimulus and food; there is the passion for an occult subtlety of which simplicity is the mask, illustrated in Heine and Turgénieff; and there is the passion for artless art of which Tolstoi is the notable exemplar.

I cannot close this section without recurring to his fondness for weaving threads, or rather threadlets, of poetical quotation into the bright woof of his own flexible and many-colored prose. They are oftenest from Shakespeare, commonly from "Macbeth" or "Hamlet" or the descriptive and melodic opulence of the fifth act of "The Merchant of Venice." Eight of his books, "A Foregone Conclusion," "A Counterfeit Presentment," "The Undiscovered Country," "The Shadow of a Dream," "The Quality of Mercy," "An Open-Eyed Conspiracy," "Questionable Shapes," "Fennel and Rue," borrow titles from Shakespeare, and a very little pressure would add "The Mouse-Trap" and "The Coast of Bohemia" to the list. It may interest a reader here and there to know that his favorite Shakespearean quotation, in my own partial record, is

"Bare, ruin'd choirs, where late the sweet birds sang." Milton is rarely specified by name in his criticism, but the Miltonic phrase variegates his tapestry, and it is curious to note that, out of twenty-six quotations I have jotted down, twelve are taken from "Lycidas." He sows his page with "orient pearl" from the imaginative passages of Tennyson and Wordsworth, and he has that exultancy in the phrases of Keats the absence of which is a blot in the 'scutcheon of any generously bred and finely tempered spirit. I am sad to think that the most recurrent phrase from Keats is the "heart high sorrowful and cloy'd" of the "Ode to a Grecian Urn."

Mr. Howells was a copious and a constant reader, constant, I mean, in the sense of recurrence to the books he esteems; but his principle in reading was the avoidance of principle, and he sometimes found himself simultaneously in advance and in arrear of the academic standard of thoroughness. For example, in 1895 he had read most of Thackeray twice, and parts of him twenty times, but had never succeeded in finishing "The Virginians." At the same date he had not yet read one of Shakespeare's most esteemed plays. In 1901 he "confessed" that he had never "read a novel of Blackmore's, or a novel of Stevenson's, or more than one novel of Mr. George Meredith's." One can hardly see how the mere vanity of knowledge should have failed to enjoin a perusal of widely known and much-debated writers, unless indeed a compensation was supplied in the vanity of ignorance. The courage of omission and the courage of admission have each its engaging side, and certify the genuineness of the man's relation to the books he had actually read. To read an author perfunctorily had for him the horror of a *mariage de convenance;* the reluctant perusal which reviewing demands is one of the outstanding counts in his sharp indictment of that "wretched trade," and the reading of an old author to stop a gap in knowledge is described as "beggarly."

II

CRITICISM AND FICTION

As a critic Mr. Howells has evolved; but experiment has shown me that an attempt to study his criticism in the time-order means prolixity and repetition. I shall accordingly group the facts in relation to the principle they embody, with references, at opportune points, to the changes his beliefs and feelings underwent. I shall begin with "Criticism and Fiction," and shall take up afterwards the beliefs and practices illustrated in the "Atlantic," "Harper," and "North American" reviews, and shall reserve for the conclusion "Modern Italian Poets," 1887, and "Heroines of Fiction," 1901.

The little book called "Criticism and Fiction" is a series of extracts from the "Editor's Study" critiques in "Harper's Monthly" between the years 1885 and 1892. The book omits particular reviews and epitomizes the author's philosophy. In calling it great criticism I do not allow myself to forget that its bulk is insignificant and that its dicta are unoriginal.

The principles with which this book of ninety pages is occupied had been affirmed with energy before, as Mr. Howells's magnanimous citations clearly prove. The credit is freely, nay eagerly, relinquished to Symonds, to Farrar, to Emerson, to Valdés, to Carlyle. Mr. Howells is content with the sure burdens and doubtful recompense of the devoted subaltern.

When all has been conceded, it is somehow Mr. Howells who has done the work. The honor he diverts to others flows back ineluctably to its source. The supremacy of simple truth in fiction had been avouched by other men; it was *implanted* by Mr. Howells. The distinction between his predecessors and himself is the distinction between explorer and settler. The speculative idea and the illustrative practice, hitherto largely divided, were to effect their convergence in a mind which should invest the cult of realism with the double dignity of a business and a gospel. Mr. Howells massed and squared the idea, brought to its defence perfect clearness of head, perfect sureness of conviction, absolute unity of purpose; the election was final; the self-committal unreserved; the will added its stay, the conscience its mandate; a life, in a sense, flowered in an undertaking in which intelligence at its crest became the voice of manhood at its acme, and the culminant phase of an incomparable style supplied the apt and peerless instrument for both.

Mr. Howells's principle is truth. He believes in the transference of life to the page with as little alteration as is compatible with the difference between being and discourse. This is the kind of proposition that commands a cordial assent from everybody — including the unbelievers and antagonists. He might have uttered dicta of this sort through a tranquil and honored lifetime without hurting or helping anybody. Mr. Howells, however, was not the man to rock a somnolent race in the cradle of its ancient habits, to the lullaby of pointless generalizations. He specified sins, and, as if this effrontery were not enough, he named sinners. He woke the English novel-reading world with a declaration like the following: "The art of fiction, as Jane Austen knew it, declined from her through Scott, and Bulwer, and Dickens, and Charlotte Brontë, and Thackeray, and even George Eliot." His principles had an impudent appearance of cogency; his tests were vexatiously simple; and he had a willingness to reason on the subject which, in a person so manifestly unreasonable, it was really difficult to forgive.

The censure in the book is abundant and sometimes contemptuous, though the contempt is always transitory, and never endangers the vigilant and provident self-poise. Even in the exceptional charter of blame which Mr. Howells has here allowed himself, two restrictions are inflexible: the censure of the living falls upon classes only, and the censure of individuals is restricted to the dead. There is no tenderness for reputations, or for the reader's literary partialities, a field in which it is not inappropriate to remark that the sufferings bear no proportion to the moans.

In "Criticism and Fiction" theory is minimized; indeed, the absence of abstractions, of firstlys and secondlys (things perennially obnoxious to Mr. Howells), of therefores and accordinglys, is as noticeable as the relish for the concrete in things and people. We are always in the flux of things; the study overlooks the street. The practical bent of the topics is unmistakable. What shall Americans do? Shall the scale of fiction be large or small? Shall sex be emphasized? Shall lurid sensations be expelled, or merely discouraged? What shall critics do? Shall authors rebut critics? Everything is forward-looking; it is not *review*, but *preview*. The world seems beginning, and literature is emergent from nonage.

I have already observed that the strong speculative bent of Mr. Howells has the peculiarity of arresting its excursiveness at one remove from the fact. This barrier is a bulwark. The love and practice of theory seem to disable men for successful theorizing. Speculation in thought resembles speculation in finance in the weighty particular that the passion seems almost to imply the abeyance of the faculty. The value of the spare and wary generalization which ripens slowly in the humid warmth of a lifelong saturation with the facts is signally exemplified and confirmed in this volume.

Mr. Howells's object is truth, and truth is universal, or rather has its universal side. But truth, to be verified, must be observed, and observation belongs to a spot and a moment. The truth in fiction will tend to be national, even provincial; America will supply materials and standards for Americans. As thoroughness hardly permits extension, the soundest fiction tends to be praiseworthily "narrow." But observation must handle *present* material. Tradition and convention are overset. The matter reduces itself to an almost unimaginable simplicity. A man, a fact, and honesty — that is the sum of the essentials, the nucleus of literature.

This is a daring and impressive simplification. If it simplifies overmuch, the excess may be error, but is hardly a misfortune. Integrated views are commonly one-sided, but integrity in the grasp of a truth is precious. There are always palliations of evil, abatements of good, which it is well that the man commissioned by destiny to oppose that evil and to advance that good should not too perfectly distinguish. There are blindnesses that subserve vision.

I am not sure that Mr. Howells has written better English than that of "Criticism and Fiction," and I should hardly know whither to betake myself in the search for finer specimens of grave, vigorous, and supple prose. How rich is the cargo of felicities! How complete the release from any subservience to felicity! How *upright* the style is! With a finish unsurpassed in other work, it unites a vigor, a serene mastery, as of some great chancellor in the empire of literature, which only the ripe man in the utterance of his ripest convictions could command. The language was worthy of the critic who was to give, not originality, but finality, to the enunciation of a master truth.

This is what I say in my severer moods, but at other times I know that, of course, no one is going to hold all fiction to such strict account. There is a great deal of it which may be very well left to amuse us, if it can, when we are sick or when we are silly, and I am not inclined to despise it in the performance of this office. Or, if people find pleasure in having their blood curdled for the sake of having it uncurdled again at the end of the book, I would not interfere with their amusement, though I do not desire it. There is a certain demand in primitive natures for the kind of fiction that does this, and the author of it is usually very proud of it. The kind of novels he likes, and likes to write, are intended to take his reader's mind, or what that reader would probably call his mind, off himself; they make one forget life and all its cares and duties; they are not in the least like the novels which make you think of these, and shame you into at least wishing to be a helpfuller and wholesomer creature than you are. No sordid details of verity here, if you please; no wretched being humbly and weakly struggling to do right and to be true, suffering for his follies and his sins, tasting joy only through the mortification of self, and in the help of others; nothing of all this, but a great, whirling splendor of peril and achievement, a wild scene of heroic adventure and of emotional ground and lofty tumbling, with a stage "picture" at the fall of the curtain, and all the good characters in a row, their left hands pressed upon their hearts, and kissing their right hands to the audience, in the old way that has always charmed and always will charm, Heaven bless it!

In a world which loves the spectacular drama and the practically bloodless sports of the modern amphitheatre the author of this sort of fiction has his place, and we must not seek to destroy him because he fancies it the first place. In fact, it is a condition of his doing well the kind of work he does that he should think it important, that he should believe in himself; and I would not take away this faith of his, even if I could. As I say, he has his place. The world often likes to forget itself, and he brings on his heroes, his goblins, his feats, his hair-breadth escapes, his imminent deadly breaches, and the poor, foolish, childish old world renews the excitements of its nonage. Perhaps this is a work of beneficence; and perhaps our brave conjurer in his cabalistic robe is a philanthropist in disguise.

Within the last four or five years there has been throughout the whole English-speaking world what Mr. Grant Allen happily calls the "recrudescence" of taste in fiction. The effect is less noticeable in America than in England, where effete Philistinism, conscious of the dry-rot of its conventionality, is casting about for cure in anything that is wild and strange and unlike itself. But the recrudescence has been evident enough here, too; and a writer in one of our periodicals has put into convenient shape some common errors concerning popularity as a test of merit in a book. He seems to think, for instance, that the love of the marvellous and impossible in fiction, which is shown not only by "the unthinking multitude clamoring about the book counters" for fiction of that sort, but by the "literary elect" also, is proof of some principle in human nature which ought to be respected as well as tolerated. He seems to believe that the ebullition of this passion forms a sufficient answer to those who say that art should represent life, and that the art which misrepresents life is feeble art and false art. But it appears to me that a little carefuller reasoning from a little closer inspection of the facts would not have brought him to these conclusions. In the first place, I doubt very much whether the "literary elect" have been fascinated in great numbers by the fiction in question; but if I supposed them to have really fallen under that spell, I should still be able to account for their fondness and that of the "unthinking multitude" upon the same grounds, without honoring either very much. It is the habit of hasty casuists to regard civilization as inclusive of all the members of a civilized community; but this is a palpable error. Many persons in every civilized community live in a state of more or less evident savagery with respect to their habits, their morals, and their propensities; and they are held in check only by the law. Many more yet are savage in their tastes, as they show by the decoration of their houses and persons, and by their choice of books and pictures; and these are left to the restraints of public opinion. In fact, no man can be said to be thoroughly civilized or always civilized; the most refined, the most enlightened person has his moods, his moments of barbarism, in which the best, or even the second best, shall not please him. At these times the lettered and the unlettered are alike primitive and their gratifications are of the same simple sort; the highly cultivated person may then like melodrama, impossible fiction, and the trapeze as sincerely and thoroughly as a boy of thirteen or a barbarian of any age.

I do not blame him for these moods; I find something instructive and interesting in them; but if they lastingly established themselves in him, I could not help deploring the state of that person. No one can really think that the "literary elect," who are said to have joined the "unthinking multitude" in clamoring about the book counters for the romances of no-man's land, take the same kind of pleasure in them as they do in a novel of Tolstoy, Tourguenief, George Eliot, Thackeray, Balzac, Manzoni, Hawthorne, Mr. Henry James, Mr. Thomas Hardy, Señor Palacio Valdés, or even Walter Scott. They have joined the "unthinking multitude," perhaps because they are tired of thinking, and expect to find relaxation in feeling — feeling crudely, grossly, merely. For once in a way there is no great harm in this; perhaps no harm at all. It is perfectly natural; let them have their innocent debauch. But let us distinguish, for our own sake and guidance, between the different kinds of things that please the same kind of people; between the things that please them habitually and those that please them occasionally; between the pleasures that edify them and those that amuse them. Otherwise we shall be in danger of becoming permanently part of the "unthinking multitude," and of remaining puerile, primitive, savage. We shall be so in moods and at moments; but let us not fancy that those are high moods or fortunate moments. If they are harmless, that is the most that can be said for them. They are lapses from which we can perhaps go forward more vigorously; but even this is not certain.

My own philosophy of the matter, however, would not bring me to prohibition of such literary amusements as the writer quoted seems to find significant of a growing indifference to truth and sanity in fiction. Once more, I say, these amusements have their place, as the circus has, and the burlesque and negro minstrelsy, and the ballet, and prestidigitation. No one of these is to be despised in its place; but we had better understand that it is not the highest place, and that it is hardly an intellectual delight. The lapse of all the "literary elect" in the world could not dignify unreality; and their present mood, if it exists, is of no more weight against that beauty in literature which comes from truth alone, and never can come from anything else, than the permanent state of the "unthinking multitude."

Yet even as regards the "unthinking multitude," I believe I am not able to take the attitude of the writer I have quoted. I am afraid that I respect them more than he would like to have me, though I cannot always respect their taste, any more than that of the "literary elect." I respect them for their good sense in most practical matters; for their laborious, honest lives; for their kindness, their good-will; for that aspiration towards something better than themselves which seems to stir, however humbly, in every human breast not abandoned to literary pride or other forms of self-righteousness. I find every man interesting, whether he thinks or unthinks, whether he is savage or civilized; for this reason I cannot thank the novelist who teaches us not to know but to unknow our kind. Yet I should by no means hold him to such strict account as Emerson, who felt the absence of the best motive, even in the greatest of the masters, when he said of Shakespeare that, after all, he was only master of the revels. The judgment is so severe, even with the praise which precedes it, that one winces under it; and if one is still young, with the world gay before him, and life full of joyous promise, one is apt to ask, defiantly, Well, what is better than being such a master of the revels as Shakespeare was? Let each judge for himself. To the heart again of serious youth, uncontaminate and exigent of ideal good, it must always be a grief that the great masters seem so often to have been willing to amuse the leisure and vacancy of meaner men, and leave their mission to the soul but partially fulfilled. This, perhaps, was what Emerson had in mind; and if he had it in mind of Shakespeare, who gave us, with his histories and comedies and problems, such a searching homily as "Macbeth," one feels that he scarcely recognized the limitations of the dramatist's art. Few consciences, at times, seem so enlightened as that of this personally unknown person, so withdrawn into his work, and so lost to the intensest curiosity of after-time; at other times he seems merely Elizabethan in his coarseness, his courtliness, his imperfect sympathy."

III

ROMANCE AND ROMANTICISM

I call Mr. Howells a great critic, a great legislator, if I may venture the term, in criticism; I do not call him a great reviewer. No doubt he would associate great reviewers with great costermongers or great chimney-sweeps; and, while his own reviewership is competent and strong, there is sufficient inconsistency and error in the application of his principles to individual books to debar him from supremacy in this field. The inconsistency begins perhaps in his attitude toward romance and romanticism.

In his denunciation of romanticism Mr. Howells is tireless. He calls it a mania; works of its class are compared to conjuring or the puppet-show or ground and lofty tumbling or the circus or negro minstrelsy or the ballet or prestidigitation or an opium-joint. All this is natural and consistent in a realist, and its violence, which is usually impersonal or retrospective, need not be censoriously viewed. The embarrassment is furnished by Mr. Howells himself. He has a passion for Hawthorne for which he must find room in the fissures or the outskirts of his aversion to romanticism. The address of his self-extrication is incomparable. In "Heroines of Fiction" he discriminates romance from romanticism. "Romance, as in Hawthorne, seeks the effect of reality in visionary conditions; romanticism, as in Dickens, tries for a visionary effect in actual conditions." But this is not all. The high priest of realistic orthodoxy carries still other heresies in his scrip. In "My Literary Passions" he declares: "I have always had a great love for the absolutely unreal, the purely fanciful in all the arts, as well as the absolutely real; I like the one on a lower plane, but it delights me as a pantomime at the theatre does, or a comic opera, which has its being wholly outside of the realm of probabilities." In the shelter of this principle Tasso's "Aminta" and Guarini's "Pastor Fido" may dispose themselves in such comity as they can establish with "Pinafore," "Patience," and "The Mikado." Whether Maeterlinck, whose early mortuary plays are dear to him, finds admission on the plane of visionary conditions or of absolute unreality, I am at a loss to say. I am equally puzzled to determine whether Mr. Shaw, whose plays are "my daily, my nightly joy," is approved on the score of the acceptance or the defiance of reality.

Mr. Howells as a man is the more likable for the tastes which overlap or overleap his theories and for the frankness that avows these tastes undauntedly; indeed, a nature so various could hardly have compressed itself within a philosophy so simple as that set forth in "Criticism and Fiction." Moreover, the defence of Hawthorne is very able, and that of pantomime and pastoral has undoubted plausibility. Still, the reader, who delights in logical simplicity where other people have to pay the charges, would have found the criticism of Mr. Howells more available, more applicable, if he had clung to Tolstoi, and forborne this perplexing enthusiasm for Hawthorne and this condescending but eager relish for "Aminta" and "Pinafore." We seem to be playing into the hands of our antagonists. So many things can be jockeyed into a semblance of reality in visionary conditions, and not a few things, if hard pressed, might take shelter in the covert of the absolutely unreal. Where is exclusion to begin? The situation resembles that in "The Princess," after the tournament, when all the wounded cavaliers find admission to the woman's college through the cleft made by the reception of the Prince.

"Ay so," said Ida with a bitter smile,
"Our laws are broken; let him enter too."

Questions flock to one's mind. Is not the absolutely unreal in fiction itself a fiction? Is the absolutely real itself a reality? If mixtures are detestable, are they not omnipresent? Are not the purely realistic novels impure in the sense in which our so-called "solid silver" is an alloy?

Mr. Howells's liberality is innocent, though it is undoubtedly troublesome; what is questionable is the intolerance which he chooses to combine with that liberality. He is truculent with Rostand; he cannot away with the magnanimous deceits of Cyrano or what he regards as the morbidities and juvenilities of the Duke of Reichstadt. I should have thought that Rostand's high purity, which is rare enough among French dramatists to be comparable only to the amenity of Mr. Howells among English reviewers, might have pleaded in his behalf with a critic equally well known as a lover of gentleness and a hater of lubricity. Again, he is without mercy, without measure, in his condemnation of the recent workers in historical romance. In the light of his own tolerations and unbendings, these rigors savor a little of the stringencies of Angelo in "Measure for Measure." Is not his true part that of the generous Duke? Or, to vary the figure, if he can play with Tasso or Gilbert while waiting for Tolstoi, very much as he fondles the lapdog before the arrival of its mistress in the drawing-room, why should the reader, in the stress of a like situation, be forbidden to play with "Cyrano" or "L'Aiglon," or even, at a pinch, with the historical romance of contemporary America?

The true welfare of realistic criticism would seem to lie in the generous and comprehensive admission of all forms of artistic romance to the outer court or ground level of the literary edifice, while the precincts are reserved for the disciples of reality. For Hawthorne an exception to the latter inhibition might possibly be made; the Hawthornes will not embarrass us by their multitude.

I am sometimes doubtful whether romanticism proper is the true object of Mr. Howells's antipathy. He abhors stale tricks; he detests the morbid in morality and immorality alike. These things are not infrequent in romance, but it is not clear that they constitute its essence, or that to its essence he is inherently hostile.

IV

ART AND STYLE

Mr. Howells's criticism is inadequate in its appraisal of art. In his maturity he came close to the identification of art with truth. "Jane Austen," he affirms, "was the first and the last of the English novelists to treat material with entire truthfulness. Because she did this, she remains the most artistic of the English novelists." If the obvious import of this passage be its real import, then the excision of the word "art" from the critical vocabulary might be a useful economy and a furtherance to that honesty which the same page commends to the reverence of readers. But Mr. Howells is as sensitive as the rest of us to the spell of that decorative word, which seems to enchase or enamel the sentence in which it figures, and no critic reverts to it with a more affectionate persistence. But the meaning in his mouth is peculiar. When he says that a work lacks art, he usually means one of two things: either that it contains romanticism, mechanism, or melodrama, in other words, is untrue to reality, or else that the author sermonizes or gossips.

The traditional view of art is altogether different; it is a trifle multifarious, but its main constituent is the presence in the copy of life of a structure, an organism, not present in life itself; it is, in plain English, a departure from truth. What most of us call organism, and uplift on a pedestal, Mr. Howells calls mechanism, and consigns to the junk-heap; only in recrudescent moments he visits the junk-heap to recover his lost property, as in that indulgent hour when he confessed his pleasure in the craftsmanship of Augustus Thomas's "Arizona," or even in the forcible-feeble carpentry of Pinero's "Gay Lord Quex." "A Sea-Change" and "A Likely Story" prove that, in the lighter forms of comic opera and farce, he was himself capable of a resort to mechanism.

Whatever were the exceptions in his own judgment or practice, Mr. Howells seemed latterly drifting toward a conception of art which should exclude all form except the form preëxistent in the matter. His metres aspire to freedom; his style undergoes a form of deliquescence; he praises authors who escape from their first intention; he approves the sauntering essay; he reports with a sympathy that barely stops short of indorsement Mark Twain's adoption in literature of the inconsecutiveness of life; he believes that the American drama will be "more and more a series of sketches, of anecdotes, of suggestions"; he visits irrelevancy and episode with that faint blame that blesses almost as effectually as faint praise damns; he suggests the ultimate displacement of fiction by transcripts of actual reality.

He defends the evasiveness of Mr. James in these terms: "Ought we not rather to praise him where his work confesses itself, as life confesses itself, without a plan? Why should we demand more of the imitator than we get from the creator?" To which the assenting or non-assenting reader might pertinently add: "Why write books at all?"

A student of contemporary views and methods is almost moved to say that, according to the new code, the difference between art and its opposite is resolved into a difference of intention. If a congeries or discrepancy is premeditated, it is art; if it is inadvertent, it is botchwork. It might be likened to the utterance of an unpleasant truth in society, which in one person might be an act of heroic probity, in another an unpardonable awkwardness. Mr. Howells, however, who has no admiration of the "stupid" truth and no rebuke for the "mechanical" falsehood, should be tolerant of those literary unveracities in which the gain in amenity far exceeds the loss in truth.

Life is undoubtedly formless, and the theoretic perfection of realism would include the reproduction of this want of form. But truth to nature in this regard impresses me as a refinement of realism, which, like many other refinements, is essentially luxurious, and has no vital bearing on its sustenance or well-being. The formlessness of life is a fact, but it is an obvious, a monotonous, and an unpleasant fact; and I see no reason why the novel should encumber itself with the indefinite and mechanical repetition of a truth which has three good reasons for keeping out of sight. At this point science, which pursues truth quite as seriously and successfully as realism, supplies the instructive analogy. Science is classified knowledge, that is, it is nature verified but rearranged; and neither the validity nor the usefulness of science is impaired by the circumstance that its facts are presented in an order differing *toto cælo* from the order of life. There is as much difference in form between a page of Darwin on bees and the order of business in a bee-hive as between a page of Turgénieff and the section of life it reflects and rearranges. It is good to mix common sense with conscience, even literary conscience.

I do not say that Mr. Howells lacked this restraining common sense. His difficulty lay in the fact that he was drawn two ways in his criticism, and that he failed to choose definitively between prescription and anarchy. In his practice and in his theory alike, he yielded a point here and a point there, and never decided on a consistent plan for the rectification of the shifting frontier. He was a wavering, a tentative extremist, and his judgments on the organic or structural side of fiction are weakened by this uncertainty. The ways of Tolstoi were dear to him; he had a covert or backstairs fondness for the structural laxities of Mark Twain; but he rejoiced also in the cunning ways of Turgénieff and Thomas Hardy, and the artist in him never quite capitulated to the truth-teller.

If we turn from art to style, we shall find that in this associate field his views, like his practice, suffered a disintegration which never quite completed or confirmed itself. It is very interesting to hear the author of the beautiful periods in "Criticism and Fiction" discoursing on Sterne's English in the terms that follow:

> Sterne's English is the most natural English that ever was written, or "wrote," as he would have written; it is the very manner of the spoken language; it halts, it hesitates, it turns upon itself; it puts the preposition last where it belongs; it emulates the beauty of a tree or flower rather than the symmetry of animal life; it has no care for antitheses; it balances itself only from the thinker's brain, and flies along the swaying thread of sympathy to the reader's mind, where it lights easily, softly, joyously.

The above passage is an arrowhead marking direction rather than a milestone noting the terminus of a journey. I think that Mr. Howells outgrew his faith in style in the old sense without outgrowing his love for it, that his criticism never finally took the plunge in the expectation of which it was always swaying and poising on the spring-board. I think that he permitted — perhaps persuaded — himself to ignore the immense difference in æsthetic value that might separate two styles whose diction and syntax were both simple and whose superficies were very much alike. He may have blurred the distinction between the cheap and the plain, and failed to remember steadily that literature may journey toward the spoken word more fitly and securely than it may start from it. I imagine he felt the discomfort of uncertainty in this field, and that the rarity and brevity of the allusions to style in his later criticism is a consequence of this unrest.

V

PERSONALITY

There is another matter in which I imagine a want of clearness in the self-adjustments of Mr. Howells. If you ask him whether he dislikes the photographic novel, he will tell you that objections to photography are "silly." But if you thereupon conclude that he proposes to follow nature with a canine rather than a human faithfulness, there is consolation in the announcement that literature is to interpret life, and in frequent reference to the "meaning," the "beauty," or the "poetry" of life as the goals of the artistic quest. The subjective element is explicitly acknowledged in one passage: "The first thing of his which I read seemed to me so very life-like that I knew it was not merely a transcript, but that sort of truth which fact precipitates after passing through the alembic of a friendly imagination."

The reassurance seems final, but much reading provokes the suspicion that Mr. Howells expects to have the meaning, the beauty, and the poetry of life on the same terms of unqualified certainty and unanimous assent on which he may possess, for instance, the law of the square of the hypothenuse, the diameter of Saturn's rings, or the preamble to the Constitution of the United States. The existence of a quality of truth answerable and accessible only to a similar quality of human nature, perceptible only in combination with a mind, and warranting and necessitating the study of personality in criticism, is a conception which Mr. Howells is disposed to slight, or, in his own diction, to "minify." I struggle throughout this discussion with the indocility of my own words — words which in spite of me give wholeness to the partial, permanence to the fluctuating, and definition to the implicit, failing altogether in justice to the subtle diversity of the nature they abridge and simplify. A rough simile must crudely illustrate the difference between the customary attitude and the conception of Mr. Howells.

Imagine a blood-stream with various neighboring glands, each extracting from the blood its own fluid, one milk, one oil, one tears, one serum, one bile. Imagine next a great sponge immersed in a body of water, in which one type of fibre everywhere absorbs one quality of fluid. It is quite obvious that, in the first instance, biology is pledged to faithful study of the glands, while, in the second case, it is not bound to *particularize* the knowledge of the fibres. The first, or gland, image suggests the average critic's reason for emphasizing the personality of writers. The second image, in which the sponge is the human race and the body of water is all truth, indicates Mr. Howells's reason for regarding fiction as, in a sense, an affair between universal truth and universal man, instead of as a question of the gifts of individuals. Mr. Howells is wider than his theory, or rather than his tendency or implication, and his hero-worship, his author-worship, is in certain aspects highly notable; but for him the soul of authorship is truth, and truth, as he thinks, is won, in literature as in daily conduct, not by rare and costly endowments, but by the clear sight and faithful record which are feasible to every honest man.

Let us suppose that a realistic author paces Michigan Avenue by the lake shore in Chicago, and observes that the lamp-posts carry six burners. He records the fact in his novel. The realistic critic reads the book, paces Michigan Avenue, verifies the fact, and commends the author. The wheel has come full circle. The example is an exaggeration, almost a caricature, and the number of lamps is really a mere *x* which may represent the subtlest truth in psychology; but the supposition crudely defines a type of criticism into which the criticism of Mr. Howells might logically have developed.

He intimates his attitude in a comparison of Jane Austen and George Eliot. "The only observer of English middle-class life since Jane Austen worthy to be named with her was not George Eliot, who was first ethical and then artistic, who transcended her in everything but the form and method most essential to art, and there fell hopelessly below her." This amounts to saying that George Eliot was the bigger woman (he calls her "that colossal George Eliot woman" in another place), but that bigness of character and soul is an insufficient counterpoise to faulty method. The method is paramount; the man is secondary. Among English novelists he exalts Jane Austen and Trollope, among Russians, Turgénieff and Tolstoi; and all of these, though in different degrees and fashions, may be classed as impersonal or objective writers. But we must not strive too hard to unify his views. Mr. Howells is heretic enough to entertain a passionate fondness for Henry James and Thomas Hardy, in whom the dominance of personality is undeniable.

The mention of Mr. James recalls a consequence of the attitude in question which I cannot but regard as a curtailment of insight. The differences between realists are minimized. Read the critiques of Henry James and of Tolstoi without previous cognizance of those writers, and you would suppose them to be almost as near to each other as Tolstoi is to Turgénieff or Henry James to Mrs. Wharton. The chasm that divides the writers has a breadth which nobody could infer from the crevice that parts the estimates. I should overstate the case, but I should not grotesquely overstate it, if I said that in this criticism all the realistic novels have an effect of being the work of one author. I should not wish to say that Mr. Howells did not perceive the differences; I should prefer to say that his criticism did not perceive them. When he tells me that Miss Jewett is a finer writer of short stories than Maupassant, I am conscious of the same dismay that I should feel if I were told in all seriousness that an anemone was more delicate than a Roman candle.

The quality of writers, if I may use the word in a sense distinct both from function and desert, is sparingly noted in the later criticism of Mr. Howells. To clarify my meaning: in an "Atlantic" review, he selects "graciousness" as perhaps the word most expressive of Longfellow's spirit. Now "graciousness," in its application to Longfellow, is a word that reveals, a word that educates. Or take the following from "Heroines of Fiction": "Anthony Trollope with his immense, quiet, ruminant reality, ox-like cropping the field of English life and converting its succulent juices into the nourishing beef of his fiction." Again, for a satiric flick, the phrase, "hat-cocked-on-one-side, wink-tipping sketches" disposes effectually of the crude beginnings of Mr. Kipling, for whose later work amenities were waiting. The touch is exquisite in the reference to Lowell's "flower-like delicacy of feeling that in his robust and vigorous poetry makes you think of a tree in blossom." There is no poverty of these invaluable touches in his work, but there is no plenty; the habit of viewing an author as a witness whose testimony was to be assayed by the critic's independent knowledge of the facts disposed him to be unmindful and sparing of these delicacies of characterization. One's regret that a man who could do so fine a thing so finely should have taken the doing of it so little to heart is heightened by the remembrance that touches of a kindred type lend grace and mastery to his fiction.

I have nothing but cordial indorsement for the verifying process, the process of referring the copy to the original; what I would deprecate is a devotion to that process so exclusive as almost to merge the witness in the testimony. There are times when this tends to induce a real or apparent confusion of levels. When the incentive of Mr. Howells's praise has led me to the perusal of minor novelists, the result has seldom been commensurate with his promises or my hopes. I have not so often questioned the truth of the picture as I have doubted the weight and depth and force of the author's response to his own truth. Mr. Howells can dispense with this incitement; truth itself is spur enough for him. But sleepier minds need to be taught to love truth by the same hand that teaches them to see it, and this love is naturally infused by contact with an enlarged and generous spirit. I cannot take even truth from everybody; the spokesman pervades the fact. If he is common, he cheapens the fact. It may, of course, be a lurking vulgarity in myself that is nourished by the discovery of commonness in others. A spirit of perfect temper, a Jesus, a Socrates, would almost automatically do away with the word "common" in the sense of "cheap" by the very fervor of emphasis which it would lay upon the same word in the sense of "universal."

The sin, I repeat, is very possibly mine, but I suspect that my fellow-sinners are plentiful in the class to which Mr. Howells appeals, and that their number is a factor in the usefulness of his critiques. The criticism may be exact for the high class of men whom it addresses, but that class in America numbered one individual, while Mr. Howells was alive. His unconcern, if it be really unconcern, for personality, for breeding and mettle, in a novelist, may exalt his stature as a man, but it scarcely qualifies him to speak for his clientage.

VI

BENEVOLENCE

This limitation is the other side of one of his noblest peculiarities — belief in the omnipresence of good. Wherever there is man and fact, wherever there is eye and object, there is nascent art, there is the augury of literature — such is the faith of Mr. Howells. In these matters a passive liberality tolerant of merit from any quarter is insufficient. To be liberal, one must be generous. Expectation is the parent of discovery. The belief that every truth is a potential theme and every man a potential artist begat a hope in the unknown and the untried which found its recompense in a discovery of merit hardly surpassed in the annals of criticism. Toward the past, indeed, he was mainly tepid, or reserved his cordiality for the masters. But no man has more stoutly, more fervidly and pertinaciously, upheld the significance of artists of the second and third classes in his own day. He speaks impatiently of that "worst kind of bore who is always exacting supreme and final beauty in art." The principle is altogether sound, and, if the application is sometimes over-liberal, the type of mind and soul disclosed in this excess of liberality carries us far beyond the grudging days when literature was a closed and guarded precinct, the true passports to which were often illegible to the purblind doorkeepers.

The indication of grades of desert is a trying problem for the critic. Grammar provides three degrees of intensity — positive, comparative, and superlative — in contempt of the obvious fact that Nature does not confine herself to three grades of excellence or defect. The niggardliness of language is one embarrassment; the lavishness of our vocabularies is another; the poor are often thriftless. The superlative in diction is employed to denote the positive in feeling, and the weaker form suffers an abatement in both currency and value. When literature wishes to discriminate between, let us say, five or six grades of merit in authorship, the wherewithal is absent. Industry or pedagogy solves the problem instantly and perfectly: it grades wheat by numerals — one, two, three, four — or college papers by letters — A, B, C, D. If criticism were earnest, perhaps it would adopt the suggestion; but a dislike of formality, which possibly veils an incapacity for precision, has hitherto prevented the experiment.

It follows that, when an appreciative man endeavors to express his admiration for a poem of the fourth class, — a phrase whose connotations differ absolutely from those of a fourth-class poem, — he is apt to use language which lifts that poem to the second or third rank in the mind of the unclassifying reader. Mr. Howells, in whose mind superlative pleasure can be induced by something far short of superlative merit, is prodigal of friendly hyperboles. An artistic holiday gift-book whose merits the adjective "charming" would probably encompass and exhaust is "very charming indeed." A poem of humorous cast called "Iron Quill" is "unutterably delightful." The acting of American actors is of "a very high grade." Bryant is "a very great man." The phrase might encircle Shakespeare. The reviews in the "Atlantic Monthly" of New England masters whom he personally knows are fondly reverent to an extent that brightens our estimate of the human nature generative of such homage; and the love which they embody, while it never contravenes sincerity, fashions sincerity in its own likeness. The attitude is rather trust than vision, and he has little that is pointed to say of Lowell, Longfellow, Whittier, and Holmes. I will not stop to chronicle the raptures and ecstasies which dance through later commentaries in Corybantic exuberance. One almost wonders how the authors themselves sustained this immersion in panegyric, but in such ordeals their robustness is proverbial. Mr. Howells can orient himself, in a fashion, after these excursions, but the reader regains the high-road with more difficulty.

We may deprecate this incontinence of laudation, but its nobler aspect is unmistakable. The man was untouched by the barbarity of his craft. He had small respect for criticism in any light. He felt that the critic was arrogant and unfair in his claim of universality for a judgment which was merely individual, and of authority for a judgment which was merely tentative, a stricture in which all sensible men — even sensible critics, should they emerge from their lurking-places — will heartily concur. But the thing in criticism which he absolutely could not away with was malignity. Referring to the time when his adolescence exulted in the critical ferocities of Poe, he says: "I think that hardly less immoral than the lubricity of literature, and its celebration of the monkey and the goat in us, is the spectacle such criticism affords of the tigerish play of satire." He puts the case with irresistible force when he condemns the torturing of a writer "for no offence but the wish to produce something beautiful, and the mistake of his powers in that direction."

The sincerity of these declarations has been tested and attested in "Editor's Study." The old motto, *De mortuis nil nisi bonum*, Mr. Howells has amended by adding "*de moribundis*." Through seven years he adheres almost undeviatingly to the magnanimous alternative, silence or praise. Sometimes anonymity — the victim's anonymity — is substituted for silence, and sometimes ample praise is qualified by meagre blame. With respect to the large mass of obscure and secondary literature, this stand seems as sound as it is Christian. The immediate award for worthless books whose ultimate portion is oblivion should be that silence which is at once doom and mercy. The dilemma offered by another class of books, too conspicuous to ignore and too faulty to commend, presents itself rarely to Mr. Howells, or is solved by expedients which leave no scar upon his pages. That these pages have lost some piquancy by this forbearance is highly probable. There is a curious irony in these matters. Tolstoi with his abhorrence of war and his revulsion from sex achieves his unrivalled successes in sexual and military scenes; and Mr. Howells, who advocates and practises amenity, is never so amusing as when, in the case of dead authors or authors grouped in classes, he gives play to his satire and invective. The sacrifice of this piquancy in ordinary cases gives distinction to his forbearance. Even with this handicap of decency and kindness, his wit is not disqualified for victorious competition with those gentlemen who prove that the pen is mightier than the sword in the sword's own specialty of hacking and slashing. In many cases his benevolence is clairvoyant: the sunbeam is an aid to vision.

VII

ETHICS AND DECORUM

A sentence from Mr. Howells on John Hay is descriptive of his own probable experience in the field of art and ethics. "I venture to think rather than say that, from the stress in which his tendency toward the æsthetical and his tendency toward the ethical were pitted against each other, he found no peaceful issue, no entire reconciliation, except in 'The History of Abraham Lincoln.'" So sharp is the similar antithesis in Mr. Howells's own mind that he is capable in the same article of declarations that, on the surface at least, are self-contradictory. In the paper on Tolstoi, in volume 188 of the "North American Review," he says categorically, on page 847: "A great gulf, never to be bridged, divides the ethical and the æsthetical intention." Eight pages farther on, he speaks of the novelist in this fashion: "If he had represented the fact truly, as in his conscience and intelligence he had known it really to be, he had treated it ethically and of necessity æsthetically; for as you cannot fail to feel in every piece of his fiction, the perfect æsthetics result from the perfect ethics. . . . Where the artist and moralist work together for righteousness, there is the true art." The disparity is manifest; and even if subtlety could harmonize the contradiction, the appeal to subtlety is a half-capitulation.

If Mr. Howells were asked if morality is not a *parti pris*, and as such, adverse to the impartiality of realism, I think he would reply that morality is Nature's *parti pris*, and that the distillation of truth which we call realism can never be inconsistent with the other distillation which we call morals. For him the morality is tacit or implicit in the facts, and from this he deduces two interesting conclusions: that fiction must be universally moral, and that the author must never moralize. The position is one of great logical strength and of the utmost practical difficulty. The facts are good moralists, but they are bad preachers. Their case is sound, but their exposition is clumsy and obscure. The beneficence of morality may be hard to establish in a world in which the bulk of the inhabitants are baddish, for precisely the same reason that the value of cleanliness might be hard to demonstrate in a shiftless tropical seaport, where the mass of the population was bedded in dirt. The beneficence of either merit would remain intact, but their demonstration by example would be restricted.

It requires some hopefulness to assume that the uncolored and uncommented picture of the facts will exert a moral influence on readers who have proved impervious to the daily and hourly spectatorship of the facts themselves. A moralist is usually driven, however reluctantly, to distort or to discuss the facts, and Mr. Howells, to whom both these proceedings are anathema, is forced in his own practice to comply with the hard alternative. He prefers the discussion to the distortion, and some of his fictions, "A Modern Instance" and "The Quality of Mercy," for example, are bent double under the weight of ethical reflection. He tries to elude his conscience by putting the disquisition into the mouths of the actors in the drama; but this is admissible only on the supposition that the comments illustrate nothing but the minds of the commentators. In point of fact, they influence the reader's view of the problem.

In the criticism of others his virtue is less wavering; he is zealous for pure drama, is not unfaithful to his own dictum that "the artist's business is to be the colorless medium through which the reader clearly sees the right and wrong." Even here, however, he yields so far as to place among the transcendent illustrations of the moral law the "Romola" of George Eliot, a book whose great but highly checkered merits do not include the repression of commentary. There is deviation from standard here, but I suspect that the inconsistency is helpful.

It is good that Mr. Howells should discipline the moralists, who are so often pragmatists and busy-bodies, and it is good that he should feel the ethical impressiveness of "Romola." If a writer is primarily moralist, — as Mr. Howells pretty clearly is, — it is certain that he can have no better safeguard or counterpoise than an exquisite or even an exaggerated sensibility to the obligations of artistic reticence. It may be said, of course, that the artist loses as much as the moralist gains by their fraternization, but I doubt if the inference be sound. An artist in such company will lose no more in the nicety of his workmanship than he will recover indirectly through the subsidy to his manhood. I think that the criticism of Mr. Howells has profited in soundness and breadth, at the expense no doubt of logical consistency, by the equality of the stress it lays on moral tendency and artistic method.

One further topic cannot be ignored. Mr. Howells is distinguished among his contemporaries for reserve of speech, and for a long time his demand for restraint in others was regulated by his own chariness. In "My Literary Passions," published in his fifty-eighth year, he recommends that "what is lewd and ribald in the great poets shall be kept out of such editions as are meant for general reading, and that the pedant-pride which now perpetuates it as an essential part of those poets shall no longer have its way." It is a very curious fact that at a later period this rigor in criticism, without any retraction of the above dictum or alteration of his private practice, should have undergone a modification so drastic as to be almost tantamount to disappearance. The earlier criticism now and then exhibits a severity in which my own acquired and mature taste — which may or may not be one's sounder taste — has a difficulty in keeping pace with him. But in his later critiques he has words of homage, not to say veneration, for novels and plays which even the latitude of my riper taste approaches with grave misgiving. Such books are "The Gay Lord Quex" of Sir Arthur Pinero, "Pepita Ximenez," where to my mind the fornication is revolting because needless, "Jude the Obscure," in which Mr. Hardy's "supreme mastery" is reached, and "Madame Bovary," which is characterized as "one impassioned cry of the austerest morality." I do not put Brieux's works in this group, but I note with interest that, while Mr. Howells cannot read "Les Avariés," pretty much everything else in Brieux, including "Maternité," is indorsed and commended, and the objection to "Les Avariés" is rather a matter of personal hygiene than of public morals. It must be perfectly understood that there is not the slightest relaxation in the demand for ethical tendency.

I suppose a very sensitive person who is firm in his determination not to be shocked will often endure more than a hardier or tougher nature unprovided with the armor of resolution; fortitude may go further than recklessness. I suppose, again, that a man who took to wine after fifty would be unlikely to become a connoisseur in vintages; and I feel that Mr. Howells does not discriminate too sharply in the shades and tints of that freedom to which his autumnal taste, if I may risk the word, offers a belated welcome. He was poignantly alive to tendency, but, in the growing objectiveness of his criticism, he came to measure tendency too exclusively by the dole of good or ill which the result dispensed to the actor, and made light of the atmosphere in which the author's sympathy or satire or indifference enwraps the portrayal of the fault. In "The Gay Lord Quex," for instance, the awards are tolerably moral, and Lord Quex is fairly innocent in the transaction that sustains the drama, but a callousness pervades the work which petrifies the sensibilities in the fashion that supplied Burns with his main objection to illicit love. That callousness is either unobserved, or, if observed, is unrecorded, by Mr. Howells.

VIII

MODERN ITALIAN POETS

In the above general estimate of Mr. Howells's criticism, I have referred sparingly or not at all to two collateral volumes, "Modern Italian Poets" and "Heroines of Fiction." It is time to repair this omission.

"Modern Italian Poets," the fruit of that consular leisure at Venice for which Mr. Howells was so largely indebted to the forbearance of the Confederate privateers, was not completed or given to the world until 1887. It is in essence a work of the earlier Howells, the studious, beauty-loving, receptive, and deferential young man, who reminds us a little of Coleridge's wedding-guest before the hour when the Ancient Mariner called "life" had imparted to him the full measure of the deep and melancholy import of his tale. The maturer voice, audible here and there in the work, never ruptures the habitual mood; and one is glad that the legacy of the slighter and blither man was preserved in much of its primal grace by the piety of his executor and successor.

The earlier Howells must not be imagined to be lacking in independence of mind. He is low-voiced, soft-footed, self-depreciative; quotes admiringly Italian judgments which are not much better grounded or better worded than his own; but his humility is quite aware of its own mind, and quite capable of giving to that mind a meek but explicit utterance. The "Perdoni" which he seems always addressing to the Italians imparts to contradiction something like the charm of acquiescence. For him Italy is lovable in the very faults of her poets, as her weeds were beautiful to Filicaja. In the criticism, as in the early travels, one feels how strongly the general deference and homage qualifies the particular remonstrance. Was this word tame and that artificial? What matter? It was Italy that spoke.

The book, according to its preface, forms "a sketch, however slight and desultory, of the history of Italian poetry during the hundred years ending in 1870." Literature at that time and place retraversed the road taken by nationality; and, as that history was *drama*, so that literature is a *story*, in senses hardly justified by the politics or the literature of other epochs. The dip of the author's sympathies was preordained. To sympathize with Italy in her struggle was a form of loyalty to America; he is never demonstrative, however; he is permeated with that unquestioning sense of the holiness of a cause which makes rhapsody an impertinence.

IX

"HEROINES OF FICTION"

"Enjoyment" is the key-word to "Heroines of Fiction." It neither formulates a creed nor defends a thesis; it is a record of happy experience, an autobiography, in which, in George Eliot's phrase, the arm-chair is brought to the proscenium. He chats interestingly about interesting things; there is conscious, and there is unconscious, frankness. He reports of his tastes much that we had expected and some things that we had failed to expect. We see that his nature was wider than his theory. If we try to tuck his nature into his theory, some loose ends refuse to be inserted; and if we substitute a theory of our own, the result is hardly more satisfactory: the parcel threatens to escape its string.

He tells us that power in the delineation of women is the test of artistic mastery in fiction. He tells us, again, that inconsistency and variation are the soul of feminine identity, and this conception becomes perfectly clear when we associate it with the recoils and rebounds, the fluid receptiveness, the passionate inconsequence, of the women who dominate his own fictions. Granting this ideal, the authors whose heroines he should logically prefer are Reade and Hardy, and to this forecast he is measurably true. Between vilification and idolization of Reade he very nearly suffers intellectual rupture, but on the whole he upholds the Reade women staunchly. The same notion of women will sustain him well enough in his liking for Maggie Tulliver and Gwendolen Harleth, in his preference of Hetty Sorrel to Dinah Morris and of Effie to Jeanie Deans, in his admiration of Emily Brontë's Catharine and of Hawthorne's Zenobia. It will indulge, if it will not expressly sanction, his equable and far from exuberant regard for Dora Spenlow, Bella Wilfer, and even Miss Burney's Evelina. He likes little "geese" (the word is his own), if there is sufficient variegation in their plumage and flutter in their gait. But a formula of this kind must stand agape at the spectacle of Lily Dale's apotheosis, must question the credentials of Hester Prynne, and I do not see how it can possibly adjust itself to the critic's immeasurable delight in such quadrilaterals and hexagons as Elizabeth Bennet and Emma Woodhouse. These young ladies whose characters are rather diagrammed than drawn (I admit, for my own part, a fondness for diagrams) afford unspeakable pleasure to a critic for whom passionate waywardness is the measure of reality in woman.

I am treating this inconsistency as a fault, but at bottom I am far from sure that it is really blameworthy. One is naturally a little vexed to see that Mr. Howells's hoop will not encircle his cask, that his generalization cannot house his examples. But, "at the end of the ends," as he likes to say, the liberality which the inconsistency discloses is probably a more useful possession than the logical coherence which it oversets. There are other liberalities for which he feels bound to apologize incessantly, with the effect of imparting the disquiet rather than the reassurance to the reader. Such is his hospitality to Kingsley's Hypatia and Bulwer's Nydia, who are allowed to block the way for their betters, while Mr. Howells is copious in his explanations of the accident that stops the flow of traffic. Early affection may have had its share in the homage offered to Olivia and Sophia Primrose, and later association may have influenced the allotment of twenty-three pages of concentrated eulogy to Daisy Miller, the heroine of a short story a little longer than the critique. In spite of her high parentage and high sponsorship, the average human nature which Mr. Howells delights to praise will not hesitate to call Daisy Miller impossible.

There is a second point in which Mr. Howells's personal experience has a difficulty in finding lodgment within the straitened confines of his theory. He believes in truth, the plain, firm, quiet truth, and disowns sensation and theatricality. Yet the list of passages which he cites as fine or distinctive includes the following: the Ivanhoe-Rebecca sick-chamber scene; two hectic passages from "Belinda"; the invasion of the parsonage by Heathcliff in "Wuthering Heights"; the murder scene in "Hypatia"; the portrait scene in "Peg Woffington"; the expulsion scene in "Janet's Repentance"; the reception of the diamonds by Gwendolen Harleth in "Daniel Deronda"; the Steyne-Crawley fracas; the explanation of Edith Dombey with Carker at Dijon; the murder of Nancy Sikes.

It is true, no doubt, that a critical or passionate moment in experience may be as capable as any other reality of yielding its store of truth to the vigilant and conscientious observer, but the remark is by no means applicable to all these passages. The Gwendolen Harleth passage, for example, contains only one such demonstrable insight; the rest is passion and skill. The critiques were written for "Harper's Bazar," and the case may be referable to Macaulay's observation in a letter to Napier that the fly which the angler selects is determined, not by the taste of the angler, but by the taste of the fish. If the assumption be correct, the fish, in this instance, liked pepper.

When the selections are quieter (and they are often quiet), I note with interest that the author's favorite passages contain few of those subtleties for which his own work is notable, few of those absolute novelties which reward the explorer of unsounded depths or of unknown combinations. The object of admiration is often less originality than fitness, the trait, in itself often familiar, which suits both the fact and the frame. This points to the interesting conclusion that the rarity and subtlety which figure so largely in the reader's consciousness of Mr. Howells's work enter very slightly, if at all, into his own impression of his novels. He is himself original and pungent and clever in rare abundance, but he does not ask other truth-tellers to be original or pungent or clever; he asks them only to be true. This is why the pursuer of these qualities often rises discouraged from the perusal of fictions which Mr. Howells has dignified with his approbation.

"Heroines of Fiction" contains some notable generalizations. I have already quoted the acute distinction between romance and romanticism. A remark on the second page of the first volume deserves a still warmer recognition: "The best thing in the expression of any sort of modernity is a voluntary naturalness, an instructed simplicity."

The generalities are firm enough, but in the treatment of particulars there is much demure tentativeness, much courteous and calculated indecision. The temporizing suavity is one mood; another is pathos, fatherly, considerate, of restrained poignancy; still another is severity, the more searching perhaps for the conservation of the key of mildness; a fourth is sunny homage with a sort of playful arrogance in the assertion of the right to revere.

The style has lost in shapeliness and speed. Its figure is impaired, and with its figure, by natural consequence, the elasticity of its gait. To call the style journalism would be impossible; but perhaps I should keep within bounds in defining it as an artistic style in a mood of journalistic relaxation. If the feet are not elevated, the back is comfortably depressed, and there is something in the tentativeness which really suggests the balancing (for the moment only) of a chair on its hind-legs.

I do not know whether "Heroines of Fiction" has enjoyed the popular favor which seems the just recompense of its many tactful and engaging qualities. Its themes are vivid and familiar; its citations are effective; the lights and shadows are both strong, and the lights far outnumber the shadows; the topics are persons, and the tone is steeped in personality. If these attractions have failed to enlarge its public, I am constrained to wonder if Mr. Howells's fame is not the hindrance to his popularity.

X

CONCLUSION

Mr. Howells achieves a greater formal excellence in the brief critiques of the "Editor's Study" than in the ampler estimates which he contributes to the "North American Review." His material in later years is circumscribed by the slightness of his allusions to style, by a novel definition of art which made it almost a section of truth, and by a reluctance to accentuate personality. The comparison of the picture with the fact becomes the staple of his discussion, and his material is further straitened by the high-minded refusal to be copious or strenuous in blame. In his long essays, moreover, the plan is a little relaxed and the outlines uncertain. The old school of criticism had the guaranty of a certain elementary shapeliness and proportion in the division of its matter into four or five clear-cut, commensurable topics: plot, character, style, ethics, and the like. The removal of two of these elements, plot and style, disturbs the effective symmetry of the ground-plan, and Mr. Howells, to whom squaring and measuring are distasteful, is content to let the essay shape itself. As offset to this drawback, the larger

"North American" papers, the "Zola" and the "Ibsen" and the "Henry James," contain not a few of his weightiest and most striking declarations. In the "Atlantic Monthly" reviews the style is attractive but unsure; in "Editor's Study" the felicity is unerring and unceasing; in the "North American" papers disintegration is traceable. In "Editor's Study," where personality twinkles at us through impersonality, like an eye through a keyhole, there is a charm which the formalities of the "Atlantic" and the "Review" naturally fail to rival. It is a curious fact that the five or six social and political essays in the "North American" average higher in force and interest than the fifty or more reviews of authors.

Mr. Howells's judgments of poetry are good, and his choice in kinds is significant of the realist. It is in brief lyrical outcries and pictures of landscape that the superficial quarrel between poetry and actuality is most readily intermitted or concealed; and it is to poems of this type — with a friendly nod here and there for satire — that the critic affectionately turns. He has an ear for that inwardness of poetry which is so curiously imbedded in its outwardness, as if somehow its heart lay in its cuticle; and, while his eulogy is wide and warm, the passage he quotes in its defence is commonly equal to its responsibilities. He understands that not all good lines or stanzas, or even poems, are produced by the transcendent poets, just as not all the *bon mots* are assignable to the wits or all the divinations to the seers.

It is time to summarize briefly. Mr. Howells is a great critic because, in "Criticism and Fiction," he voiced with power and authority the principle to which the fiction of the future may look for its standard and inspiration.

The greatness is evinced in principles. In the applications, his discerning and genial criticisms fall short of absolute primacy, and the reasons for the insufficiency are clear.

Mr. Howells's realism tended to complete itself, but failed

absolutely to complete itself, in three notable directions. The first, if carried out, would have meant the absorption of art by truth, in other words, the conscientious and intentional reproduction, in the imaginary world, of the formlessness of the world of actuality.

The second tendency, in its completion, would have sacrificed style, as criticism habitually knew it, to ideals of spontaneity and transparency.

The third tendency, if unchecked, would have led to the effacement of the author's personality, the establishment of a purely objective criticism serving—not dominating—a purely objective art. Knowledge would become the equipage of author and reviewer alike, and criticism would pass into auditorship.

Not one of these tendencies mastered the man. The influence of all three was advanced to a point where it ceased to be purely beneficial, but its progress was limited by two strong checks — the inherited and inbred literary instinct, and the sanity in which few Americans of his time were comparable to Mr. Howells.

I think the novelist-critic remained strongly sensitive to the spell of art and style and personality, even when he redefined the one and stinted his acknowledgments to the other two. I should compare him to some severe Puritan lover who, stoutly asserting that he values nothing in his lady but her virtue and piety, is far from insensible to the grace of her figure or the bloom on her cheek.

As an offset to these handicaps, he brought to the craft of reviewing a catholicity of reception and a humanity of procedure which conduced to its renovation and to his own honor.

His objective ideals, his catholicity, and his humanity tended to a breadth and warmth of appreciation, a latitude — I use the word in both its radical and its derived sense — of panegyric which sometimes threatened the confusing of levels and the exaltation of mediocrity.

The question arises, however, if these latter effects are not more apparent than real. Mr. Howells has praised warmly persons who came to little, but while the depth of his obeisance to literary rank hardly discriminates between the simple baronet and the prince of the blood, a careful survey proves that the people he most loves and praises are people who have won the approval of the elect few, and even of the common voice when that voice has had time to distill and calm itself. I remember only two poets whom he hailed as discoveries, Archibald Lampman and Emily Dickinson; and the wise, or, at least, the influential, seem now to have ratified these judgments. The American novelists whom he has preëminently and constantly praised, Mr. Cable, Miss Wilkins (Mrs. Freeman), Miss Jewett, Miss Murfree, Mark Twain, have demonstrated for the most part that his judgment was sounder than his theories and his perceptions clearer than his language. His error has lain only in loving truth and men a little too well; and if, as the exponent of a great truth, he has incurred the liabilities of his mission, the soundness of his inherited fiber and the sanity of his early taste have always been on the ground to shield him from the harsher penalties of truth and magnanimity.

CHAPTER VII

Style

I

Diction and Grammar

MARK TWAIN, in an essay on Mr. Howells's style, once declared that other men, including himself, *sometimes* found the right word; Howells *always* found it. I do not know that, if vocabularies were counted, Mr. Howells's footings would humiliate all his competitors. But hardly a man of our own times has been on easy terms with so many words, has had the familiarity, the confidence, of so many words, as W. D. Howells. There are troops of useful words which the average writer barely knows because they dwell but in the suburbs of his good pleasure; more literally, because the occasions for their use are too far apart to keep them within easy call of the scatter-brained memory. The arrival of these words at the opportune moment is viewed as a windfall or providence, and is fêted with thankful acclamations. Now in Mr. Howells there is no question of arrival: the words are *in situ;* they are housed in the establishment. No doubt, this happy readiness owed something to the early drill that made him a skilled compositor at thirteen, and more to the rigorous self-discipline in reading and writing that marked his aspiring and diligent youth; but it came mainly, I believe, from a profound sensibility to the savor of all sorts of words, and from the copious drafts upon language made by a ceaseless mental activity to which expression was as natural as perception and perception was as natural as breath.

Mr. Howells was a word-maker, but the words which were his by invention or discovery rather than by inheritance should possibly be classed, as inventions commonly are, among liabilities rather than assets. This word-coinage is distributed pretty evenly through his long career; it is mature in "Venetian Life" (the edition I use is revised), and it is not decadent in "Roman Holidays." Here are specimens from "Venetian Life": potenter, reverendest, Constantinopolitan, proprietarians, sentimentalizer, superation, tableclothy. Here are specimens from "Imaginary Interviews": usurperesses, been-abroads, songy, villaginosity, debarking, ancestored, laughability (in speech), heroinically, parallelable.

I shall show more mercy to the reader than Mr. Howells shows to the language, which indeed quite staggers under the weight of these benefactions, and shall not reproduce the extended lists with which his fecundity in this point has gorged my note-book. I think this coinage was largely whim; it is difficult to believe that he felt himself to be repaying his obligations to his mother-tongue by the gift of a vocable like "Constantinopolitan" or "tableclothy." Let us frankly confess that there was an antic element in Mr. Howells which found pleasure in "trying on" prefixes and suffixes if a stem chanced to be available, with a feint of demureness for the guileless reader and an arched eyebrow, possibly, for the shuddering philologist.

The whimsicality is more evident and more excusable where the word is clearly a nonce-word, as someone calls it, a saltation, or a caprice. Most people who know Mr. Howells at all know him as a highly decorous and dignified writer, and they are just in this appraisal; but I wonder if they will believe my word or even my reference when I tell them that he says "packaged, bundled, bagged"; "not manned but *girled*"; "tongueyer"; "drinky, smoky, and sweary"; "onliest"; "hot-scotching and beef-teaing"; "hatiness and cloakiness"; "their betters or their richers"; "lawn-mowered and . . . garden-hosed"; "umbrellaed"; "mothering and daughtering"; "elders and youngers"; "elders and fatters." The contradiction, if you choose to call it such, penetrates Mr. Howells everywhere. He is primarily and mainly fastidious, he is even finally fastidious, but there is a moment before the finality when he is just perceptibly relaxed. The place is exquisitely kept, but there is always a servant in the varied retainership who leaves a corner unswept or a shutter unfastened. This can be traced from his neologisms to his attitude toward slang, toward grammar (less emphatically here), toward the mention of unpleasant things, toward style and art in their entirety. I should add, in fairness, that the facts are no worse than my specimens, and their appearances are dispersed and occasional.

Mr. Howells's response to what may be called the physique of words is apparent in his fondness for bringing into intellectual relation words that have material or vocal affinities. I do not mean puns, or mean them very secondarily. It is very characteristic that Mr. Howells, for all his love of verbal coincidence, should very nearly exclude puns, and yet should not quite exclude them. The Marches call their silver wedding journey in Germany their German-silver-wedding journey, and in the hotel elevator they go higher to find something lower. If a man is lighting a cigar while he discusses a love-affair, it would be superhuman in a novelist to abstain from a modest emphasis on the word "match." But though temptations must have been numberless, transgressions are singularly few. "The round-bodied men . . . with hair and vowels clipped surprisingly short" is a confusion of applications rather than of meanings. More often he couples words that concur in sound, like "chance and change," "chance and choice," "enfolded and enfeebled," "detecting and deterring," "flashing and flushing," "spacious, if specious, palatiality," "petted and patted by her inventor" (of Dolly Varden), "imperative and importunate as the Great Stone Face itself," "born into and borne out of the house." Sometimes the phrase is longer: "surfaces almost impassable to the foot and quite impossible to the nose"; "their strength was rather of the tetanic than the titanic sort." Sometimes the correspondence is rhyme: the squirrel has "a beady, greedy eye"; Mr. Gage is a "prim little, grim little man"; people are not to write "barely or sparely"; "March conspired and perspired"; "Charlotte Brontë's life is divided between native solitude and alien multitude." The following is not mere rhyme, but is enlivening: when Thackeray "painted a saint, he wanted to paint 'Saint' all over the halo."

I may throw in here the remark that Mr. Howells seems not to have minded those accidental chimes in proximate or correspondent syllables which the normal artist prides himself on avoiding. There are two examples of what I mean on the first page of "Annie Kilburn": "He had married late, and in her thirty-first year he was seventy-eight," and "He was lying in the Protestant cemetery, and she was trying to gather herself together." An ear more sensitive or differently sensitive would have avoided the approximation in one couple and one title of the tinkling names, Florindo and Lindora. It will admit the positive din of the last four words in the following: "a form [the short story] which I have great pleasure in as a reader, and pride in as an American." I think he must have liked these consonances, which affect the normal artist and average reader as dissonances. Otherwise, could he have written: "for opulence of invention and perfect expression of intention"? My own list, made rather casually, includes thirty-five examples.

The interesting point in Mr. Howells's relation to slang is the fact that, having felt its witchery keenly, he should so seldom have participated in its sabbaths. Here, as elsewhere, great continence specked with rare indulgence is his practice. I have a fairly buxom list of transgressions, but I should not call them criminally numerous; in respect of his temptations, I should call them virtuously few. He has an affection for "swells," but he disproves the charge of snobbishness by showing almost equal favor to "jays." "Give away," a phrase that overcame the reserves of Mr. James, proved equally effectual on his one-time compatriot. His "nerve" in linguistic crises has been frequently demonstrated, though he is known, in extreme urgencies, to have "thrown up the sponge." He mentions the advance of "come off" into "merited favor," and commends it to the lips of a cherished heroine. It is needless to say that he places the accumulations which his own temperance cannot utilize at the disposal of the receptive and unscrupulous Mr. Fulkerson. But, to my mind, he has observed a certain chariness in the use of slang, even in dialogues where its use would be verisimilar. It is odd that his refined people are most subject to its lure; the cosseted Bostonian, Mr. Otis Binning, finds it instantly penetrating his dialect, his Englishmen approach it with grave deference, and his virtuous Altrurian cannot deny himself a lawless comfort in its "vulgar vigor."

It is worth noting that provincialisms, or vulgarisms other than slang, are of the rarest occurrence in Mr. Howells's personal English, and that, while peculiarities in the writings of others are very often mentioned and passingly illustrated, the extended use of dialect is infrequent in his work. One can scarcely lament this rarity in recalling the most salient exception in the faithful record throughout "Ragged Lady" of that New England parlance in which the *r*'s are all boiled down to the consistency of gelatine. Let no one infer, however, that Mr. Howells is not highly, is not astonishingly, sensitive to languages, to dialects, to pronunciations, to intonations, to every property and aspect of human speech. The precision of his ear is a main factor in his subtle divination of the *race* of foreigners, and he recognizes his countrymen in Europe, "as the blind man knows the cuckoo, by the bad voice." A habit like the following never escapes record: "He dropped his aspirates everywhere, and when he picked them up he put them on in the wrong places." "In his parlance I was a bird of night [Howells = owls], or several such," etc. Archaisms are very rare, and he is cautious, without being timorous, in the matter of quartering foreign words on the English sentence. He stooped once to "laissez-faireist."

His ear was everywhere attentive and retentive. The verse he read became embedded in a memory which readily gave it forth to incrust his own prose with its jewelled fragments. But, apart from these elegances, he was obsessed by all he heard, by the locutions of the newspaper, by the platitudes of eloquence, by the flourishes of advertisement, by the catchwords of politics, by the blandishments of society. One appreciable source of his humor is the reproduction of the stereotyped phrase in the novel context, and another is the De-Morgan-like proclivity for harking back — or hearkening back — for the literal sense in phrases which the later conventional meaning has dulled for conventional ears.

Mr. Howells's grammar demands a moment's attention. Many years ago Richard Grant White, himself a purist in many matters, having ventured to praise the fine precision of Mr. Howells's English, drew down upon himself vigorous, even violent, reprisals from that acrid and rigid critic, Fitz-Edward Hall. The truth is that the English in question is delicate without being impeccable. Neither the logical nor the philological instinct was ascendant in Mr. Howells; his early practice, though good, was not inerrant; he liked forms he did not quite esteem; and in points on which literature was divided, he was disposed to follow his pleasure. He tells us with his beautiful candor that Lowell corrected his early interchange of "shall" and "will," and his attitude toward these forms is a very curious illustration of the great extent and the occasional limitation of the self-evolving, self-reshaping process in his life. He acquired an expertness in the delicacies of this idiom — a rare victory for the adult man. He was true to the idiom where truth was all but heroic. For instance, he allows a young girl to say: "Do you think, you shall see me at his feet before the evening is over?" This is stoic grammar, and the grasp of the idiom is apparently impeccable. But in "Venetian Life" he writes, "I would have been glad"; and in "Roman Holidays," more than forty years later, he writes, "We would have liked." Many of his "I should like's" and "We should like's" would have been current even at Elmwood, but in this phrase and its kindred the longitude of his birth is prone to declare itself in the latitude of his usage. He can even do the incredible: he can use the idiom with admirable delicacy in one clause, and violate it in another verb of the same sentence. "'We must n't keep Mr. Breckon from his friends, mother,' she said, brightly, and then he said he *should* like the pleasure of introducing them, and both of the ladies declared that they *would* be delighted." (Italics mine.)

In questions like that of the desirability of superlatives where only two things are compared, or of expressions like "Mrs. Sewell and himself," "Mrs. Thrall and myself," Mr. Howells takes the side of tradition, which in grammar, paradoxically enough, is often the side of liberality. For this others must chide him, if they will; I reserve what displeasure I can feel with Mr. Howells for the unlovely "that much more," and the illogical "I must try and realize," and the slouching "that kind of a man." I recall only one use of the split infinitive. It seems very odd to write sixty or seventy books and use the split infinitive once. One might have saved the purchase-money for the hatchet. The following instance of corrupt logic vexes me in the ratio of its security from average censure: "He gave way to an irascibility which he tried to check, and to ask with indifference." To sum up, Mr. Howells's grammar would satisfy the educated man; it might sometimes amuse or trouble a scholar; it might enrage a pedant.

II

PERIODS AND PHASES

The style of Mr. Howells may be roughly sketched in three periods. There is a time antedating the earliest of these periods which hardly pertains to the present study, since the data it includes are either out of print or have never emerged from the shelter of the magazines. Mr. Howells could write very unconcernedly in his youth. In a review in the "Atlantic Monthly" for the year 1866, he writes as follows (I choose the worst sentence that offers itself without research): "We confess to a deeper respect for Mr. Taylor's power than we have felt before, when we observe with what masterly skill he contrives by a single incident to give sudden and important development to a character which, however insignificant it had previously seemed, we must finally allow to have been perfectly prepared for such an effect." This verbose and clumsy sentence, amid many things fitly and happily said, may suggest the sound inference that Mr. Howells, though an adept in style, — far more an adept than many or most precisians, — was not himself a precisian. With this preface, let us pass on to the three periods.

The first may be illustrated from a passage in "Their Wedding Journey," the date of which is 1872.

> It was deadly hot, and most of the people saddened and silenced in the heat. From time to time the clouds idling above overhead met and sprinkled down a cruel little shower of rain that seemed to make the air less breathable than before. The lonely shores were yellow with drought; the islands grew wilder and barrener; the course of the river was for miles at a stretch through country which gave no signs of human life. The St. Lawrence has none of the bold picturesqueness of the Hudson, and is far more like its far-off cousin the Mississippi. Its banks are low like the Missis-

sippi's, its current swift, its way through solitary lands. The same sentiment of early adventure hangs about each: both are haunted by visions of the Jesuit in his priestly robe and the soldier in his mediæval steel; the same gay, devout, and dauntless race has touched them both with immortal romance.

This is plainly an excellent style. It has a gleaming, a lustrous, clearness; the freshness of youth exhales in its always unshackled, though never unguided, motion; it maintains a high decorum never stiffening into propriety. Its serene and high art is evident chiefly in the flawless sculpture of the sentences in which clause answers to clause with the sureness of brow to nose or arm to trunk in a statue of the Phidian era.

Even at this period, when the style is robing itself in beauty and magic, the delicacy is not absolute. Here is a slight asperity: "They hailed the first car that passed, and got into it." It would have been easy to avoid the prickles in the last phrase by saying "and mounted the steps"; perhaps Mr. Howells preferred an obvious defect to a facile correction. Whether the fault be voluntary or not, it remains true that the sentences are not uniformly or meticulously patterned; and that distinction is not evenly distributed like a stucco.

I must offer two passages in illustration of the mid-period. The first is from "An Imperative Duty" (1892).

He would not have been ready to say that one of the negro waiters, whom he wished they had at his hotel, would not have been just as greedy of money; but he would have clothed his greed in such a smiling courtesy and such a childish simple-heartedness that it would have been graceful and winning. He would have used tact in his ministrations; he would not have cumbered him with service, as from a wheelbarrow, but would have given him a touch of help here, and a little morsel of attention there; he would have kept aloof as well as alert. That is, he would have had all these charms if he were at his best, and he would have had some of them if he were at his worst.

In fact, the one aspect of our mixed humanity here which struck Olney as altogether agreeable in getting home was that of the race which vexes our social question with its servile past, and promises to keep it uncomfortable with its civic future. He had not forgotten that, so far as society in the society sense is concerned, we have always frankly simplified the matter, and no more consort with the negroes than we do with the lower animals, so that one would be quite as likely to meet a cow or a horse in an American drawing-room as a person of color.

This is again admirable writing. If the youthful coloring is a little dimmed, the youthful figure is intact. The contours are firmer, not less fine; the main difference is the rise of a new element into parity with form, an element which an Elizabethan would have curtly called wit and a modern Frenchman, I suppose, might still call *esprit*, but for the denotement of which the modern "wit" is too narrow and the English "spirit" too ambiguous. Let us make shift with the word "point," meaning by that a stimulation which may appear in half a dozen forms, of which humor, simile, contrast, parallelism, allusion, may be offered as examples. Styles of this type are wont to be a little noisy and strutting; the crackle accompanies the flash. In Mr. Howells, as in Mrs. Wharton and in Anatole France, the flash is noiseless. Imagine a feat performed with the ease and quietness of a gesture, and you have a perfect image of this medial phase of the style of Mr. Howells. By a curious paradox, taste, measure, and tranquillity are the saliencies in this author's work; the brilliancy seems an afterthought or adjunct.

To be just, however, to the range of Mr. Howells's manner, I must quote a second passage, which I select from "The Minister's Charge" (1886).

At last the wagon came to a place that he saw was a market. There were no buyers yet, but men were flitting round under the long arcades of the market-houses, with lanterns under their arms, among boxes and barrels of melons, apples, potatoes, onions, beans, carrots, and other vegetables, which the country carts as they arrived continually unloaded. The smell of peaches and cantaloupes filled the air, and made Lemuel giddy as he stood and looked at the abundance. The men were not saying much; now and then one of them priced something, the owner pretended to figure on it, and then they fell into a playful scuffle, but all silently. A black cat lay luxuriously asleep on the canvas top of a barrel of melons, and the man who priced the melons asked if the owner would throw the cat in. There was a butcher's cart laden with carcasses of sheep, and one of the men asked the butcher if he called that stuff mutton. "No: imitation," said the butcher. They all seemed to be very goodnatured. Lemuel thought he would ask for an apple, but he could not.

This reveals progress on another line. The object is here clearly to throw up or relieve the fact; point is shut out, and style is, so to speak, in hiding. Nevertheless, the exercise of choice in the matter is patent to a receptive ear, and form or contour in the sentences is screened rather than slighted. The black-cat sentence is an outstanding exemplar of perfect finish in absolute simplicity. Elegant and subtle writer as Mr. Howells was, we must never forget that his hold on realities was powerful, and that this power was predestined to mark his style.

There is another point in Mr. Howells's narrative which has attracted the elect in the measure in which it has repelled the untutored. To him, as to most disciplined minds, the time-order in its nudity or crudity is a little wearisome, and he allays its harshness by the constant introduction of relations of contrast or resemblance or causation. To effect this end, he sometimes obscures, sometimes very slightly inverts or displaces, the order of particulars in time. This substitution of finer for cruder relations is an inspiration and refreshment to the trained mind; but the untrained mind, for which the bare time-order is imperative and sacrosanct, rejects brusquely this encroachment on its rights. A sentence or two may exemplify the point.

The mill property had been a long time abandoned before Libby's father bought it, and put it in a repair which he did not hasten to extend to the village. This had remained in a sort of picturesque neglect, which harmonized with the scenery of the wild little valley in which it nestled.

Now the facts in their plain order are simply these: Libby's father bought a mill property in a village in a wild little valley, repaired the property, and neglected the village. But Mr. Howells wishes to suggest two subtler relations, the contrast between property and village, and the resemblance between village and valley; and, to attain this end, he has postponed the normally antecedent fact about the wildness of the valley to a point where its affinities would be seasonable. The result is admirable for Mr. Howells's parishioners, and they do not worry about the fact that the competition of such a craftsman will never lessen the profits of Mr. Winston Churchill or of Mr. A. S. M. Hutchinson. They are not troubled by the circumstance that the point in the sentence which is logically supreme is sometimes grammatically subordinate; they know that Mr. Howells can be undeviating in the midst of circuits, that he has carried into subtlety an ease and life which were once supposed to reserve their companionship for artlessness.

The first passage illustrative of the third period is extracted from "The Son of Royal Langbrith" (1904).

Anther noted in himself, with curious interest, the accomplished adjustment of the spirit to circumstances that once seemed impossible, and the acceptance of conditions which before had been intolerable. He had gone on to the end of a certain event, strongly willing and meaning something which then he no longer willed or meant. With a sense of acquiescent surprise he found himself at peace with desires and purposes that had long afflicted him with unrest, and it was not they, apparently, that differed, but himself. To the young this will be a mystery, but to those no longer young it will be of the quality of many experiences which, if still mysterious, are not more so than the whole texture of existence.

He had foregone a hope that had seemed essential to his life, but that, once foregone, was like other things outlived — like something of years ago, of his early manhood, almost of his boyhood. He was still baffled and disappointed, but he perceived that he did not care, did not suffer, as he supposed he should care and suffer. It was his compensation that what was ignoble in his regret was gone from it. Neither resentment nor the selfish sense of loss tinged it.

Let the reader with a sensitive ear note the abrupt and ridgy terminations of the first four sentences and the scarcely credible dissonance of the brief sentence that closes the extract, and he will perceive that, while clearness and vigor still persist, the form of this style has disintegrated.

If the reader will tolerate a classification that does no justice to the delicacy and diversity of the phenomena, we may tabulate the three periods as follows:

In the first period, we have form with incipient point; in the second, form and point both eminent; in the third, point with decadent form.

We have seen in our treatment of the criticism of Mr. Howells that, in his increasing acquaintance with life and Tolstoi — two powers that were almost bi-cameral in the constitution of his universe — he came more and more to depreciate style in the traditional sense, and to advocate an uncompromising and undeviating directness and honesty of expression. There are philosophers in our day, called the new realists, who believe that the thought of an object in the human mind may be hardly more than an extension or spur of the object itself. Mr. Howells believed that by absolute straightforwardness and disinterestedness on a writer's part an object might be virtually lifted, transported as it were, from the field of reality to the reader's mind. The writer's function corresponds to that of the central operator in the telephone office, who has merely to establish a circuit and to avoid interference.

There was a time in Mr. Howells's career when it seemed as if the effect of these ideas upon his own practice was to be the advent of a new, sound, and forcible method. A passage from "The Kentons" (1902) seems to me to illustrate the possibility of a felicitous compromise between his earlier ideal and his later theory. It pleases me rather less than his second manner, but I think it almost unrivalled in its suppression of what I may call the author's *brokerage*, in the sense it conveys that the thought is shaped by its own life and moved by its own energy. It is not the *author's* manner, but the *thought's*.

She had certain provincialisms which he could not ignore. She did not know the right use of will and shall, and would and should, and she pronounced the letter *r* with a hard mid-Western twist. Her voice was weak and thin, and she could not govern it from being at times a gasp and at times a drawl. She did not dress with the authority of women who knew more of their clothes than the people they buy them of; she did not carry herself like a pretty girl; she had not the definite stamp of young-ladyism. Yet she was undoubtedly a lady in every instinct; she wore with pensive grace the clothes she had not subjected to her personal taste; and if she did not carry herself like a pretty girl, she had a beauty which touched and entreated.

For a parallel in the essay form to this narrative method in which the story becomes in a sort the novelist, the studious reader may turn to the first paper in "Literature and Life." But Mr. Howells did not pursue this manner with consistency. He fell into other ways; he neglected form; he declined in impact; he sometimes, I fear, became a prey to that carelessness which lies in wait to betray the preacher of spontaneity. The later group of travels exhibit the dissolution of form and the thinning-out of substance; they rely on feeling and point, and the charm of the feeling and the point is evinced in the fact that the books do not pine, and sometimes actually thrive, on this limited and insecure nourishment.

In these later travels Mr. Howells has a pretty habit of figuring his younger self in quaint proximity and dramatic contrast with the older self who handles the pen. I cannot help wondering what that younger self who wrote "Venetian Life" would have said to the author of this sentence in "Roman Holidays": "I recall a brother in a cutaway coat, and a daughter in a tie-back, embraced in their grief and turning their faces away from their mother toward the spectator; and doubtless there were others whom to describe in their dress would render as grotesque." Again, I should be glad, or rather I should be sorry, to hear, what that young critic would have thought of the following bit from "Seven English Cities": "It was a pleasant place, with a play ground before it, which in the course of generations there must have been a good deal of schoolboy fun got out of." Again, I wonder what would have happened if an essay on Oxford, submitted to the editor of the "Atlantic Monthly" between the years 1867 and 1882, had begun with the following sentence: "The friendly gentleman in our railway carriage who was good enough to care for my interest in the landscape between London and Oxford (I began to express it as soon as we got by a very broad, bad smell waiting our train, midway, in the region of some sort of chemical works) said he was going to Oxford for the Eights."

Let me quote one more sentence, which shall be taken from "Imaginary Interviews and Other Essays":

> Only the other day we were reading a paper by a man of that science which deals with life on strictly physical lines, and drawing from it an immense consolation because it reaffirmed that the soul has not only its old excuse for being in the unthinkability of an automatic universe and the necessity of an intentional first cause, but with Evolution, in the regard of some scientists, tottering on its throne, and Natural Selection entering the twilight into which the elder pagan deities have vanished, is newly warranted in claiming existence as that indestructible life-property or organizing power which characterizes kind through kind from everlasting to everlasting.

This is not Tolstoi. This is not simplification. This is mere laxity, the line of least resistance. Now in Mr. Howells the line of least resistance is not simplicity, as it might be in a cruder man, but a formless complexity; when he is heedless, he becomes involved. He falls into what I have called the snowball sentence, the loosely accumulative aggregate, which, in the uncertainty of its route, appears to invite suggestions from any idea or object or phrase upon which it stumbles in the meanderings of its course. The loose and casual intricacy of this later style has a perceptible, though not a close, relation to the less fortunate moments of his unformed style of which an example is quoted on page 311.

Let it be clearly understood that here the theory of intellectual decay is quite untenable. The vigor of the thought is intact, the scintillations have not paled; the faculty of style is still dominant in sentences of Phidian profile, or even in whole papers like "The Counsel of Literary Age." The loss, then, is voluntary. Whether the trouble-saving impulse has affected that volition I do not know. The wish to spare one's self is a dissembling motive, and may have cloaked itself in the form of a homage to truth, especially in a case where that homage was very strong and undoubtedly sincere. In other points one searches in vain for an abatement of watchfulness or energy.

A modest parallel may be drawn between the fortunes of the two elements of art and style in Mr. Howells. At their meridian both were exquisite, but to some extent both suffered — the art more continuously and lightly, the style more gravely and more narrowly — from realism or the kindred cult of spontaneity. I think the circumstance unfortunate. The passion for form is ineradicable, and the fewer the depredations that the pursuit of truth can make on things which the race cherishes so earnestly as art and style, the better not only for art and style, but for the pursuit of truth likewise. The greater part of Mr. Howells's work seems to lend salutary and vigorous support to the idea that the differences between realism and art, between sincerity and style, are not irrepressible conflicts but adjustable and curable misunderstandings; I am sorry that another part should lend a semblance of color to the adverse conclusion. It pains me to see him throw his style overboard; I cannot willingly see him "scatter all his spices on the stream, enrobe the roaring waters with his silks." I loved that precious and fragrant merchandise, and cannot persuade myself that it was really contraband, even in a ship whose masthead floated the realistic pennon.

Style is a perishable commodity, and the high-bred, high-strung styles seem especially subject to reactions of distrust or recoils of satiety on the part of their versatile practitioners. Such men feel sometimes, no doubt, that mastery in these lines is another name for thraldom; they dread to be subject, or abject, to style. In this matter the analogy between Mr. Howells and Mr. James is interestingly close. In the work of both men the impression of literature is transcendent; both had what Lowell would have called *costly* styles; in both, the composition was distinguished by a delicate exactness of contour and a fine, not to say proud, reserve of tone. In the later life of both, this perfection of form and fineness of reserve underwent a marked disintegration, though both processes were carried to burlesque excess by Mr. James, who apparently lost his head and "broke the good meeting with most admired disorder." If one chooses to associate this parallel with the difference in style between Mrs. Wharton's "House of Mirth" and her "Custom of the Country," — a difference which shall not tempt me to prophesy or generalize in relation to Mrs. Wharton, — he will be half moved to affirm that the most subtle styles are the most evanescent.

One further observation must be made. The style of Mr. Howells, in its ripe and unflawed excellence, is no trick, no separable accomplishment, no masterpiece of naked virtuosity. The style has a preëxistence in the psychology, is in essence the ingress of that psychology into language. The peculiarity of the writing might be defined as a rare ease and quietness in the setting forth of delicately intricate relations. But this trait merely images, merely registers, the lasting condition of its author's mind. The impartial and almost universal curiosity of Mr. Howells made it natural that, in his perception of one object, he should become vividly conscious of all its kinsfolk and neighbors; and his eye for relation enabled him to traverse instantly and readily the manifold threads of connection which fastened it to the surrounding world. Since he was adept in all the leanings or inflections of a thing, his options in expression were numerous, and, in this spaciousness of choice, it was easy for him to solve the recurrent problem of style, to discover the doubly apt phrase which at once fills up the measure of the thought and integrates the contours of the sentence. I transcribe a few lines: "It was not a question of Dryfoos's physical presence: that was rather effective than otherwise, and carried a suggestion of moneyed indifference to convention in the grey business suit of provincial cut, and the low wide-brimmed hat of flexible black felt." Now the average novelist's spontaneous perceptions would stop short at the grey suit and the felt hat and their unmistakable relation to Mr. Dryfoos, and the lack of alternatives would force him into a directness of expression which would no doubt further his prospects with the average man. But a man who, without search, could relate that suit and hat to a moneyed indifference to convention could have related them without trouble to half a dozen other things, and, among these various approaches to the thought, some one approach will probably signalize itself by the fitness of the correlative phrase to dignify and harmonize the sentence. This is artifice only in the sense that, being the final choice among several routes, it has not the inevitableness which belongs to the choiceless acceptance of one. It has its basis, its complement, in a state of mind, the state of mind of a man who sees each object as the point of intersection for many highways, and who utilizes this variety of approach and departure to indulge his predilection for rhythm and symmetry in the fashion of his English. Whether Mr. Howells found the task burdensome is a point on which I am both curious and doubtful; I know it would overtask me and my associates to produce a third-rate imitation of his style; but that fact has no bearing on the question.

CHAPTER VIII

Humor

THE topic we now approach is capital. I believe that certain great traits in Mr. Howells — his breadth, his humanity, his spontaneity — are unperceived by the public at large through the failure to appraise justly the humor which chances to be the supreme, not to say the sole, vehicle for the exposition of these traits. What is the common notion of Mr. Howells? That he is a writer whose distinctions are subtlety of matter and elegance of form. If he has humor, its form will be a refined and polished irony with which these high-bred virtues can freely coalesce. Now these estimates are sound enough, if they are viewed as beginnings or inclusions; if viewed as conclusions or exclusions, they are equally unsound and unjust. There is much in Mr. Howells besides subtlety and elegance, and this sterling residue found its main expression in a humor which the phrase "courtly irony" could not encompass or exhaust. I believe that his humor became the bulwark of the Ohioan in him against the Easterner; of the American in him against the cosmopolitan; possibly, though of this I am more doubtful, of the human being in him against the man of letters. It was his humor that stood out unshakable against that process of refinement and subtilization active in Venetian and Bostonian days, a process which remained salutary because it remained partial, and which would have lost its beneficence in its subjugation of the man. You are safe from becoming an aristocrat, literary or social, if every other man you meet on the pavement, in tatters or in broadcloth, exhales a humor which you helplessly and incorrigibly love.

It is a lastingly impressive fact to me that the liegeman of Oliver Wendell Holmes should have been the devotee of Mark Twain. Measure the distance from Holmes to Mark Twain, and you have found the diameter of the mind of Mr. Howells. The arch that spanned this chasm was his humor.

I

IMPORTANCE OF HUMOR

Mr. Howells is not, of course, the first of humorists, though his place on the roster is high; but he is first among all writers of fiction that I can recall in the importance — the stature, the compass, the weight — that is allotted to the joke in his estimate of life. A joke in his novels has the dimensions of an incident, not because it is a rarity (a tax on jokes would have sent Mr. Howells to the poorhouse, especially if it were levied *ad valorem*), but because everybody makes way for it, takes off his cap to it, treats it as an appreciable and estimable fraction of life. This quite fairly represents the author's attitude. His father was incurably humorous, and the son speaks, in "My Year in a Log Cabin," of the "blessed" jokes that leavened and sweetened the hardships of the straitened boyhood in Ohio.

The heroes with whom he sympathizes most keenly in his stories are men so susceptible to humor that they are beset by temptations to laugh in situations where laughter would be impolitic or indecent or inhumane. I do not speak of pathologic laughter, in which horror and sorrow find self-defence or self-indulgence, but of cases where the laugher's nerves are not in question. A girl, gasping with anguish and despair, confides her problem to a high-minded and generous clergyman. His feelings are thus described: "At fifty it is hard to be serious about these things, and it was well for the girl that she was no longer conscious of Sewell's mood." Mr. March is brought to the verge of a smile (these verges are sometimes precipitous) by a serious woman's formulation of certain views on the future life, the fun of which is imperceptible to the groping reader. A sentence like the following is no surprise in Mr. Howells: "Olney's heart ached for her, but he could not help his laugh." Or take this: "There was something in this explanation, serious, tragic, as it was to Mrs. Bowen, which made Colville laugh." These persons are serious after their laugh or under their laugh, but their perception of incongruity is not in the least checked by the incongruity of the fact of perception.

Humor is sometimes the decisive weight in courtship. Penelope Lapham's jokes find the young Tom Corey defenceless; and in "The Kentons" the charms of one joker turn out to be the only means of extricating a foolish young girl from the toils of another. The humor of a despised blackguard in "The Coast of Bohemia" cajoles an excellent young woman into acts that compromise her self-respect.

The rôle of humor in the life of Mr. Howells himself may be inferred from a pregnant sentence in "Imaginary Interviews," in which the author's identity with the spokesman is fairly presumable: "Speaking selfishly, as we always do when we speak truly, I have not had a great deal of happiness, though I have had a good deal of fun." Humor, in other words, is the rebate on the heavy liability known as life.

The psychology of an artist's mind is insoluble or, at least, unverifiable, but I ask sometimes if Mr. Howells's realism did not reinforce his humor by debarring the caprice and fancy which were one phase of his being from any serious or sentimental outlet, and turning their whole efflux into the channel of his mirth. Humor is homespun romance, that is to say, it agrees with romance in falsifying reality in the interest of pleasure. If Shakespeare's literary conscience had forbidden the presentation of Oberons or Titanias, the release of creative energy in this quarter might have resulted in a still larger procreation of Bottoms, Snugs, and Quinces.

II

COURTLY HUMOR

I shall begin my illustrations with a passage of the refined humor which everyone can instantly relate to his preconceptions of the author. The passage is from "Criticism and Fiction."

It is certain, however, that the Christmas season is meteorologically more favorable to the effective return of persons long lost at sea, or from a prodigal life, or from a darkened mind. The longer, denser, and colder nights are better adapted to the apparition of ghosts, and to all manner of signs and portents; while they seem to present a wider field for the active intervention of angels in behalf of orphans and outcasts. The dreams of elderly sleepers at this time are apt to be such as will effect a lasting change in them when they awake, turning them from the hard, cruel, and grasping habits of a lifetime, and reconciling them to their sons, daughters, and nephews, who have thwarted them in marriage; or softening them to their meek, uncomplaining wives, whose hearts they have trampled upon in their reckless pursuit of wealth; and generally disposing them to a distribution of hampers among the sick and poor, and to a friendly reception of chubby gentlemen with charity subscription papers. Ships readily drive upon rocks in the early twilight, and offer exciting difficulties of salvage; and the heavy snows gather thickly round the steps of wanderers who lie down to die in them, preparatory to their discovery and rescue by immediate relatives. The midnight weather is also very suitable to encounter with murderers and burglars; and the contrast of its freezing gloom with the light and cheer in-doors promotes the gayeties which merge, in all well-regulated country-houses, in love and marriage. . . . We need not point out the superior advantages of the Christmas season for anything one has a mind to do with the French Revolution, or the Arctic explorations, or the Indian Mutiny, or the horrors of Siberian exile; there is no time so good for the use of this material; and ghosts on shipboard are notoriously fond of Christmas Eve. In our own logging camps the man who has gone into the woods for the winter, after quarrelling with his wife, then hears her sad appealing voice, and is moved to good resolutions as at no other period of the year; and in the mining regions, first in California and later in Colorado, the hardened reprobate, dying in his boots, smells his mother's dough-nuts, and breathes his last in a soliloquized vision of the old home, and the little brother, or sister, or the old father coming to meet him from heaven; while his rude companions listen around him, and dry their eyes on the buts of their revolvers.

This is the irony of the salon, and its restraint is emphasized by the surprise with which, at the end of the passage, we stumble upon the momentary roguishness of the grotesque image, "dry their eyes on the buts of their revolvers."

Waiving the grotesqueness for a moment, the irony which forms the staple of the passage is sufficiently delicate, but it pales, or rather it flushes and purples, beside another form of irony from the same hand — an irony which faithfully and literally records the facts, and equivocates only in the implications of the tone. I quote from "A Woman's Reason":

It was to this period that her passion for the German language also belonged. She had studied German at school, of course, but it was not till after leaving school that French was relegated to its true place as something charming enough, but not serious; and German engrossed her. She read Goethe's and Schiller's plays with her teacher, and Heine's songs with one of her girl-friends. She laid out a course of reading in German, which was to include Schopenhauer's philosophy, already familiar to her through the talk of a premature Harvard man, who rarely talked of anything else. But it never really came to this; German literature presently took the form of drama, and after Helen's participation in a certain number of German plays, it yielded to the pleasing dance of the same name; though not till it had superseded Italian as well as French in her affections. Dante, of course, one must always respect, but after Dante there was so little in Italian as compared with German!

Where Dickens or Thackeray would have inverted the *fact* or the *diction*, Mr. Howells's subtler art, which has analogues in "Sir Roger de Coverley" and "The Vicar of Wakefield," is content with the inversion of the *attitude*.

III

WHIMSICALITY

So much for the academic pleasantries. Before passing to the grotesqueries, which invite us by their contrast, I must reserve a moment for a third variety of humor, distinct from both and not less piquantly characteristic. It might be known as gay and tender whimsicality; its mood is delicately personal, and the fancy which ministers to its needs is, in the words of Coleridge about Mercutio, "busy and procreative as an insect." I shall draw my illustrations chiefly from the books of travel, because it is a fact worth remembering that Mr. Howells is never so idly or irresponsibly whimsical as in these books where his theme is himself. The characters in his novels are grave and weighty personages with whom a sober historian must hazard no liberties, but there is no reason why that chimera known as W. D. Howells should not be abandoned to the freakish convoy of his brother gnomes.

The fancy is curiously multiform. His favorite assumption of meek passivity, the attitude of the babe in the hands of Fate, I have mentioned in an earlier page, but the playfulness has many variations. He coquettes with his double, his youthful self of earlier times or previous journeys, with whom the riper self of to-day engages in a pretty game of hide-and-seek or airy "Comedy of Errors." But there are multiples as well as doubles of himself, whose main occupation is to buy and hold properties in various corners of the earth, with a special eye to piazzas in Rome and to houses appropriated right and left in "every eligible and memorable quarter of Bath." He has a footing of social acquaintance with monuments and works of art, with busts that recognize their admirer and even recall his book, with villas that remain stiffly elusive of what they clearly regard as the doubtful honor of an encounter with Mr. Howells, with Rome herself, who follows his departure on her "poor, broken aqueducts," "like some fond cripple pursuing a friend on crutches." In the freedom of wayfaring he delights to parley with his reader (a practice of untold enormity in fiction), whom he refuses to admit to a carriage already full, despatches to Spain for the purpose of making up the shortage in two or three miscalculated tips, and debars from the privacies of Hampton Court with the meagre solace of promenading, if he likes, in the court proper, where he looks, to the condescending eye of Mr. Howells in the gallery above, like a figure in a water-color.

The shimmer of this fancy is pervasive. If the weather is gloomy in Manchester, it copies the grimness of the "Manchester School." If March is cold in Rome, the overthrow of the temporal power has left the seasons neglected and indifferent. A tourist, chilled in a gallery, retires to "thaw out his love of the beautiful." If cows at Llandudno obey the dog rather than the boy, it is explained as "their Old-World convention." On a page of glowing newspaper eulogy the print all but smokes to his excited imagination, and he can even conceive himself to be Early English or Perpendicular Gothic when the explanations of his verger approach those topics.

IV

THE AMERICAN ELEMENT

This blend of wit and fancy might recall a similar vein in Rostand, as the drawing-room irony, in its explicit form, might suggest Voltaire, or, in its latencies and innocencies, Pascal. But in Mr. Howells there is another humor, a bolder, freer, half-rollicking American humor, which affects us in relation to the refined quiet of his daintier personality like a child laughing out in church. Would any reader imagine beforehand that Mr. Howells was the sort of man to say that a hotel was, on a rough calculation, about a hundred miles by omnibus from the station, that an English family demesne was about as large as

Connecticut or New Jersey, that a train gave every promise of arriving five hundred years behind time, that a spectator in St. Peter's rivalled the dome in rotundity, that a cab arrived from Mount Ararat encrusted with "the mire of the subsiding Deluge," or that a stench in Spain was dire enough to reach across the Atlantic?

When Marcia Gaylord says, in reply to Bartley Hubbard's wish that the ride might last forever, "Forever! That would do for a beginning," or when Wallace Ardith, after a humiliating scene, wonders that he did n't go out through the keyhole, since there would have been room enough, we seem to hear the robust laughter that heaves the ribs of our own lusty continent rather than the clear, fine tone of the diplomatists and satirists of Europe.

But this is by no means all. Mr. Howells uses with effect the burlesque simile, the simile that both defines and diminishes its object. He will compare serried breakers tossing their white caps against the sky-line to so many cooks abandoning the hotel kitchen. His theme is the closing of a hotel. In another closing hotel, the last bell-boy "winks out." "At Berlin the horses look like old hair trunks and the drivers like their moth-eaten contents." Here is a gauge of his reverence for the wonders of Pisa: "The Duomo a vast and beautiful pudding; the Baptistery a gigantic *charlotte russe;* the Campo Santo an exquisite structure in sugar; the Leaning Tower a column of ice-cream . . . weakened at the base."

There are grotesqueries that make us turn back to the title-page to see if the name it bears be not Richter or Carlyle or Dickens. The west of England, in early spring, looks "as if wringing it out and hanging it up to dry in a steam-laundry could alone get the wet out of it." In one of his similes a person, trying to soak up a rainstorm, stands "with his blotting-paper in his hand, in a puddle over his shoe-tips." There is an animated description of Charles Reade firing in all sorts of attitudes (metaphorically, of course), firing "lying down and standing on his head," and finally leaping into the air and clicking "his heels together with a whoop of triumph." On a clamorous night in Seville a "maniacal" bell clashes out: "Hello! Here 's a bit of silence; let 's knock it on the head!" In "Literature and Life" three American ladies are said to pin a gardener to the wall by their cruel interrogations. This is surely grotesque enough, but let us read a little further. The "barbed points" are "buried in the stucco behind him," and the "feathered shafts . . . stick out half a yard before his breast." We should call this excessive — in Mark Twain. I cannot quote indefinitely. Let the reader look up for himself, if he has the time and the inclination, that passage in "Italian Journeys" where reeking silks invite dress-coats to look over dripping photographs. I know not whether finally I shall have the courage to insert or the magnanimity to suppress that passage in "Imaginary Interviews" in which the guest at the dinner is represented as "streaming drawn butter from every limb."

People who talk about gibbering (by cable) at a shilling a gibber are delightful company, but shall we group them with the dignitaries or the madcaps? Let no one suppose that Mr. Howells reserves these audacities for jocular occasions when outbreak is permissible. There is a decorous paragraph where Hilary, the unimaginative banker, in his preoccupation with Northwick, seems "to be eating and drinking him at every course."

The grotesque in incident is somewhat rare in the novels; I recall the bedroom scene in "Their Wedding Journey" and Kinney's floury paws in "A Modern Instance," which baffle his attempts to detain the offended Bartley. But the farces rather abound in these enlivenments, as the reader of "Room Forty-Five," "The Sleeping Car," "The Smoking Car," and "The Garroters" will readily, perhaps a trifle ruefully, attest.

Their appearance, even in this sportive form, completes the evidence, since it implies their preëxistence in Mr. Howells.

There remains, finally, the provisioning, if I may so call it, of fantastic and ebullient humorists like Fulkerson in "A Hazard of New Fortunes." For the qualities or the opinions of a dramatic entity his creator is not properly responsible, but the imagination and the vocabulary of a character are loans from the author of his being. No fictitious character pays his own way, nor are his expenses paid by his original and counterpart in real life; for the speeches and actions, which are the equivalent in his case of board and lodging, the child reverts helplessly to his parent. The parent shows a readiness that is not wholly sacrificial in joining with the child in sports which in other relations his maturity might disown. It is universally conceded that a father may go to the circus if he goes in the company of his child.

In the mere aspect or exterior of Mr. Howells's mind there is something misleading. He has a polished tranquillity which represents sufficiently well one half or two thirds of his character, and which overlays or enamels the fraction of his nature which it fails to represent. The gentleman in him is so high and absolute that he is a little unfair to the man. It is as if the firm-name reproduced only the appellation of the more genteel and self-contained of the two partners, as if the stationery had been headed "March and Company," instead of "March and Fulkerson." At this point humor intervenes with its redress of the failing equipoise, its vindication of the slighted man. It reveals that element of impulse, of boyishness, of nimbleness, of plasticity, that reversion to the liberality of nature, which, in the dormancy of humor, the student of Mr. Howells might have failed to perceive, or perceived with inadequate distinctness. I have emphasized the freer humor, not because I find its quality preferable, but in recognition of the greater pregnancy of its disclosures. The smile of Mr. Howells may be a ceremony, but his laugh is a confidence.

CHAPTER IX

The Future

On the question of Mr. Howells's future status in the court of letters, I am averse to dogmatism. In my view, justice has not yet been done to his power and service as a critic. No approach to justice has been done to the singular merit of his later poems. I doubt, moreover, if due recognition has been accorded to three great elements in his fiction — its vitality, which seems to be inadequately felt, the surpassing distinctness and variety of its characterization, and its firm grasp of some of the rarer and more elusive aspects of everyday reality.

His fortunes in his own day have by no means equalled his deserts; but to feel this strongly is not to be overconfident that the future will side with the deserts against the fortunes. I doubt if his later poems will ever be justly rated: their bulk is slight and their gloom does not prepossess. I feel much more hopeful of an ampler and juster recognition of the soundness of his critical achievement. The vogue of romance will doubtless fluctuate, but in the absence of any arrest or reversal of the broad movement of our world-civilization, the place of realism in the lasting esteem, if not the steady favor, of the better public seems tolerably secure. The establishment of realism may ensure reverberation, or at least remembrance, for the courageous voice which was not the first to announce the principle, but the first to give clarity and sonority to the proclamation of its worth. The travel and autobiography are the passengers in the ship; if they are saved, they will owe their safety to the crew.

About the novels two things may be confidently averred: they will be perennially valuable to scholarship, and they will never be valuable to Philistine middle-class humanity; the point of interesting doubt is whether they will retain a value for culture undefiled with scholarship. Will they be read by the Coreys and Bellinghams, the Hallecks and Athertons, the Westovers and Anthers, of 1950 or 2000? As realism, their chances exceed those of an equal bulk of romance, if the decline of Scott in relation to Jane Austen and of Reade in relation to Trollope, and the curious strengthening of the position of the amphibious Balzac in our day are to be accepted as criteria. The profundity of these fictions in dealing with some of the most signal interests and aspects of life should plead for the continuance of their hold on the doubtful loyalty of a forgetful race.

There is, however, a ground of misgiving which I may fitly embody in a supposition. If a Japanese — a cultivated Japanese — who knew nothing of America by travel or reading, were to ask me whether he could repair that defect by a perusal of the novels of Mr. Howells, I should hesitate, and I can imagine myself ending with the recommendation that he get his *elementary* schooling in American life from the works of some inferior writer. The cultivated American or Englishman of a century hence might find himself in the position of this Japanese. A very considerable part of Mr. Howells's fiction deals with a highly specialized variety of Americans. The *man* in him is not eccentric, not exotic: the man is human, sane, poised, generous; after you have rounded the bend — to utilize the vernacular — he is simple: simple in his criticism, simple in his religion, simple in his economic theory. But his simplicity is *ultimate*, not obvious; and it requires a dash of subtlety in the reader to grasp the fact of his normality. He is not wholly unlike those girls of his who want the same things at bottom as other girls, and who succeed, at last, in simplifying themselves, but only after a process whose intricacies and sinuosities fill the unaccustomed onlooker with dismay. This seems the fit place to remark that, in a series of novels which woman dominates, the fact that the woman-type is extreme and borders on eccentricity will cast its vote in the final arbitration of his fame. These things have undoubtedly checked the enlargement of his vogue among his homespun and artless contemporaries; and, unless posterity should evolve in his particular direction, it is rash to assume that the obstacle will vanish. His lot in relation to his endowment has been singular. He is rich, not only in strength of mind and force of conscience, but in the gifts that captivate; the Graces almost outsped the Muses to his cradle; he is the master, the exemplar, of charm; but the public, impatient of the slightest transcendence of its own limitations, puts him by for the sake of novelists who offer, not only fewer benefits, but fewer pleasures.

Amid these inauspicious signs, there is one proffer of encouragement. Mr. Howells holds a position among his contemporaries which is far superior to his vogue. A sense of worth, of fineness, of service, has penetrated to the minds of many persons who know "The Rise of Silas Lapham" only by title, and who would scarcely care to commit themselves on the question of the authorship of "The Landlord at Lion's Head" or "The Son of Royal Langbrith." Homage of this type, discerning in ignorance, is capable of transmission to later times, and I see no reason why Mr. Howells should be denied the atoning good-fortune of men like Petrarch, like Dryden, like Landor, like Goethe himself, in a measure, who became widely known and honored on the *credit* (I use the word almost in its mercantile sense) of works that were vaguely known and scantily read. I assert no parity or imparity of Mr. Howells with these masters; I merely indicate a type of fame. Such an outcome would not satisfy those to whom the work and teaching of their great compatriot are so dear that they could not willingly see a valuation replace a value; and it is always possible that the future may be wiser than its sonship to the purblind present would lead us to assume. But, in the absence of a larger fulfilment, it would be something to know that the memory of Mr. Howells will add to the glory of America beyond the date, which our hope and love indefinitely postpone, when that rare and high intelligence shall no longer be listed among forces that nourish and impel.

BIBLIOGRAPHY

BIBLIOGRAPHY

THE bibliography which follows is selective, not complete. An attempt has been made to supply a clew to the whereabouts of every novel, tale, and play published by Mr. Howells and to every *book* (exclusive of reprints, anthologies, and rearrangements) in the fields of travel and miscellany. Of periodical writing by Mr. Howells and of commentary on Mr. Howells in books and periodicals, nothing more has been attempted than a selection of the more prominent or valuable material. Under "periodicals" no article afterward reprinted in a book has been included; this explains the meagre lists under "Atlantic Monthly" and "Harper's Monthly." The shortened firm-names ("Harper" for "Harper and Brothers," etc.) are self-explaining for any person likely to concern himself with these lists. "Harper" under "periodicals" means "Harper's Monthly" unless "Weekly" or "Bazar" is specified. No attempt has been made to list the books which Mr. Howells edited, or to which he furnished prefaces. Dates are, or should be, the dates of first editions. It may be well to add that the novels usually cost two dollars or two dollars and a half.

The Library Edition of Mr. Howells's works, the publication of which has been stopped or suspended, includes only six volumes: (1) A Hazard of New Fortunes; (2) The Landlord at Lion's Head; (3) Literary Friends and Acquaintance — My Mark Twain; (4) Literature and Life; (5) London Films — Certain Delightful English Towns; (6) My Literary Passions — Criticism and Fiction. The publisher is Harper.

Novels

Annie Kilburn........................ Harper 1889
April Hopes........................ Harper 1888
A Chance Acquaintance................ Houghton 1873
The Coast of Bohemia................ Harper 1899
The Day of their Wedding.............. Harper 1896
Dr. Breen's Practice................... Houghton 1881
A Fearful Responsibility............... Houghton 1881
(With two tales: At the Sign of the Savage, and Tonelli's Marriage.)

Fennel and Rue	Harper	1908
A Foregone Conclusion	Houghton	1875
A Hazard of New Fortunes	Harper	1890
An Imperative Duty	Harper	1893
Indian Summer	Houghton	1886
The Kentons	Harper	1902
The Lady of the Aroostook	Houghton	1879
The Landlord at Lion's Head	Harper	1898
The Leatherwood God	Century	1916
Letters Home	Harper	1903
The Minister's Charge	Houghton	1887
Miss Bellard's Inspiration	Harper	1905
Mrs. Farrell	Harper	1921
A Modern Instance	Houghton	1881
New Leaf Mills	Harper	1913
An Open-Eyed Conspiracy	Harper	1897
A Parting and a Meeting	Harper	1896
The Quality of Mercy	Harper	1892
Ragged Lady	Harper	1899
The Rise of Silas Lapham	Houghton	1885
The Shadow of a Dream	Harper	1890
The Son of Royal Langbrith	Harper	1904
The Story of a Play	Harper	1898
Their Second Wedding Journey	Harper	1900
Their Wedding Journey	Houghton	1871
Through the Eye of the Needle	Harper	1907
A Traveler from Altruria	Harper	1894
The Undiscovered Country	Houghton	1880
The Vacation of the Kelwyns	Harper	1920
A Woman's Reason	Houghton	1882
The World of Chance	Harper	1893

See also "The Whole Family," twelve-author novel, to which W. D. H. contributed the opening. Harper, 1908.

Dramas (in book form)

The Albany Depot	Harper	1892
Bride Roses: A Scene	Houghton	1900
A Counterfeit Presentment	Houghton	1877
The Elevator	Houghton	1885
Evening Dress	Harper	1893
Five O'Clock Tea	Harper	1894
The Garroters	Harper	1894
An Indian Giver	Houghton	1900
A Letter of Introduction	Harper	1892
A Likely Story	Harper	1894

The Mouse-Trap	Harper	1894
The Night Before Christmas, with A Daughter of the Storage[1]		
Out of the Question	Houghton	1877
The Parlor Car	Houghton	1876
Parting Friends	Harper	1911
A Previous Engagement	Harper	1897
The Register	Houghton	1884
Room Forty-five	Houghton	1900
A Sea-Change or Love's Stowaway	Houghton	1888
Self-Sacrifice: A Farce-Tragedy, with A Daughter of the Storage[1]		
The Sleeping Car	Houghton	1883
The Smoking Car	Houghton	1900
The Unexpected Guests	Harper	1893

The Mouse-Trap and Other Farces, containing, besides the title-piece, The Garroters, Five O'Clock Tea, and A Likely Story, was published by Harper in 1889. The Library of Congress catalogue mentions Minor Dramas (D. Douglas, 1907, Edinburgh) in two volumes, containing nineteen plays (practically all the best minor dramas). Ten or more farces have been separately reprinted by Samuel French, Boston.

DRAMAS (in periodicals, not reprinted)

		Vol.	Page
Her Opinion of his Story	Harper's Bazar	41	429 (May, 1907)
The Impossible: A Mystery Play	Harper	122	116
A Masterpiece of Diplomacy	Harper	88	371
Saved: An Emotional Drama	Harper's Weekly	52	22 (Dec. 12, 1908)
A True Hero: Melodrama	Harper	119	866

DRAMAS (in verse). See "Poems."

POEMS

Poems	Houghton	1873
The Mother and the Father: Dramatic Passages	Harper	1909

Contents:
After the Wedding
The Father and the Mother
The Mother

Stops of Various Quills	Harper	1895

See also "The Daughter of the Storage" for scattered verse.

[1] See under "Tales."

TALES

At the Sign of the Savage (printed with A Fearful Responsibility)

Between the Dark and the Daylight...... Harper 1907

Contents:

- A Sleep and a Forgetting
- The Eidolons of Brooks Alford
- A Memory that Worked Overtime
- A Case of Metaphantasmia
- Editha
- Braybridge's Offer
- The Chick of the Easter Egg

Christmas Every Day and Other Stories .. Harper 1893

The Daughter of the Storage............ Harper 1916

Contents (nothing but tales listed):

- The Daughter of the Storage
- A Presentiment
- The Return to Favor
- Somebody's Mother
- An Experience
- The Boarders
- The Mother-Bird
- The Amigo
- The Critical Bookstore
- A Feast of Reason
- Table Talk
- The Escapade of a Grandfather

The Flight of Pony Baker............... Harper 1902

A Pair of Patient Lovers................ Harper 1901

Contents:

- A Pair of Patient Lovers
- The Pursuit of the Piano
- A Difficult Case
- The Magic of a Voice
- A Circle in the Water

Questionable Shapes.................... Harper 1903

Contents:

- His Apparition
- The Angel of the Lord (same as At Third Hand, in Century, 61, 496)
- Though One Rose from the Dead

Tonelli's Marriage (printed with A Fearful Responsibility)

TALES (in periodicals)

		Vol.	Page
The Fulfilment of the Pact........	Harper's Weekly	56	9 (Dec. 14, 1912)
The Pearl......................	Harper	133	409
Rotational Tenants..............	Harper	133	770
A Tale Untold..................	Atlantic	120	236

TRAVEL

Title	Publisher	Year
Certain Delightful English Towns	Harper	1906
Familiar Spanish Travels	Harper	1913
Hither and Thither in Germany	Harper	1920
Italian Journeys	Houghton	1867
A Little Swiss Sojourn	Harper	1892
London Films	Harper	1905
Roman Holidays	Harper	1908
The Seen and Unseen at Stratford-on-Avon: a Fantasy	Harper	1914
Seven English Cities	Harper	1909
Tuscan Cities	Houghton	1885
Venetian Life	Houghton	1866

MISCELLANIES

Title	Publisher	Year
Boy Life (selections by P. Chubb)	Harper	1909
A Boy's Town (autobiographical)	Harper	1890
Character and Comment	Houghton	0000
Criticism and Fiction (from "Editor's Study")	Harper	1892
A Day's Pleasure and Other Sketches	Houghton	1881
Buying a Horse — Flitting — The Mouse — A Year in a Venetian Palace		
Great Modern American Stories	Boni and Liveright	1920
Heroines of Fiction	Harper	1901
Howells Story Book	Scribner	1900
(compiled by M. E. Burt and Mildred Howells)		
Imaginary Interviews (from "Easy Chair")	Harper	1910
Impressions and Experiences (essays)	Harper	1896
Literary Friends and Acquaintance	Harper	1900
Literature and Life	Harper	1902
A Little Girl Among the Old Masters	Osgood	1884
Modern Italian Poets	Harper	1887
My Literary Passions	Harper	1895
My Mark Twain	Harper	1910
My Year in a Log Cabin	Harper	1893
Sketch of the Life and Character of Rutherford B. Hayes	Hurd and Houghton	1876
Stories of Ohio	American Book Co.	1897
Suburban Sketches	Houghton	1871
Mrs. Johnson — A Doorstep Acquaintance — A Pedestrian Tour — By Horse-Car to Boston — A Day's Pleasure — A Romance of Real Life — Scene — Jubilee Days — Flitting (Some Lessons from the School of Morals, added 1872)		
Three Villages	Houghton	1884
Years of My Youth	Harper	1916

CONTRIBUTIONS TO PERIODICALS

North American Review

	Vol.	Page
Recent Italian Comedy	99	364
Henry W. Longfellow	104	531
Are We a Plutocracy?	158	185
The New Poetry	168	581
The New Historical Romances	171	935
A Hundred Years of American Verse	172	148
Mark Twain: an Inquiry	172	306
The Recent Dramatic Season	172	468
The New Poetic Drama	172	794
Emile Zola	175	587
Frank Norris	175	769
Mr. Henry James's Later Work	176	125
The Personality of Hawthorne	177	872
English Feeling Toward Americans	179	815
English Idiosyncrasies, I, II	181	649, 897
Henrik Ibsen	189	1
The Fiction of Leonard Merrick	185	378
On Reading the Plays of Henry Arthur Jones	186	205
Lyof N. Tolstoy	188	842
Robert Herrick's Novels	189	812
The Fiction of Eden Phillpotts	190	15
Literary Recollections (W. D. H. and H. James)	195	550
Recent Russian Fiction	196	85
"Part of Which I Was" (History of N. A. Review)	201	135
The Plays of Eugène Brieux	201	402
Why? (1915 — World War)	201	676

A complete list of the contributions to the *North American Review* is given in that review, volume 212, pages 14–16.

The Atlantic Monthly

	Vol.	Page
A Glimpse of Genoa	19	359
The Next President (Grant)	21	628
The New Taste in Theatricals	23	635
An Obsolete Fine Gentleman	36	98
Four New Books of Poetry	37	105
Edward Bellamy	82	253

See also "The Holmes Breakfast" (*Atlantic*, vol. 45, Supplement) at which W. D. H. was toastmaster.

The Century

Equality as the Basis of Good Society	29	63 (new ser.)
Pictures for Don Quixote................	34	177

The Forum

The Nature of Liberty..................	20	401

Harper's Monthly

A Bermudan Sojourn....................	124	16
Confessions of St. Augustine.............	134	680, 877
In an Old-Time State Capital...........	129	593, 740, 921
The Modern American Mood............	95	199

The practical absence of reprints in the *North American Review* articles explains its preponderance in numbers over the *Atlantic* and *Harper*.

ABOUT HOWELLS

Books on Howells, or Associated Topics

Cooke, Delmar G.	William Dean Howells	E. P. Dutton	1923
Harvey, Alexander	William Dean Howells	B. W. Huebsch	1917
Howells, W. C. (the father)	Life in Ohio from 1813 to 1840	R. Clarke	1895

Sections of Books

Higginson, T. W.	Short Studies of American Authors	Lee and Shepard	1880
Macy, John	Spirit of American Literature	Doubleday	1913
Peck, H. T.	Personal Equations		1898
Phelps, W. L.	Essays on Modern Novelists	Macmillan	1910
Robertson, J.M.	Essays toward a Critical Method	T. F. Unwin, Lond.	1889
Trent, W. P.	Authority of Criticism	Scribner's	1889
Vedder, H. C.	American Writers of To-Day	Silver, Burdett	1895

Periodical Articles on Howells

		Vol.	Page
Certain Overlooked Phases of American Life (M. H. Vorse)	*Critic*	43	83
Chronicle and Comment (*wise in parts*) ...	*Bookman*	35	451
Contemporary Novelists (W. D. H.)...... (H. T. and W. Follett)	*Atlantic*	119	362
Heroines of Fiction (from London Times) .	*Littell*	232	760
Howells and Trollope .... (*interesting*) (J. F. Muirhead)	*Littell*	308	304
James, Crawford, and Howells (Indian Summer)...........................	*Atlantic*	57	850
Life, and a Man of Letters..............	*Academy*	63	553

Title	Periodical	Vol.	Page
Literary Recollections (H. James, F. B. Sanborn)	*North American*	195	550
Literature and Life (reviewed)	*Athenæum*	1	393
Living Critics (*racy*) (H. T. Peck)	*Bookman*	4	529
Lowell's Appreciation of Howells (*interesting*) (Viola P. Franklin)	*Methodist Review*	62	112
Meetings with Howells (H. Garland)	*Bookman*	45	385
Mr. Howells and his Brother (W. Fawcett)	*Critic*	35	1026
Mr. Howells as a Critic (*judicious*) (B. Matthews)	*Forum*	32	629
Mr. Howells and American Aristocracies (*good*) (A. van Westrum)	*Bookman*	25	67
Mr. Howells at Home (W. H. Bishop)	*Critic*	9	259
Mr. Howells at Work at Seventy-two (*good data*) (V. W. Brooks)	*World's Work*	18	11547
Mr. Howells Interviewed (T. C. Crawford)	*Critic*	21	36
Mr. Howells's Literary Creed	*Atlantic*	68	566
Mr. Howells's Style (*energetic*) (Mark Twain)	*Harper*	113	221
Mr. Howells's Way of Saying Things (*good on style*) (Edith M. Thomas)	*Putnam's*	4	443
A Modern Instance	*Atlantic*	50	709
New York in Recent Fiction	*Atlantic*	65	563
The Novels of Mr. Howells (W. C. Brownell)	*Nation*	31	49
On Mrs. Farrell (*curious fact*)	*Bookman*	21	201
The Passing of William Dean Howells (E. Gosse)	*Living Age*	306	98
The Sanity of Fiction (H. Garland)	*North American*	176	336
Social Consciousness of W. D. Howells (*substantial*) (A. L. Bass)	*New Republic*	26	193
Tribute to William Dean Howells (birthday dinner)	*Harper's Weekly*	56	27 (Mar. 9, 1912)
W. D. Howells (*thoughtful*) (J. Erskine)	*Bookman*	51	385
Why Have We Not More Great Novelists? (comment on the Gertrude Atherton interview)	*Current Literature*	44	158

INDEX

INDEX